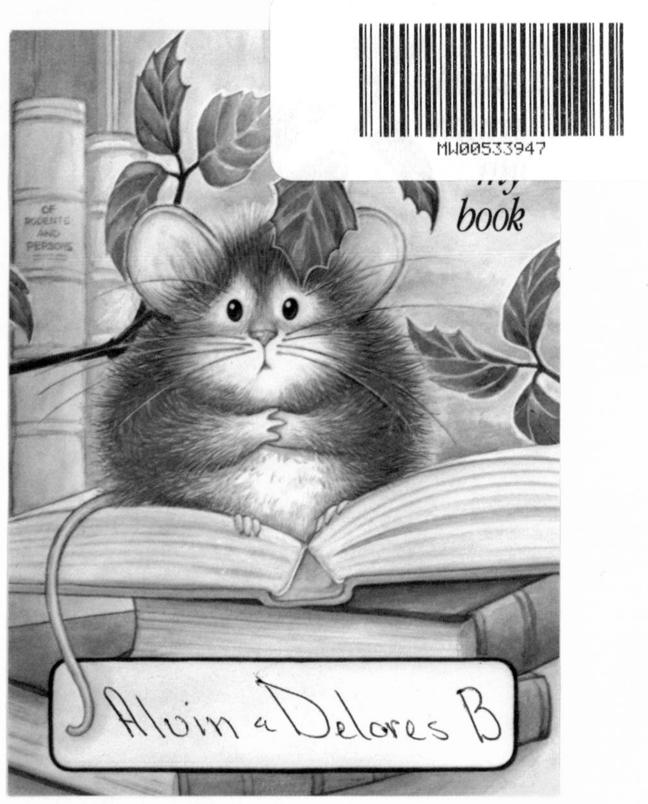

Prophecies Of Pale Skin

Prophecies Of Pale Skin

D.S. Phillips

ISBN 978-0-988545-007

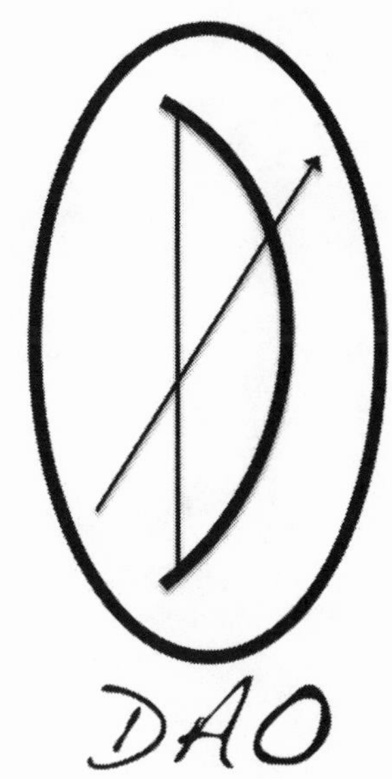
DAO

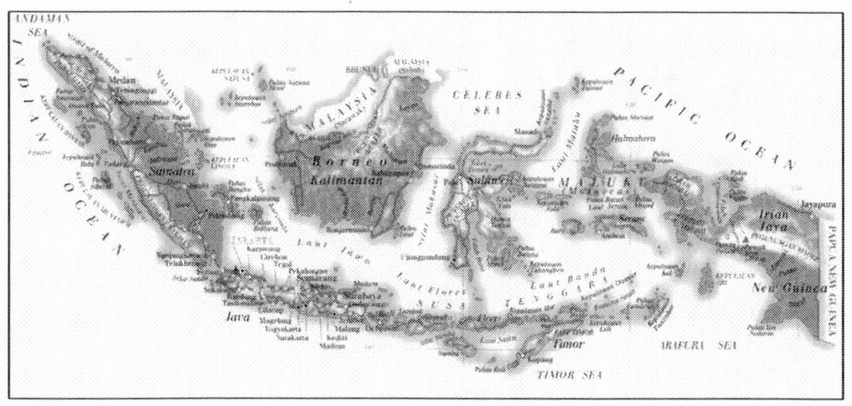
ANDAMAN
SEA
INDIAN OCEAN
Medan
Sumatra
MALAYSIA
BRUNEI
CELEBES
SEA
PACIFIC
OCEAN
Borneo
Kalimantan
Halmahera
Laut Jawa
Laut Flores
Laut Banda
Java
Surabaya
Malang
Timor
Irian
Jaya
Jayapura
PAPUA NEW GUINEA
New Guinea
ARAFURA SEA
TIMOR SEA

Indonesia

For my sons Moses and Job,
so that if the Great Creator decides to take me while I am still young, you will have a way to know about your Dad, the love I have for your mom and the adventures we have had together.

And for Wikipai,
I look forward to the day we are reunited my brother.

CONTENTS

Chapter 1

Vine Bridges and Raging Rapids

It is not the critic who counts, not the man who points out how the strong man stumbles or where the doer of deeds could have done them better. The credit belongs to the man who is actually in the arena, whose face is marred by dust and sweat and blood, who strives valiantly, who errs and comes up short again and again. Because there is no effort without error and shortcomings, he who knows the great devotion, who spends himself in a worthy cause, who at the best knows in the end the high achievement of triumph and who at worst, if he fails while daring greatly, knows his place shall never be with those timid and cold souls who know neither victory nor defeat.

Theodore Roosevelt,
Citizenship in a Republic

We stood on the edge of the churning jungle river and watched the worn vine bridge bounce and sway above the rapids. In a world overrun with cellphones, droids, computers, gadgets, and the latest space-age technology, it seemed that we had perhaps stumbled into one of the only places left so remote that even its location was just a blank space on the Indonesian maps. Its coordinates hidden beneath a reoccurring void that read over and over again: "Relief Data Incomplete." Though we had nothing to go by on this long lost jungle trail: no maps, no compass, and no GPS, we had Paatoma. We had been in these Stone Age jungles long enough, however, to know beyond a shadow of a doubt that Paatoma was all we need.

Probably in his late twenties, covered with veiny muscles from his broad shoulders all the way down to his long, slender legs, Paatoma stood to our right, his forehead wrinkled with concern. Usually a very playful and jocular individual, in this moment sweat beaded and dripped from his protruding, concerned brow and ran down onto his bare chest. After a short pause he finally broke the silence. "*Anii keta pakaanaka,*" which in English meant: "I'll climb up first and test the old vines so I can see whether or not they are strong enough." Within seconds he was scurrying up the twisted jungle tree that held the tattered rattan vines to the jagged, rocky riverbank.

We were out of breath from the long jungle trek, and our arms were dotted with the bites of flies and mosquitos that gathered and swarmed any warm-blooded creature that was unfortunate enough to get caught in their path. Our socks were rimmed with bloodstains from the numbing anticoagulant effect of the leeches that had been taking turns latching onto our bodies and feeding until they were fat and bloated and could suck no more. It hadn't been an easy trek by any means and we welcomed the opportunity to rest a bit as Paatoma checked out the bridge. We slid our packs from our shoulders and collapsed onto the mossy-green rocks beside the rapids and sucked in lungfuls of air as we tried to catch our breath. Our shirts and clothes were soaked from the spongy jungle humidity and nearly six hours worth of sweat. The blazing tropical sun was now at full height. Our knees ached from scaling mountain ridge after mountain ridge since before first light.

Despite the hardship of these jungle trails, it only took but a few minutes of sitting in silence to be reminded of the beauty and pristine nature of this place. The cool breeze rolled off the river and onto our skin, refreshing every pore after the harrowing descent down the slippery, twisting trails of a forty-five-hundred-foot rainforest mountain. This was the jungle that captured our hearts years before when we first set foot in the Dao territory during our initial attempt to contact this nearly undiscovered mountain tribe. This place had a hold on us like no other. It had become our home and these people our family. We sat in silence and watched the swift jungle river crash and whirlpool its way down the broad ravine.

We had barely caught our breath before Paatoma scurried back down that twisted jungle tree and rejoined us on the river's edge. While raising his voice to be heard over the sound of the churning river rapids, he shouted, "*Eto, daamaa*!" "It will be okay now," he assured us. "They did a good job tying the old vines back together and reinforcing the bridge with fresh green vines after the flood knocked it down a couple moons ago. Don't be afraid friends, I will watch as you cross and then come behind you after you're on the other side!" He could tell by the looks on our tired faces though that neither of us was excited about the crossing.

It seemed like whenever we came to one of these tattered bridges or to a sketchy tree crossing high above a rocky ravine, or when we were getting ready to set out on a long jungle trek such as this one for that matter, there was always the same ominous feeling looming in the background: The feeling of inadequacy. The feeling that leaves us asking ourselves: "Is this really a good idea? Or are we perhaps finally biting off more than we can chew?" Often times once we were well into a journey such as this, we would find that we really had gotten in over our heads. It really was more than we could handle or just downright unhealthy and even borderline insane to keep going. But sometimes in these jungles, there was no turning back. Other times we were just too stubborn to give up.

"I guess I will go first, that way if anything happens to me or the bridge breaks again, you and Paatoma will at least still be on the same side of the river." I yelled to Jennie. "Be careful!" she yelled back "And know that I love you." she added in as I began climbing the tree to get up to the bridge. Those words..."I Love You" we always knew why we were saying them in these moments. Almost like it was a disclaimer, just in case it was our last chance to say it.

The bridge, swaying from the winds that race down through the ravine, hangs about fifteen feet up above the grey, rocky riverbank. Cold spray mists up off of the rapids below. As nice as it would have been to spend a bit more time on those cool mossy river rocks we knew we had to keep moving. We had nearly another four thousand foot jungle mountain to work our way up before sundown. That is, if we wanted to make it to a village with food and shelter and not sleep the night in the open jungle.

Not to mention that Paatoma's older brother and my very close friend Wikipai was said do be deathly ill. The medicines in our backpacks might save his life if we got to him in time and this really was the only trail, the only way to get to Wikipai. Besides this tattered vine bridge, there is no other way past the central Dago River: A river that begins as just a small trickle at the top of a valley surrounded by the cold, wet ten thousand foot jungle mountains of the highlands. The Dago starts out as just the smallest of streams, fed by one side stream after another as it works it's way down through the valley. Many of the small streams and creeks that feed into the Dago are so far up in the unpopulated mountains that they remain unnamed to this day. But then eventually as the stream gains velocity it is joined by bigger streams such as the Matauwoo, and then the Epeadee and the Degeuwo and finally the muddy Taane from the west.

One by one various streams and small rivers both named and unnamed join the Dago until it is so violent it is virtually unstoppable. A raging class four stretch of rapids devouring and pulling under anything in its path. It races, churns and angrily crashes through the mountains until eventually it finds its way down into the hot, blistering lowlands. It winds and snakes its way through mile after mile of muddy jungle towards the northern coast until it eventually begins to slow, only to finally be devoured itself by the great salty Asia Pacific Ocean.

While slowly climbing my way up the twisted jungle tree to get onto the rattan vines, thoughts raced through my mind of what I would do were I to find myself in those class four rapids below the bridge in the next few minutes. They were moving too fast to think I had a good chance of surviving if the vines broke underneath my weight. Not to mention the swirling white and brown whirlpools I could see spinning below. As I looked down I could see swirling torrents twisting their way through the jagged boulders like little tornadoes. I could also see ancient looking broken trees poking their ugly pointed heads up from below the water's surface. As I reached up and grabbed ahold of the first vine, the rattan itself wet from the cold mist that was coming off the churning water below, I began cautiously inching my way onto the vine bridge.

It was built in the typical Dao way. There were only two vines about as thick as a man's wrist running across the breadth of the river, one about four feet above the other. There was one vine for my hands and one vine for my feet. I would have to sidestep across the bridge sideways one baby step at a time. The whole bridge began to sag a few feet closer to the rapids as I began to inch my way across. The tallest Dao person didn't even come up to my shoulder in height and probably didn't weigh much more than half my weight. It became evident that this bridge was not designed for people like me at six feet two inches and nearly two-hundred pounds!

A few more feet across the bridge and I was slowly approaching the center point. Then I heard it. "Snap!........Snap! Snap!" some of the small vines used to hold the bridge together began to break under my weight. Frozen in fear I glanced back behind me at the riverbank towards Jennie and Paatoma. I could see the panic on Jennie's face. Emotion flooded my chest and chills ran up my spine as the bridge began to creak and sway even harder under my weight.

Now that I was at the center point of the bridge, it would have been the same difference whether I turned around or kept going forward. I continued to inch my way forward, the sweat once again flowed down my forehead and burnt my eyes as it trickled down my face. A sharp burning sensation started in the fingers of my right hand. I looked down to see a string of bright red fire ants had also decided to use the vine bridge on that day. Another yard of distance gained and I could feel the sting of the fire ants in my left hand as well as they took turns biting my arms and letting me know of their disapproval that I was trespassing on their bridge.

As I glanced down at my hands again and tried to shake a few of them off I saw that a huge pointed boulder about the size of a small car was waiting to impale me if I were to stumble and fall. I tried to speed up my pace but the faster I went, the more the whole bridge bounced up and down under my weight. Finally, a few more snaps and creaks and I found myself nearing the other side. Coming to the jungle tree holding the other side of the bridge I finally was able to step off of the vines and grab a hold of something solid again. I gave the tree a big bear hug like it was my new best friend and began to work my way down it and onto the other mossy riverbank.

I was nearly sick to my stomach from the swaying and bouncing of the rattan bridge. I turned and gave a victory shout with one fist up in the air then waved to Jennie to go ahead and begin making her way across behind me. As she scaled the tree to begin across the bridge I quickly scurried down below the bridge and onto the riverbank and grabbed a hold of one of the vines which broke during my crossing. Wrapping it a couple times around my forearm I pulled it taunt, trying to help steady the bridge as well as I could for Jennie's crossing.

While scanning the river and rocks to my right as the raging river rushed by, I began searching for a good place to jump in the rapids and try to reach her should she fall from the swaying bridge up above. Jennie being much smaller than I and much more like the Dao people in her weight and height seemed to have better chances than I on a bridge like this but this didn't give me any relief or settle my nerves in the least. As I watched her sidestep onto the rattan vines, to my relief the bridge didn't sag as much under her weight as it had under mine. Flint-faced and undeterred, she inched her way across the vines a little bit at a time.

The look of concern from earlier transformed into a look of sheer determination as she steadily worked her way across the bridge in record time. For her, the bridge remained intact. There was not a single snapping noise during her crossing as there had been for mine. Yet when she neared the end of the bridge and as I climbed back up to the base of the tree to help her down she began to cry. "Why are you crying! You made it! You made it!" I said in a loud voice so that she could hear me above the rapids. As I pulled her close and hugged her there on the riverbank, with the tears streaming down her face she said, "I heard the vines snapping under your weight Scott. I saw the bridge sagging. I thought you were going to fall into the rapids and I am not ready to lose you!"

A few minutes later Paatoma was joining us on the riverbank and laughing with joy that we have all three made it across. Not only had he crossed the bridge with no problem at all but he had done it with one hand! He had decided that he wanted to also carry our faithful little dog Mili across the river as well so that she could also continue on the journey with us. Tail wagging full speed, Mili excitedly pranced circles around us and licked our ankles in amusement that she was reunited with us as well.

Despite our aching knees and tired bodies, it was only a moment before we had our backpacks strapped on and were headed up our second mountain for the day. We were determined to make it to the next hamlet: Todi, before sundown. We knew we would be cutting it close but the thought of sleeping along these trails in the open jungle with the leeches, swarms of biting flies and malaria carrying mosquitos of these lower elevations, combined with the prospect of having no shelter from the nightly jungle rains and winds wasn't the least bit appealing to any of us.

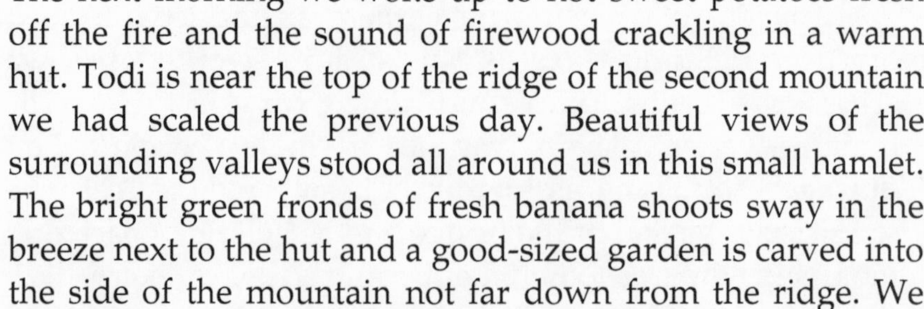

The next morning we woke up to hot sweet potatoes fresh off the fire and the sound of firewood crackling in a warm hut. Todi is near the top of the ridge of the second mountain we had scaled the previous day. Beautiful views of the surrounding valleys stood all around us in this small hamlet. The bright green fronds of fresh banana shoots sway in the breeze next to the hut and a good-sized garden is carved into the side of the mountain not far down from the ridge. We had straggled in just barely before sunset the evening before. Despite the hard ground, we had no problem sleeping the night through thanks to our being completely exhausted from that day's events.

As much as it would have been nice to spend the day there in Todi, we knew that if he was still alive, Wikipai along with his wife and children would be awaiting our arrival. "Paatoma, we better get going. We need to get down to Wikipai as soon as possible" I said. He nodded in agreement as we quickly scarfed down a breakfast of sweet potato and cassava root along with a few cooking bananas. It wasn't long before we were back on the trail making our final descent down the second mountain and towards the village called Taomi .

Only a few years before Taomi had been nothing but a small clearing on the bank of the swift, coffee colored Taane River. The only consistent inhabitants were screeching jungle birds, some tree kangaroos and perhaps an occasional wild pig rooting around by the cool waters edge. Only one small lean-to dotted the lonely stretch of sand and not a single garden as the shelter was only used for people merely passing through: Travelers that were perhaps on hunting trips or on their way to the mountain ridges on the other side of the river. Being the farthest out dwelling place of the Dao people and one of the only hamlets in what was considered the lowlands, it had very few visitors. Some of the Dao people had found out the hard way that this was not the best place to permanently reside.

Some of them had become deathly ill with malaria and other lowlands diseases after making trips to this area for hunting and trading purposes. They had stayed too long and the cerebral malaria of the lowland mosquitos had taken its toll. Traditionally, the Dao people being seminomadic are mountain dwellers moving from hamlet to hamlet and gardening in the cooler, higher elevations of the four to eight thousand foot mountains. They are not used to spending large amounts of time in the lowland areas where the sun beats down much harder and hotter than in the highlands.

Now Taomi was developing into one of the largest Dao villages in existence. The outside world was moving in fast. Traders from other more developed parts of Indonesia were traveling up the lowland rivers seeking to make their profits from the resources of the mountain people's lands. The Dao people themselves knew that there is only one main river by which these outsiders could enter their territory and it was for this very reason that many of them were moving down to this area called Taomi despite the life threatening lowlands diseases and scorching lowland heat.

It was an attempt to control what resources were being taken from their lands. To rightfully demand payment of these outsiders for what was being stolen from their people and to stand up for their tribe against those that would exploit them. Only a few short years after our first entrance into the Dao territory, Taomi had developed into a bustling trade center with over thirty houses and more being built almost every month. These houses were not built by the Dao people but by those that were finding their way the Taane river and looking to make their fortune from the land and people of these once seemingly impenetrable jungles.

Wikipai had long been one of my best friends. Although we didn't know him at the time, he was one of the first to greet us on the riverbanks of the muddy jungle rivers when we stepped foot into Dao territory for the first time. I will never forget the first day I saw him standing there on the edge of the jungle. A lean muscly man with dark eyes and curly black hair, he was sporting the traditional dress of his people: naked with the exception of a gourd on his privates held up by a thin bark string tied around his waist. He also wore a tattered head band of old faded blue cloth to keep the sweat out of his eyes, making him look more like a nearly naked early nineties glam rock singer than a primitive tribesman in the backwoods of Indonesia. He was almost stylish but in an unintentional sort of way.

He looked strong and intimidating as he stood there on the riverbank with his fist full of arrows and a dark wood bow nearly six feet in length. A gleaming white nose bone made of the shinbone from a recently killed cassowary protruded from his nostrils. The soot of ash from the cooking fire darkened his body but at the same time a sweet wide toothed smile beamed from his face as he motioned us closer and invited us to follow him into a small lean-to on the riverbank next to the warm crackling fire.

As we continued to make our descent and get closer and closer to Taomi memories flooded my mind of the adventures Wikipai and I had taken part in together over the years. We had hiked the jungles together many times. He had taught me the Dao ways and spent hours upon hours helping me to learn the culture and language of his people. Many a day we had spent relaxing around the smoldering fire in the men's hut having conversations late into the night about the great Creator Spirit and His leaf book. Both about the same in age and both of us newly married, he had become like a brother to me and now I was proud to see him becoming a leader in his people group.

He had made the long hike down to Taomi not merely to represent his people to the outsiders for the sake of material gain but mainly to begin teaching his people about a new talk that they had not yet heard. He wanted the people that had gathered there to also hear the things he had heard about the great Creator Spirit. With his whole heart he desired for them also to know about the words of the leaf book that had changed him and revolutionized his life. Wikipai knew that what his people ultimately needed was not the leaf paper money of the outsiders. There was way more at stake than just material gain. They needed the words from the leaf book of the Creator One even more. He had set out to bring them these words.

Wikipai had been down in this lowlands village for over a month. According to his younger brother Paatoma the lowlands sicknesses were taking their toll. Jennie and I had been looking and waiting for a good opportunity to hike down and take some much needed supplies, medicines and teaching materials to Wikipai and his family. We wanted to support him in his efforts to help his people but we knew that the two-day hike wouldn't be any easy one. We had been told stories of people that died along this same trail and another young tribesman named Kogipiyaa had even told us how his father had a few years earlier died from falling from the same bridge that we knew we would have to cross to get to Wikipai. We had been waiting for the right time to take the journey. When we heard of Wikipai's sicknesses setting in it seemed like there couldn't be a better or more necessary time.

We were finally on the last descent into Taomi. One last corner to turn and we would be walking along a small stream that led down to the village. What a relief to think we were finally almost there. The trail was definitely taking its toll on our bodies, both of us felt the affects of what we jokingly refer to as "sowing machine legs": With each step our legs would involuntarily rapidly shake up and down and quiver because our knees were so tired from the final descent. Our backpacks with the medicines and supplies seemed to press down on our shoulders ten times as heavy as when we initially started the journey. It would be so nice to put our knees in the cool stream beside Taomi and drink some cool, fresh water after that long and grueling trail.

"We are almost there friend! Just a little ways to go!" I yelled up the trail to Paatoma in my excitement. Jennie smiled at the thought of finally getting to rest for a few days. We rounded the last corner and I looked down to my left towards the riverbank to see if I could get a glimpse of anyone from the village. There was a little shelter off separate from the village a few hundred feet from us: a newly built structure that I had not seen before. "Paatoma, it looks as if there is someone lying in that shelter? Who is that?" I asked. Stopping by the stream and turning to face me, "I think that's Wikipai. They must have built a small shelter for him closer to the stream so that in his sickness he could find a little relief from the cool breeze that comes off the fast flowing water." he replied. We picked up the pace, it had been months since I had seen him last.

Another couple hundred feet and we were approaching the structure and the one laying in it. Then as we came within a few feet of the one laying there no one said a word at first. I could hardly recognize him but unfortunately Paatoma was right. It was Wikipai. With the skin hanging off his bones he looked like a completely different person. His eyes were sunken in with dark circles around them and his face gaunt. He looked like not much more than a shallow breathing skeleton. He didn't even have enough strength to sit up and greet us. In that moment, all the sudden it hit us for the first time just how serious his situation was. Neither Jennie nor I could say a word as we watched Paatoma help his older brother Wikipai to sit up so that he could greet us. A feeling of desperation flooded my chest as I stared at Wikipai there in such a state. I couldn't believe that the situation was so bad.

Subconsciously I guess I hadn't come to terms with the fact that he could be this bad off. Sure, I knew that he was sick but in my mind I still pictured him as the strong, bow and arrow clenching, muscle covered tribesman I had always known. Now, he had withered away to the point where he seemed he was on the verge of death itself. Trying my best not to break down I tried to swallow the lump in my throat and shake the feeling off but I couldn't hold back the tears any longer. I placed my hand on his shoulder as his brother Paatoma helped him up and began to uncontrollably weep at the thought of losing him. I just couldn't process that it had come to this.

With the little bit of strength he had remaining he motioned to us he wanted to speak. Very slowly and in almost a whisper he began: *"Oh friend, do not cry for me. Do not cry for me. Yes, it is true that my body is wasting away. I am like a jungle stream that has not been fed by the rain for many days. But although my body is very weak, my spirit is strong. I know what the Great Creator One's Son has done for me. And if I die here in this place, then that is what the Creator One has chosen for me. I am ready to go. Do not cry for me."*

He said every word with such a sweet smile on his face. But whether he was ready to go or not, I was not ready for him to go! Surely he would live. Surely this Great Creator Spirit he had spoken of would not take him. Of all the people that He could take, surely He would not take Wikipai, one of the only members of the Dao tribe that cared at all about helping his people.

In an attempt to check his hydration level, Jennie reached over and lightly pinched some of the skin on Wikipai's arm and it stood straight up even after she let go. This told us that he was severely dehydrated and that we needed to get as much fluids in him as quickly as possible. His wife arrived a few minutes later from the garden and told us Wikipai had not been able to keep any food down for days. We immediately began taking the medicines and some food supplies out of our bags to begin treating him. Paatoma got some wood together and started a fire so that we could cook him some of the food rations we had carried down. We all knew that Wikipai's only chance of survival was to get the antibiotics working as soon as possible and to get him eating and drinking again. We would try to get him back into the highlands to his village two days hike away. We prayed as we administered the medicine and began pleading with God to spare his life. I had never prayed so hard in my whole life but only time would reveal to us if Wikipai would survive.

Chapter 2

My Highway to Hell : A Sinner's Prayer

We are never living but hoping to live. And whilst we are always preparing to be happy, it is certain we shall never be so, if we aspire to no other happiness than what can be enjoyed in this life.

Blaise Pascal,
Thoughts On Religion And Philosophy

That city was so exciting and animated at night. The world felt like it was mine on nights like those. Late in the evening after everyone else in the house was seemingly asleep I would climb out the second story bedroom window of our brown and white Dutch style house and stretch out under the stars on the rough sandpaper shingles of the roof. The cool evening breeze brushed up against me as the distant roar of crowds going wild with cheers loomed in the background from the baseball stadium in one direction. In the other direction the dark night sky lit up with the deafening pops, colorful bursts and falling crackles of Disneyland's grand finale fireworks as the colors bounced and reflected off of the suburb rooftops all around me.

The streets bustled with the weekend traffic as news helicopters with their neon flashing taillights zoomed along a few hundred feet above the six lane freeways while giving their traffic reports. I could hear jet liners rumble in and out of the largest and busiest airport on the west coast every few minutes. Even the Good Year blimp was out lazily drifting around among the glittering high rises and seemingly trying to get in on the Saturday night action.

I loved that city. The beautiful beaches were on one side and the snow capped mountains were on the other side. Los Angeles was so big to me. The air and atmosphere so full of emotion and movement. So many different types of people from so many different places in the world all in one place living life and feeding the excitement. I felt so alive here. It was all I had ever known, it was my world and Saturday night was the best of the best!

Sunday morning couldn't have been much more opposite. I sheepishly walked into the towering church building, the cathedral ceiling so high above. The tall brass pipes of the organ lined the wall like prison bars behind the pulpit. The stained glass windows refracted unnatural color patterns down on the stage as I sat in an old creaky wooden pew nervously glancing up at the preacher from time to time. The neck tie that I had been forced to wear to "Look my best for Jesus" was nearly choking me and those stiff hand me down dress shoes were killing my feet.

Then as the preacher drew the service to a close, once again the ever-present questions that had been haunting me for so long would begin: "Why is it never enough? How come I am never any better off after I pray this 'Sinner's Prayer'?" I wondered time and time again why I couldn't experience the reconciliation and freedom from fear and guilt that I longed for. I was a young teenager and there was no one that could give me an answer. Every Sunday my God-fearing parents would make sure my two brothers and I were in the local church. Every week I would sit in the church feeling the weight of God's judgment crushing down on me, knowing deep down inside that even though I knew the right answers in Sunday School, I didn't have a clue who the real God of the Bible was or what He or She might be like.

Once again the Sunday sermon was drawing to a close. "If you don't know for sure that you would go to heaven were you to die today, then just repeat the words of this 'Sinners Prayer' after me." The preacher said from his tall wooden pulpit. He seemed to be looming over me looking down on me as if I was right then and there going to be cast into the fire. I felt as if the floor was going to open up and swallow me at any moment. I felt so desperate, so heavy from the weight of my guilt and fear and I had felt this way for such a long, long time. All I wanted was release.

"Just repeat this little prayer after me" he said once again. "I pray this prayer and repeat these words every Sunday! Nothing ever changes! I still feel the same!" I thought to myself. I felt like I could stand up and scream in the middle of the congregation. "But maybe this time it will finally work. If I pray this prayer of penance just one more time maybe I will be spared," I reasoned with myself. I will try again just this one last time. *"Dear Jesus, I ask you to please come into my heart. I invite you to come into my life. I want to go to heaven…Amen."* Even after I was done praying I kept my eyes squeezed shut, waiting, hoping that something would happen. Perhaps it had worked? Perhaps I had right then and there finally been "saved". Maybe I would finally feel different this time? After a few moments I slowly opened my eyes and looked up towards the pulpit.

Was I finally a true "Christian"? Did this special prayer finally work? I hoped with everything in me that God was finally seeing me as one of His own. Then I would finally be accepted by Him and perhaps be set free from the weight of my fear of His judgment and Hell. As the days went on however those old familiar feelings of guilt and judgment weighed down on me once again. It often seemed I couldn't even look up towards the sky without being reminded that there is a great big God above those skies, looking down at me, poised and ready to cast me into the hellfire at any moment. Nothing was different. Everything was still the same. This "Sinner's Prayer" had failed me once again. "Maybe I wasn't saying the words to the prayer right or with enough feeling? Or maybe God just didn't want to save me. Maybe I should resign myself to damnation and just give up all together. Why would the great God of the universe care about someone like me anyways?"

After a week of carpooling, math tests, all the mellow dramatic episodes of the teenage life and the hassles of the Los Angeles schooling system it was finally Friday again! Every couple weeks when my mom would pick us up after school on Friday, instead of heading back home for a night of monotonous homework we would drive down to our favorite beach, Corona Del Mar and enjoy a fun filled afternoon in the Southern California sun and surf. It seemed Dad was typically gone two to three weekends out of every month on business trips but Mom would almost always find some way to make up for it.

She would pull up to the school in the families old white station wagon with that classic wood paneling down the side: the car stuffed with various beach boards, lawn chairs and that classic red and white igloo cooler. My brothers and I would all cram into the old wagon with our school bags and all the beach paraphernalia and we would head down to the golden brown sands of the California ocean side. Then we would spend the afternoon playing in the surf and combing the beach for various shells and sea creatures to add to our collection. The little Chinese immigrants with their pointy Asian hats were out collecting seaweed as usual. The old bronzed saggy skinned men with their metal detectors and gold medallion necklaces also were there scanning the sand for dropped change and jewelry from the mornings tourists and sunbathers. Mom set up her favorite lawn chair, pulled a book out of her purse and relaxed in the sun while she watched my brothers and I splash around in the surf and chase each other up and down the beach.

Often times, when I grew tired from fighting the tide currents and crashing waves I would walk around in the little shallow caves on that beach: seawater caves and craters that over thousands of years have been pounded out by the huge waves during high tide. I wandered from cave to cave feeling like an explorer or treasure hunter searching for some ancient chest full of gold coins that pirates had perhaps buried and forgotten about over time. In the little pools of the rock formations here I saw colorful and interesting sea anemones. Starfish dotted the floor just below the water's surface and little hermit crabs scurried all around the rocks, frantically running for their lives as they saw me coming. The hundreds of little turquoise colored pools filled up with salty water as the tide came in and then whirlpooled back out into the ocean again. I could explore these little caves and pools for hours.

Even in this place however there was always an ongoing spiritual battle looming in the back of my mind. I would look out at the powerful waves of the ocean crashing and barreling towards the coast and think "God created those powerful waves and they could swallow me in an instant". I felt the sand or salty ocean mist on my face and thought about how God was the One that controlled even the wind streams and ocean currents. I stared into the pools at the sea life and anemones and knew deep down inside that the same God that created all of those interesting and colorful little sea creatures was the God that had created me. He was the same God that I feared so much and couldn't feel accepted by no matter how hard I tried. The cool ocean breeze hitting my cold saltwater soaked surf shorts reminded me that the day was coming to a close. The sun started to make its way down towards the deep blue horizon of the Pacific Ocean. Mom would be expecting me to start heading back down the beach for our traditional hotdog roast about now. I stood up and brushing the powdery sand from my shorts, began running back down the beach.

This was my favorite part of the evening, the part I looked forward to the most. I knew my brothers and I would find Mom starting a fire in one of the public cast iron fire rings there on the beach and we would all together sit around roasting hot dogs and laughing as we wiggled our toes in the cold sand. We crammed our mouths with packaged mystery meat and then finished it all off with s'mores until we couldn't eat another bite. Then finally when our stomachs had hit full capacity, with the pale moon high above the ocean and it being nearly too dark to see anymore outside of the flickering fire reflecting off the deep brown sands, we would drowsily pile everything back in our old station wagon and begin heading home. The city lights flashing by the car windows one at a time lulled my brothers and I to sleep as we looked forward to Saturday morning television and no school.

We also had a family tradition that played itself out on most Saturdays. We would come running down the stairs of our big two story house and my mom would always have a five dollar bill in hand or waiting for us on the kitchen table. One of us boys would snatch the bill up and with huge grins on our faces we would run out the front door and jump on our skateboards to make our way towards Rose's Donut Shop. It was just over a mile but it seemed like only a few hundred feet as we skated down the sidewalk laughing and maneuvering our way around all the trashcans and through the various driveways and alleys. The donut shop was your typical hole in the wall little bakery but something about it seemed almost magical.

The little Asian lady behind the counter had all the best flavors with the most colorful sprinkles on top. We could smell the fresh made sugary goodness in the parking lot before we even made it to the donut shop door. She would pull out that big pink classic donut box and say in a thick Chinese accent "What will it be this week guys?" My brothers and I got four picks each, which made a dozen. We took turns choosing our favorites until we had hit our twelve-donut quota and then we were back out the door again and skateboarding home as fast as we could. Laying belly down in a circle on the living room floor, we would divide our spoils into separate piles and then eat donuts while flipping through Saturday morning cartoons and sitcoms.

One Saturday came along though that the mood of the house was different. Dad was home for the weekend, which in itself was fairly unusual but in addition to that my parents just weren't acting like themselves. Apparently Dad had brought home some important news from his last trip. They told us we needed to sit down and talk as a family about something important. We all sat down in the living room and Dad began to tell us about how he just received word that the organization he worked for wanted him to move our family from the suburbs of Los Angeles California to central Florida. He was getting a promotion and position change. My brothers and I were going to be uprooted from everything we had ever known.

At first I thought maybe things would be better there in Florida. Maybe I would somehow feel new and different in a new place. It would be quite adventurous to drive across the entire United States! I had never even left the West Coast after all! Our weekends were filled with yard sales and excited anticipation. We began making plans to move and my brothers and I huddled around maps in the evenings talking and dreaming about all the cool things we might see along the way to Florida. It wasn't long before the final days had been counted down and we were on the highway with a giant orange and white U-Haul moving truck lumbering along behind us. We were headed for our new home over two thousand five hundred miles away. Mom had packed some of her homemade specialties in tin foil for the trip and my brothers and I took turns sitting on the big leather bench seat in the moving truck with Dad.

It felt like we could see the whole world from that big high seat. The highway and the big open skies stretched out before us for miles once we got out of Los Angeles and worked our way towards the central states. I had never seen anything like it! The dry rocky gorges and bright, ancient walls of the Grand Canyon, the green, bristly, eight foot tall cactus and paint ball sized hail stones of New Mexico, the wide open golden plain lands and miles upon miles of corn and cotton fields in the Midwest. It was all so different from the city, where houses were built virtually on top of each other only a few feet apart at the most, where you would be hard-pressed to find even a little bit of wide-open empty space. After nearly a week of driving we were finally nearing the Florida border. The dry Spanish moss hanging from the old grey oak trees and swinging in the breeze looked strange. I was surprised at how flat everything was as we made our way just past the Georgia border and saw a gigantic rusty "Welcome to Sunny Florida" sign on the side of interstate seventy-five. Where were the snow-capped mountains like the ones I had grown up seeing from our front yard in Southern California?

We worked our way down route seventy-five another four hours before we finally came to our exit. An old worn highway sign had an arrow pointing to the right towards a town called Hudson. We worked our way another forty minutes or so down backcountry roads and then eventually turned right down an unpaved, dusty limestone road covered with potholes. The place seemed eerie to me and almost scary the way the big oak trees stretched out their twisted branches over the streets, the grey curly moss reaching down in large swaying clumps and getting tangled around the antenna of the moving truck. There wasn't a single street light for miles. "Surely this is not where we're moving too? Where are all the other houses and the city lights? Where are we?" I thought to myself as we finally pulled into a long curvy driveway. I could feel my heart sink as Dad sleepily announced to the family in a dry cracked voice "Here we are. Our new home!"

⟷

It wasn't but a few weeks before my parents had us boys in a local private school. They were trying to do everything they could to make us feel comfortable in this new place but I had never felt more alone. The only close friends that I had ever had in my life were back in California and were gone. Most of the teens at the podunk private school my parents enrolled us in there in Florida were very standoffish. Over our first few days there they had decided that our California accents made us socially unacceptable. On top of that, for some reason they thought that the only people living in California were homosexuals and weirdoes so they renamed me "The California Queer".

I had no idea what to think of it all. Not only did my ongoing spiritual battle leave me feeling rejected by God Himself, but it also seemed as if the entire world was turning against me, as even my peers that I was forced to spend every day with wanted nothing to do with me. I tried out for various school sports to try to find a way in and I actually wasn't too bad at them. The coach was a loud, red-faced angry man named Coach Dave. He would scream at the players and call us every name in the book if we didn't make every shot or do things exactly the way he thought they should be done. I couldn't stand him. After a few weeks of being daily verbally and emotionally abused, I came to the conclusion that this also wasn't worth my effort. I quit the sports teams not long after I had gotten on them as the last thing I wanted was a coach screaming obscenities at me all afternoon day after day.

There was only one thing that I still had that made me feel like me. Something that provided me with an outing, something I had carried with me since we left California and that still made me feel at home no matter where I was. I began to carry it everywhere with me. It was the only thing that enabled me to still feel some measure of freedom and release again. It was a little piece of California that I still had. It was my skateboard and from that point on my skateboard became my life. There were no referees or coaches to scream obscenities at me and tell me that I was doing it all wrong. I didn't have to talk to anyone if I didn't want to. I could ride for hours by myself whether I had anyone to skate with or not and just feel the way I did back in the streets and alleys of the big city.

Every day of my last couple years of high school I would sit through all the name-calling and the miserable surroundings and look forward to only one thing: When that last bell for the day would ring, I would be out the door and back on my skateboard. I even began to enter a few contests and won one of them but the competitive side of things always seemed ugly to me. All the joy of the activity seemed to be lost when I was just skating to beat someone else. So I turned my attention to the streets and would just spend most afternoons and evenings searching for old abandoned and interesting buildings I could skate in. I scavenged wood from construction sites and then built ramps in the old abandoned buildings.

It was through this I finally met some unusual people that seemed to accept me as I was. People who had also been rejected by the usual crowds of well to do locals. They were scavengers that lived in the old buildings that had been abandoned. They survived on the excess of society and lived by a different set of rules. They did what they wanted, when they wanted and talked to whom they wanted to. They didn't care what anybody thought of them and I admired them for it. Old Tom was my favorite. He stunk like stale beer and urine and had a pale yellow and white chest length beard. His face was wrinkled and darkened from years wandering under the hot Florida sun. He had the old parched raspy voice of a sea captain and a sense of humor that enabled him to laugh at even the weightiest things in life. He lived in the doorway of a closed down bank.

This old bank, though dilapidated, had an unusually smooth parking lot and some nice painted curbs sheltered from the rain by an overhang where the money tellers used to be. It was a perfect place for skateboarding. Tom could barely walk. This was partially because half the time he was too drunk to stand. The other reason though was that he was severely malnourished. He was skin and bones because of his limited diet of leftovers from dumpsters and whatever else he could find and possibly also because of his high alcohol intake. He had a couple friends named Sally and Bill that I also got to know and enjoyed spending time with.

They would all sit under the overhang of the old bank front and cheer for me when I landed a new skateboard trick I had been trying for a while.

Old Tom would hold up his beer and let out a big drunken bellow of approval with a heavily slurred "Good job Scottieeeeeee!" I didn't mind that he stunk. I didn't even mind that he and Sally and Bill were almost always drunk. I just knew they enjoyed having me around. They didn't care where I was from or what I talked like. They didn't curse at me or ever act too busy to spend some time sitting around shooting the breeze. They never had a business meeting to rush off to or a place to be at for work. They had all the time in the world. They became some of my best friends.

The business my Dad worked for was part conference center, part youth camp and part religious concert venue. Every weekend the center would hold huge concerts that sometimes thousands of people would attend. The price of the concert ticket included a four star meal cooked by professional chefs: meals that would go for at least twenty to thirty dollars a plate. After the meal was over and the crowds had gone on to the concert there was always thousands of dollars worth of leftovers. Gourmet food put in large plastic bags and thrown in the dumpster. I worked in the kitchen part time washing dishes and so I began collecting the leftovers from the meals and taking them to Old Tom and my other new found friends. After a while they had other friends also that were coming to the old run down bank in hopes of getting some free food. For a while it became almost a daily routine. I would work the dish pit, gather the leftover food that was being thrown away and in the evening head out to skate my favorite bank and hook Old Tom and his buddies up with the nights leftovers.

Then one evening as I finished up work for the night and began putting the leftovers in bags as usual for my friends, "What are you doing with that food, Scott?" I heard from across the huge brown tiled kitchen. "I am taking it to my buddies that don't have much food otherwise like usual, I have told you about that haven't I?" I replied. "Yes you have told me but we have health standards here. We can't be responsible for anybody getting sick from food that has gone cold after a meal. The health department has rules about these things and they could shut us down!" the head chef continued.

"What do you mean? The government health department would shut you down just because you're trying to make use of the leftovers?" I asked. "Yes. And that is why all that food in that bag has to go in the dumpster, it can't go to your friends." The chef said in a dry nonchalant sort of way. I couldn't even believe what I was hearing. How could the government make rules like this first of all, and even beyond that, how could it ever under any circumstances be right to throw away so much food on a regular basis when there are people that are in need of it? I mean really, how could there even be people like Old Tom and his buddies in the USA that were suffering from malnutrition when there were so many people living in absolutely grotesque excess and obesity wherever I looked?

I couldn't understand it. I was so angry at what I was hearing. I began hiding food in the bushes and behind the dumpsters in the evenings when I would take out the night's garbage from the evening meal. Who cared what the government thought. Who cared even what the old chef thought. "If they won't give me permission to take it, I will just steal it!" I concluded.

⟷

It wasn't long before high school graduation was fast approaching. I still hated Florida, not to mention that my relationship with my parents was deteriorating. I was still "stealing from the rich and giving to the poor" and spending my free time skating in abandoned buildings. Those last couple years of high school in Florida were probably when I needed my Dad the most. Dad was even busier than he had been in my younger years though. He was gone working so much every day and was so busy with his new position that I felt like I barely knew him. Mom had also taken on more responsibilities and was working part time with the same organization as my Dad and so I saw a lot less of her as well.

Those fun times we had experienced together on the beaches of Corona Del Mar were nothing but a distant memory. All I could think about was Los Angeles. I longed for the excitement and energy of the city I had grown up in. I wanted to feel happy again, I wanted to see my old friends again and skate through the streets and alleys of the suburbs like I used to. Perhaps this was where I belonged? It definitely felt more like home than anywhere else. On graduation day I told my parents of my plans to return to Los Angeles. They didn't work against me but they did request one last thing of me before I returned to California: They wanted me to spend at least two semesters at a Christian Bible college in upper state New York. "After that, your free to go where you want" they said.

This was their one last request. "Just two semesters" they told me. They even offered to provide all the funds necessary for the school: all I had to do was go. I didn't want to go but after thinking about it and counting up my savings from the part time job in the dish pit, I knew I didn't have enough money to make it back to Los Angeles by myself. After a few days I reluctantly agreed to their wishes. "Wow.... Christian Bible College" I sighed under my breath with a reluctant feeling in my chest. In the back of my mind loomed that old familiar darkness I had dealt with my whole life: Feelings of rejection by God, the failed "Sinner's Prayer", the old rituals, suits and ties, and "Lets look our best for Jesus" spiel. The Christian culture I had seen growing up literally made me sick to my stomach. I didn't want anything to do with it and the last place I would escape it was at a Christian college.

As far as I was concerned the whole idea was a disaster waiting to happen, nonetheless it would at least get me out of Florida. I packed my bags and my skateboard and my parents drove me up to New York. They dropped me off at what I thought would be the first step in my quest to get back home to L.A. Needless to say things didn't go well. Within the first couple months I had gotten into a lot of trouble, mouthed-off to superiors and was finally put on probation. The Dean of the college gave strict instructions that because of all the trouble that I regularly got into, I was not to leave my dorm room at all except for meals and classes or I would be expelled from the school. I was nearly bored out of my mind from being confined to a small college dorm room all day every day. Not to mention that this was such a conservative school that there was no TV, radio, music or anything else of the sort allowed. After rigging up a tattoo gun from an electric shaver and a sowing needle, I began giving myself homemade tattoos to pass the time. Being expelled was inevitable. It was only a matter of days.

One morning after I had put on the suit, tie, dress pants and stiff dress shoes that the Christian school dress code required, I headed out the door and began skating down the street to class. This was the only few minutes of the day I actually enjoyed at the moment, the few minutes in between my dorm room and the class room when I was on my skateboard again with my wheels under my feet and the wind whistling through my hair again. There was a new teacher there to teach us a special class for only one week but by that time I had pretty much checked out altogether mentally. For the most part I didn't care what was being taught in classes, I was just doing my time and counting down the days until this nightmare would be over and I would be free from this "one last obligation" from my parents.

Upon hearing his first words into the mic though I noticed right off the bat that this teacher was different from the others for various reasons. His name was Mr. Moyer and he had a severe speech impediment. "What is this guy doing teaching a class when he doesn't even have the ability to speak correctly?!" I thought to myself. Some of the other students even covered their mouths and chuckled to each other while he talked. This strange situation caught my attention however. I strained to understand every word and I felt respect for a man that would stand up in front of hundreds of students like that despite his physical inadequacies. Despite the fact that he could look out at the sea of college students and literally see people trying not to laugh at him as he talked. He was another one of the few I had come across in my life that really could care less what people thought of him. He was like Old Tom and my other stinky buddies back in Florida, but in a different sort of way.

His speech impediment and his "who cares if the world is laughing at me" sort of attitude made me want to strain to understand every mispronounced and stuttered word that came out of his mouth. He was so uncool that I thought he was cool. Then as he continued to teach the class that day he said something that I had never heard before. He began talking of what it really means to have faith in Jesus. "Faith", I had heard this Christian buzz word my whole life. It was a word that I had heard so many times in fact that it became stale and dry and old. But as Mr.Moyer continued on talking about what it means to have true faith, he began quoting some verses from the Bible in the book of Romans and John and then another from Ephesians saying, *"It is by grace that you are saved through faith. This is a gift from God that comes not from yourselves so that no man can brag about it".*

Mr. Moyer continued "If you are trusting in anything at all to get you to Heaven in addition to Jesus Christ alone and His finished work on the cross on your behalf, then you are looking straight into the face of God and telling Him that what His Son Jesus did on the cross isn't good enough. You are telling God that He might as well not have sent His son Jesus at all."

That statement got my attention. The more I thought about it the more it absolutely blew me away. Suddenly I realized what the problem had been all these years. All along, since I was just a kid in Los Angeles, I had been trying to gain acceptance with God through a man made ritual called the "Sinner's Prayer". All these years I had been trying over again and again to say these special words just right, just as the preacher had told me to say them. My faith never had been, even the tiniest bit, in the finished work of this man Jesus Christ. In that moment I was faced with the dark realization that I had been deceived.

This "Sinner's Prayer", this ritual, had been for me nothing more than a highway straight to hell. My whole life I had been trying to gain God's approval through a decoy that could never be anything but a shallow substitute for the real thing. Though I knew about Jesus and even many of the right answers about Him my trust was in a man made Christian church ritual that could never save me. I realized that day that the salvation of the Bible is not about this "Sinner's Prayer". It isn't about saying the right words or correctly speaking a special Christian incantation that I had been taught since I was a small child. It is not about "looking your best for Jesus", or following a set of rules, or being a good Christian American citizen. It is not about whether or not I ask Jesus to "come into my heart" or to "come into my life". These western rituals will never suffice for the finished work of Jesus Christ Himself.

Jesus was all along there waiting with outstretched arms. True salvation is nothing more than falling back into those arms and trusting Him to do what He came to do. Now I had finally realized that it is all about Jesus, not me. It is all about His death on the cross, burial and then His resurrection to prove He is who He claimed to be, God's

Son. There was no turning back from that point. No longer could I in the words of Mr. Moyer "look in the face of God and tell him that His son Jesus' sacrifice on the cross is not enough". I knew I needed to trust in what Jesus had done for me, not in anything I had done or any special magical words I had spoken in hopes of gaining His approval.

Tears began rolling down my face as this realization sank in. For the first time I felt the presence of God's Spirit inside of me. Chills shot down my spine and the hair stood up on the back of my neck as I felt the burden of judgment and sin that I had carried for so long lifted off of my shoulders. I had been in church my whole life but that was the day God decided to open my eyes. I knew that finally God now saw me as part of His family. There wasn't a doubt in my mind from that day forward that I was forgiven. The weight of fear and judgment that I had carried around with me as long as I could remember was gone. Jesus Christ had succeeded where the "Sinner's Prayer" had failed.

Chapter 3

Skate or Live

God has a plan for the world and a role for each one of us in that plan... Too many of us want to make our plans to serve God and then beg Him to come help us when we can't handle things by ourselves. God isn't looking for a co-pilots job. He is in the front seat and is offering us a position as his crew.

Steve Saint,
The Great Omission

My life was changed. All creation and the sky itself even seemed more beautiful and vibrant as I no longer saw these things as reminders of God's judgment. The magnificent Adirondack mountains there in New York lay spread out one behind another, layer upon layer of vibrant forest greens and eventually cobalt blue defiantly jutting up from the earths surface. These became reflections to me of the power and glory of a loving God that finally saw me as His own and wanted me to rejoice in his Creation.

I could see His character reflected in the fact that even the lowliest and tiniest of His creations had plenty to eat and a place to live provided by His hand. I could see His appreciation of beauty and his artistic eye in the loud bursts of color that blend together so perfectly during a sunrise or a sunset, or as the seasons change from summer to fall and then eventually to the clean gleaming white of winter. My whole perspective was different now that I had been set free to know the true God of the Bible. I wanted to know Him in ways deeper than I had ever known about him. He had changed me.

When the year was over, instead of heading back to Los Angeles I moved down to Chattanooga, Tennessee to continue studying theology and the Bible. Chattanooga was my only option for continuing on with school because there was a Christian college there with ties to my recently deceased grandfather who had been a professor there for some time. Since my grandfather had taught as a professor there for so long, they offered me tuition free education in his honor. Although I didn't care much for the school itself, all I knew was that this was a place where I could study God and in the meantime finish up college for free. While I studied, I could also work and save up money to head back to Los Angeles.

While I still had the same passion for skateboarding and other things that I enjoyed like tattoos and playing music, now I had the desire to use those things for God's glory and to make Him known. I honestly couldn't shut up about the things I was learning about Jesus. Shortly afterwards I met a few other skateboarders there in Chattanooga that were interested in studying the life and teachings of Jesus as well. So we began meeting together on Saturday mornings in different coffee shops around town to talk about what we were reading in the Bible and learning in our own studies throughout the week.

I imagine we were quite the sight to the locals walking in for their usual Saturday coffee and bagel: tattoo's, dreadlocks, beat up shoes, punk patches, skateboards and Bibles. We would sit around studying out different sections of the Scriptures and talking about what we were learning through it. For the first time in my life, I was finding release and freedom in God, instead of just on my skateboard. I had found something that was worth more to me and made me feel more loved and happy than anything this world could offer. To me, God had become someone that no activity or possession could ever be a substitute for. Someone that accepted me as I was and wanted to get to know me as a son as much as I wanted to get to know Him as a Father.

By day, downtown Chattanooga was all businessmen and bankers in starched collars and five hundred dollar suits. They would nervously run around like busy little ants. With a latté in one hand and business folders in the other they would speed walk from building to building going in and coming back out again. Late at night however, when the business hours were over and the streets were nearly empty, the city was ours! We would cruise the streets and parking garages and take turns doing tricks down the shiny marble stairs of the big business buildings and banks for hours.

One particular night, long after the sun had set and the city streets had once again transformed into a ghost town of stairs, rails and skateboarding obstacles, a couple of us decided to go downtown to skate. There was one specific skate spot, our favorite one in fact, where we had to watch the traffic lights carefully to not interfere with any late night oncoming traffic. A set of white marble stairs with ledges on both sides stood caddy cornered next to a traffic light. We could do grinds and slides across the marble ledges that lined the stairs, but the landing was right in the middle of the street under the intersection stop lights. We would watch the lights for each other and call out when it was clear to go.

When it was my turn, I took a quick glance to the traffic light on my left and since it was red, I jumped on my board and headed full speed towards the stairs. Coming to the edge of the stair set, I snapped the tail of my skateboard off the ground and locked into a solid fifty-fifty grind down the marble ledge then flew out into the street to catch my landing. I was in mid-air above the stairs about to land in the street when the traffic light turned green and the blinding white of headlights came flying across the intersection directly towards me. Everything felt like it went into slow motion as my skateboard wheels hit the pavement and I rolled out into the middle of the street.

I was met by the screeeeeeech of tires and the feeling of my heart dropping down into my stomach. Realizing I was about to be run over I yelled out loud as the car slid directly at me, now within only inches of my kneecaps. With my eyes closed I braced myself for the impact and what I thought would be my last second on earth. Wham! My hands slammed down on the hood of the car. With my knees resting against the cold steel of the front bumper I slowly lifted my head upwards toward the windshield. While standing there completely shocked that I hadn't been flattened like a piece of road kill I heard the words "Are you okay?! Are you hurt?!" being frantically yelled out the car window. I cautiously glanced up at the driver's side to look at the face of the person sitting behind the steering wheel. There sat a curly headed, blonde haired, blue-eyed girl already half way out the car.

I knew it was my fault and I thought for sure that whomever it was that was sitting behind that wheel would be irate. But for some reason the girl looked at me with concern instead of anger. Looking down I double-checked my knees while I brushed the dirt of my pants from the car bumper. Immediately the thought came to mind that had that car stopped only a few feet later I might be dead. I was grateful to be alive. "WOW! That was a close one wasn't it!" I said to the girl with a nervous laugh. "It's okay though, I know where I would have gone had I been run over!" I said to her as I picked up my skateboard and walked over to the side of the road, my hands still slightly shaking from the incident. Then the thought occurred to me that there couldn't be a better time to share with someone about my newfound faith in Jesus than in a moment like that. I looked at the girl and said with a half smile on my face "What about you? Do you know what would happen to you if you were the one that nearly got run over?" She sat there with an inquisitive look on her face, somewhat baffled by the question.

"Are you a Christian?" she replied. "That is interesting if you are because I just placed my trust in Jesus this past week and I literally have no Christian friends at all that I can talk to about these things! My name is Jennie, what's yours?" She pulled her car over to the side of the road and we ended up sitting right there on the curb close by the spot where she had nearly killed me and talked about God and spiritual things until almost midnight. "Hey, every Saturday myself and some other skaters meet together to study the teachings of Jesus and talk about this same stuff at a coffee shop down the road. You should join us if you have the time." I said as we parted ways.

To my surprise, later on that week she showed up at the coffee shop. I didn't know many other people that were as passionate about discussing spiritual things and learning about God as Jennie was. It seemed like that was all she ever talked about. She was sixteen years old the night that she almost ran me over. She was a junior in high school and I was a sophomore in college. Over the next couple years we became some of the best of friends in a small tight knit group of skaters and gutter punks there in that city. There were many more evenings just like that first one where we would all sit together and talk about everything from God to music, skateboarding and tattoos late into the night. I was encouraged to think that God was doing the same thing in other people's lives that He was doing in mine. It was so great to once again have close friendships. Friendships that were even closer than the ones I had known back in California. Friendships that were centered on a common love for Jesus and an appreciation for what He had done for a bunch of ratty little tattooed skater kids like us.

I finished up two years studying God and theology at that college there in Chattanooga, Tennessee and at the end of the second year got a call from a man in England inviting me to come over with my skateboard and travel from skatepark to skatepark and school to school doing skate demonstrations and sharing about my perspective on God and whatever else was important to me. It sounded like a great opportunity to see some of the world and travel so I told Jennie and the others goodbye and was shortly afterwards on a plane to Western Europe. It was my first time out of the continental United States and God used it to show me that there are other places in the world also where people are searching for spiritual truth. I grew a lot in my understanding of Jesus during those few months and decided that when I returned to America I would go back to that Bible college in New York for another year and continue to study the teachings of Jesus there for two more semesters.

Unknowingly to me, Jennie had also enrolled in that same Bible School in New York even though neither of us had let each other know our plans. She finished her last year of high school her junior summer and then at sixteen, she graduated from high school. She then packed all of her belongings in her old Volvo and even without the full approval of her own family in Tennessee, all alone drove over a thousand miles up to New York from Chattanooga just because she wanted to study the Bible. Her passion was the same as mine. She just wanted to know Jesus and she figured what better way to learn about Jesus then to go to a place where you only study the Bible? We were overjoyed to unexpectedly find ourselves at the same place over a thousand miles away from where she had initially almost killed me.

Over that summer traveling around in Europe and using skateboarding as a platform to share about my faith, I had thought a lot about what I should do with my life. It seemed I was at a crossroads, a time where I had a decision to make concerning what exactly I should to for a living after college. Some of the professors at the schools I attended suggested to the other students and myself that we should try to figure out what *"God's call"* for our life was and go from there. I concluded that since I liked skateboarding and tattoos, God's call on my life must be to start a skateboarding facility in Los Angeles. Perhaps I could use that facility to meet and share with other skaters that seemed to be searching for answers about spiritual things but didn't have people to talk to about it all. Maybe I could also have a tattoo parlor hooked on to the skate park as well and use my interest in tattoos to share about Jesus with others like myself.

By what my teachers at school were telling me, it seemed that I should base what I would do with my life on my own interests and what I liked to spend my time doing. My main passion since I had been a young teen in California seemed to have been skateboarding so it only made sense that this must be what God wanted me to center my life around. I would seek to use my skateboard to make Him known and never had I known or seen a place where all of the board sports from surfing to skateboarding and snowboarding were more popular than in Los Angeles, California. "What better way is there to spend my life than to use it making Jesus known back in the only place that has ever felt like home to me?" I reasoned. So this became my plan and I talked about it openly to Jennie and my other friends there at the school. I even began drawing up plans for my skate park and trying to figure out the logistics of what it would take to start such a business back in L.A.

About half way through that semester of Bible school however I encountered a man that said something very different from what I had heard up to that point concerning finding "God's call". He was a representative from an organization that specializes in finding and helping the last of the unreached tribes that are the farthest back in the jungles and the hardest to reach. His name was Mr. Dunn Gordy and he had come to the school to teach a class called "Tribal Missions". He struck me as a very odd man from the very first time he walked into the classroom and I remember raising my eyebrows at him in sheer confusion.

He had the swagger of an old John Wayne western and the costume to go with it. Clip-clopping his way through the door and up to the podium wearing cowboy boots, a good-sized cowboy hat and sporting a huge confederate army belt buckle he precariously leaned forward, removed his ridiculous hat and in a long drawn out sort of way said "Howdy y'all". With the school being located in upper state New York, his thick southern accent would have caught anybody's attention in that deep northern territory but he didn't seem to care about that in the least. He must have been the first teacher I had seen that year to not come in wearing a perfectly prim and proper suit and tie. He was his own man and proud of it.

This man had been to and was talking about places and small remote countries so far back in the jungles that most of us didn't even know they existed. He had recently returned from the South Pacific Islands and I will never forget those letters He brought with him. Stacks of letters from tribal people begging for someone to come and live with them and teach them about their Creator. He read them from the stage one after the other. He made copies of the letters and handed them out in class. I couldn't believe what I was reading. "We want to know how to go to God's good place after we die. We don't want to go to the place of fire but we have no one to teach us. Please send someone quickly before too many more of us die!" one letter said. Another letter described the Good News of eternal life as "a big jar of sweet, delicious cookies" that we Americans and Westerners are "keeping all for ourselves because they are so good that we don't want to share."

Another one of the letters from a tribal man that had recently had the opportunity to hear some of the Bible taught in his own language and village for the first time asked a very thought provoking question to the man that came to their village to teach them. "How long have you Americans known about this message you have shared with us?" the tribal man asked, to which the teacher replied "Well, I learned about Jesus and what He did for me from my father." "So who did your father learn this important message from?" the tribal man asked. "He learned of it from my grandfather who probably also learned about it from his own father and so on." the teacher replied. "Well if your people have had this message for so long and it really is important to them and true for all people, why didn't your great grandfather come and tell it to my great grandfather? Why didn't your grandfather come tell mine and why did your father not come share this with my father and mother before they died?" It was a question for which the teacher had no answer.

After Mr. Gordy read those letters from the stage and shared for a few days I remember one specific class he taught that seemed to split the student body right down the middle because of the controversial statements he was making. He had decided to tackle the concept that many of my other college professors had often referred to as *"God's call"*. Up until that point I had been completely confident in what I believed God's call and purpose was for my life and I was more than comfortable with the thought of skateboarding the rest of my life away in California while sharing about Jesus with people there. Mr. Gordy handed out to everyone in the class a form, which he called "The Great Commission Exemption Form". It had all kinds of thought provoking statements in it like "If you believe that everything that Jesus teaches in the Bible applies to you EXCEPT for His command in Matthew 28 to *'Go into all the world and preach the gospel to EVERY creature'* please check this box and sign your name here."

Many of the other students and even some of my close friends got so angry about the things that he said during that specific class and those "Great Commission Exemption Forms". It was as if they felt threatened by it all. Like their thoughts and dreams of Christian coffee shops and Christian t-shirt companies and being in a Christian rock band and whatever else were being threatened right before their eyes. For me however, it was a week that turned my whole world upside down and that I felt absolutely liberated by. It was that week that I realized for the first time that the infamous "Call of God" that I had so often heard about in my previous college classes was not something that I had to wait for. It was something that I already had. Something that was written down in ink and that I already had in my hands!

I was not exempt from Jesus command to "go into ALL the world" any more than any of my fellow classmates were. These words of Jesus applied to all of us and if I truly claimed to follow the teachings of Jesus, I should be just as ready to follow these words as any other words He said. I couldn't just pick which of Jesus' teachings and commands I liked, or that I felt fit my own plans and scrap the rest! "Surely someone like me shouldn't go to remote places like that, I rationalized. What about my passion for skateboarding? There's no concrete in the jungle. Couldn't I just start my skate park back in Los Angeles where I had grown up and talk to kids there about Jesus?" I reasoned. But I kept thinking about those letters. I couldn't get it out of my head that any skateboarder in Los Angeles could just walk into a Wal-Mart or a shopping mall, pick up the Bible and read about the message of eternal life if they wanted to. Anyone in America could with a flip of the wrist, pick up the television remote or flip on the radio or TV at any moment of any day and hear truth spoken.

The more I thought about it, the more it just didn't seem right. How could I skateboard my life away in a country and place so immersed with spiritual truth and so many churches and Christian schools, colleges and non-profit organizations, while entire people groups didn't have any access whatsoever to a single shred of the teachings of Jesus in their language. It bothered me so much that I lost sleep at night for laying awake and thinking about it all. It just wasn't fair. I didn't want to be one that tried to rationalize and sweep under the rug such an injustice. I didn't want to support any longer such a mass hoarding of spiritual truth in the midst of such a big world, much of it starving for just a few crumbs that we might drop from our big truth drenched American tables.

The next day after class, I waited around the classroom in hopes of talking to Mr. Gordy until most of the other students had already run off to lunch. "Do you really think that God could use me in tribal missions?" I asked him. "I've got a bunch of tattoos. What would the tribal people or other missionaries think of that? And I grew up in the suburbs. I don't know the first thing about surviving in remote places?" I said. "A lot of tribal people have their own form of tattooing too! And you can learn as you go about things like jungle survival. You don't need to worry about things like that. It doesn't matter what you look like or where you came from, God can use you to reach the farthest out unreached tribe in the deepest, darkest of jungles. You just have to step out! Take him at His Word because you as well as I know that He has already, with pen and ink, told you to 'GO!'" he replied with a thick southern drawl.

I found out later that day that God was also working in the same way on that curly blonde-haired, blue-eyed friend of mine who had nearly run me over a few years before. Jennie had been thinking through the same things that I was. She wasn't exempt from Jesus' command to "Go into all the world" any more than I or anyone else that claimed to follow the teachings of Jesus was. We had both come to the same conclusion: We could not with a clear conscience before God spend our lives just bringing spiritual truth to people in America or any other place in this world that already has access to God's Word and the story of Jesus as long as there are still tribes and people groups and countries in this world that still don't even know the name of Jesus Christ or have any access to the truth available to them.

This became our passion and our cause. Something that was worthy of spending our life on. Something that we were willing to live for and deep down inside we knew it was something that was even worth dying for. After all, if it isn't worth dying for, is it really worth living for to begin with?

It wasn't long before we were joking with each other, saying things like "Hey, you could build your hut next to mine" or "Perhaps we'll end up on the same island and we could work in the same tribe!" and it was all down hill from there. Since we were best friends, had the same passions in life, and knew that building one hut was much more practical than building two, we decided that the following year we would get married. We would search together for the most unreached of tribes and we would trek together through the deepest, darkest of jungles if need be, so that some of those people that were still waiting for someone to come and explain our message to them would finally have their first opportunity to hear.

Not long afterwards we were married and planning to head to a missions training school in a small town called Baker City, Oregon. We had contacted the non-profit organization that Dunn Gordy represented and they told us about their training center in Oregon where we could learn things like "how to build your own house in the jungle" and "how to feed yourself and family in remote areas". We figured it might prove helpful to spend some time there and learn about jungle living a bit while we decided which country we would move to and where we would go in search of "our tribe". As a newly married couple though, neither of us with well-paying steady jobs, sometimes it was hard to come by enough money even to meet our daily needs, but God was always faithful even if He did sometimes come through just in the nick of time.

The day came to pack up our car and begin heading west to attend the training school we had found out about. By our calculations we had just barely enough money for gas to get across the United States to the training center and we would have to trust that God would provide the rest. We worked our way from the eastern seaboard all the way across the states and to the West Coast sleeping in the back of a used station wagon. We bathed in rivers and ate mostly expired bread and canned goods from the Salvation Army and Goodwill thrift stores but we were happy and never once went hungry.

With just a few dollars and some loose change left in our pockets we checked into the old rundown army complex that was being used for the training facility. Some old veteran missionaries had tried to transform it into a school. The facility was in a farming community and the local farmers would donate any extra crops they had to the school to provide for the young families attending the training. Boy, were we grateful for those farmers! Time after time they would bring in just enough food in just the knick of time so that we could eat that evenings meal. This was just one of the many ways that God was teaching us to depend on Him for even things as simple as our daily bread.

I remember specifically one day when I didn't even have enough money for dinner and I had already gone without lunch. Jennie had to be at work and I had a day off so I had a day to myself and what a beautiful day it was! The temperature outside was perfect. It was spring and a soft steady breeze was blowing through the trees. Most the time I used an old mountain bike that a friend had given me for my transportation because I could save on car bills and gas money that way. That specific day I had an afternoon to kill and no money to spend so I settled on taking advantage of the beautiful weather and going for a bike ride. I had a favorite trail that went up the side of a mountain only a few miles away and I had been longing for an opportunity to get out in nature and enjoy God's creation for a while now. It seemed like the perfect opportunity.

I hopped on the bike and off I went, working my way down the street and towards the mountain bike trail. I had to pass through a few different neighborhoods on the side of mountain to get to the trail but it wasn't long before I was headed up one final hill and nearing the trail head. As I passed through that last string of houses a flash of white caught my eye. Looking down at the road underneath my wheels, I saw a small white envelope sitting face down in the middle of the pavement. I stopped and picked it up. The envelope was sealed and so I figured it was probably unopened mail from one of the houses a few feet away. Perhaps the wind had blown it out into the street or the postman had dropped it during his daily deliveries. I glanced over at the house numbers and then looked down to see the address on the front of the envelope but to my surprise, it had no address on it. It just had one name written in simple cursive handwriting: "Scott".

"This is really strange" I thought to myself. I quickly looked around to see if anyone was watching me as I tried to figure out why this envelope would have my name on it. There was no one. Just a couple people were out doing yard work a ways up the hill. "Well, someone here must also be named Scott" I concluded. I went over and put the envelope in the closest mailbox and continued on my journey thinking nothing of it. The mountain trails were beautiful. It had been well worth my while to come up to the mountain and I had a great time. I rode until my legs felt like rubber and then worked my way back to where I had started. The way back was easy, it was all down hill from there and I looked forward to not having to pedal for a while. As I came back off the bike trail and worked my way back down the streets I had come up a few hours earlier my stomach rumbled with hunger. I hadn't eaten lunch and I knew that I would have a hard time finding dinner as well considering I didn't have a penny in my pocket with which to buy anything.

As I flew through those same neighborhoods I had passed through earlier, the fresh spring breeze whipping through my hair and the neighborhood houses whizzing by on my right and left I came back to the place I had seen that little white envelope earlier. I glanced over at the mailbox I had placed it in with a smile on my face, assuming that those people had retrieved their mail and found the envelope, whoever they were. But surprisingly as I glanced over to the middle of the street where I had found the envelope earlier there it was again!

The same envelope, once again with the name "Scott" written on it was lying in the same exact place in the middle of the street! How had it gotten out of the mailbox? I picked it up and started laughing. It was nearly four hours later in the day! Why was it back in the street and why did it have my name on it? Holding it up to the sun above my head I tried to see if I could tell what was in it. The pale grey edges and silhouette of what looked like a green ten-dollar bill stood out in the light.

I once again looked around to see if anyone was watching me. Perhaps this was a joke someone was playing? There was no one. I opened the envelope and sure enough, there was no address, not a hint of where it belonged. Just a crisp ten-dollar bill in a plain white envelope with my name on it! I just smiled and started laughing out loud! "Well, I guess I will have some money to get a good dinner after all!" I thought to myself. I rode my bike to a local deli on the way home and enjoyed a nice big sandwich and a warm bowl of soup and thanked God for His provision. Those were lessons that we have never forgotten. Simple lessons about God's provision that we needed to learn in preparation for the jungles we were headed to.

It was a highlight of our first year of marriage also to meet other young vagabond types and travelers all gathered at that same run-down training complex to spend the following months learning things like how to survive in the jungle. The training also specialized in teaching us how to break down an unwritten language with foreign sounds and form an alphabet for the language. According to our teachers, who spoke from experience: breaking down the unwritten tribal language and making an alphabet for it paves the way for the Bible, literacy books and other school books to be translated into the tribal language for the first time. We were learning all kinds of neat things from these old experienced missionary veterans. It wasn't long however before we realized how out of place a couple city kids like Jennie and I were in a community like this.

I had been primarily vegetarian for the few years leading up to our marriage but not long after we enrolled in the missions training center we came to the rude awakening that there are no vegetarians in the jungles. "Those people will eat anything that moves! Rats, bugs, grub worms, you name it! And if they offer it to you, you better not turn it down because they don't have much to begin with. It is a privilege that they would offer anything to you at all!" said a tall lanky old missionary with a bushy mustache named Mr. Morrison. He used to serve in Indonesia and seemed to know what he was talking about. As his words sunk in I realized that he was right. If I was going into this kind of work, my days of picky eating and vegetarian meals were over.

The next week there was a class on how to kill and butcher animals for the purpose of feeding your family. I was convinced that this unique class on dismembering various animals would be taught through diagrams and drawings on the blackboard. After all, there weren't any animals there at the training center. To my dismay however, some of the local farmers graciously offered to donate two sheep, about eight chickens, two ducks, and two great big snow white, floppy eared fluffy bunnies for the class on butchering.

The training center put a big blonde haired burly looking young guy named Brooks in charge of the class because he was a missionary kid that had grown up in New Guinea and knew about everything there was to know about killing and butchering things. Brooks yelled out to the class

"Who here has never ever killed or butchered an animal before?" I figured he was asking so that he knew whom not to choose for the job so my hand was the first to shoot up. Unfortunately Brooks was asking for the exact opposite reason and as soon as he saw me awkwardly holding up my hand in the back of the class, "You! Your killing the first animal!" he yelled to me. "Oh, Lord help me!" I mumbled out loud as I slowly and hesitantly walked towards the front of the class.

Brooks watched me slowly walk forward with an almost sinister look on his face. He had decided that I would be the one to kill the cutest animal of all: the snow white, floppy eared bunny rabbit. I remembered my favorite pet I had owned as a child in California, our fluffy little silver bunny that we affectionately named Spiffy. "You will be using a hammer and a knife to get the job done." announced Brooks. "You grab the rabbit by the ears like this, then you hit it in the back of the head with a hammer so that it's body stiffens out in a temporary state of shock. Then you take the knife and quickly saw it's head off before it comes out of shock. It won't feel almost any pain." Brooks reassured me as he put the fluffy, soft, floppy eared bunny in my arms and laid out the hammer and the knife on the table in front of me.

Even the thought of such an act made me nauseous, but I had to do it. How else would I learn to survive in the jungle if I didn't even have the stomach to kill a rabbit? I took a few deep breaths to psyche myself up while I waited for the word to begin. When Brooks said "Go!" I quickly grabbed the rabbit by the ears and gave it a light but solid whack on the back of the head with the hammer. It's warm fuzzy body stiffened up just like Brooks had said, I put it down on the table and in a flash, grabbed the knife and began cutting through the neck as quickly as I could. From that point on it seemed like everything went into slow motion.

I got half way through the rabbit's neck but then the knife handle broke free from the blade. I had been pressing down so hard that the knife snapped in two! I looked at Brooks with sheer terror and right then the rabbit started coming out of shock! It began flopping around under my hand and blood was spattering everywhere! All over my face, all over my shirt and arms and I had no idea what to do! The only other sharp object close by was a hatchet. "Use the hatchet Scott!" Brooks remarked with a panicked look on his face. I fumbled around for the hatchet as quickly as I could but I could barely pick it up for all the slippery blood on my hands. Finally I got a hold of it and with one fell swoop "Whack!" the job was done. There was blood on my hands and arms, my shirt, pants and even all over my face and neck from where it has splashed up on me when I used the hatchet. I dropped the rabbit and the hatchet on the table. Feeling light headed and dizzy, I stumbled over to the side of the class thinking I was going to faint from the horror of the experience.

After dry heaving a few times in the grass I was finally able to regain my composure. I had to leave the class I was so disturbed from what I had seen and taken part in.

I decided that if possible, I would never kill anything again. I must have had nightmares for a week straight from that experience, but one thing it did teach me was that I was completely inadequate for the task ahead. If I was going to even make it to the jungle, let alone survive in it and provide for my wife in it, it would be a miracle of God. I wouldn't be able to do it on my own. I was just a city kid. I had nothing to offer in and of myself. But deep down inside I knew that was exactly where God wanted me. That was all the more reason for God to get the glory in this whole thing. He was the one that had said "Go into all the world". We knew that Jesus would not ask anything of Jennie and I that He could not give us the strength and ability to do.

⟵⟶

As we continued to work through the training course and near its completion we spent a lot of time on the Internet and in atlas books examining maps. We researched many countries and language groups trying to decipher where God would have us go when our training was over. We considered various South Pacific islands and even looked into Malaysia but when it was all said and done we had decided on Indonesia, the largest and most populous predominantly Muslim country in the world. There were said to be many animistic unreached tribal groups scattered throughout the various thousands of islands there and hidden back in the remote jungles of Indonesia. There were also said to be areas there where no outsider had ever worked and not a single word of Scripture had been translated into the local languages. The thought of having an influence in the most populous Muslim country in the world was exciting to us.

We still hadn't at any point heard the infamous special "Call of God" to go to Indonesia but we figured God probably wouldn't be too upset if we told the "wrong" unreached people group about Him. This seemed as good a place as any to spread the word about Jesus and make Him famous! When we came into class one day however we were sat down to the announcement that Muslim factions, some with ties to extremist Muslim groups that also had a presence in Indonesia, had just hijacked airplanes and flown them into the twin towers in New York City. Thousands of our countrymen had been murdered by people from the same religion that was said to be the predominant religion in the country we wanted to move to.

Not long afterwards the reports of terrorist bombing struck even closer to home as we received word that there had been explosions on two different islands in Indonesia. One in a major tourist area had been planted with intent of killing Americans and other westerners and another had been planted at the entrance to the American Embassy in Indonesia's capital, Jakarta. Fighting had broken out on other predominantly Muslim islands as well and the few followers of Jesus that there were in Indonesia were being tortured and decapitated for their faith. We were only months away from leaving for Indonesia and all the sudden we were hit with the stark realization that this was not a game. When we got on that plane to Indonesia, it very well may be that last time we would see our parents and grandparents, the last time we would see our brothers and sisters and friends.

"Were we really willing to leave behind our families? And what about my own wife? Is it worth the possibility of being tortured or even worse seeing Jennie tortured or perhaps raped or even decapitated in front of my very eyes? What is our message really worth?" I began asking myself. We had a decision to make and it was not an easy one. The reality was that when it was all said and done, we were very possibly staging our own suicide. In a Muslim country, this message of the cross we had decided to carry was exactly that: suicide. But it had been the same for this Man we claimed to follow. Jesus Himself had come to this world knowing what would happen to Him from the beginning. He knew He would be tortured and murdered on possibly the cruelest device invented by man. He knew what would happen to him from before He ever stepped foot on this earth. Still, He came anyways. Was He not also on what mankind itself would call a suicide mission?

Chapter 4

Terrorists and Tattooed Wedding Bands

Whoever asserts that he is a Christian, the same must walk as Christ walked.

Menno Simon,
The complete works of Menno Simon

It didn't make sense to most of our friends and even some of our family. They saw the reports of the attacks on television too. "Aren't there enough people that need Jesus right here in America?" some of them asked us. "Why do you have to go to the other side of the world to tell people about God? You aren't really going to go are you?" they asked us more than once. And who could blame them? They had the same fears that we did. I'm sure they also wondered if they would ever see us again. Perhaps they didn't feel that it was worth it? Deep down inside we had revisited these same questions over and over ourselves. After all, we were still young. Jennie was only eighteen and I was barely out of my teens myself. Was it really necessary that we do something so "unreasonable" and "extreme" at such a young age? We had our whole lives ahead of us, didn't we? Couldn't we just do this stuff later on in life after we had perhaps done more schooling and gained more "life experience"?

"Jennie and I aren't cut out for work like this anyways. The training center here has proven that to us, hasn't it? I feel like we are the joke of our class. We will never be able to survive in the jungle. We probably won't even make it to the jungle anyways! Terrorists will probably kill us in the extremist Muslim cities before we ever even make it to the deep interior jungle tribes that are asking for help!" I thought as I reflected on the whole thing. God never assured us that our worst fears wouldn't come true, but as we continued to wrestle with these fears He reminded us that He isn't just the God of America. He is the God of the universe. Even with all the other things we would be leaving behind, we would never be leaving Him behind. He would be with us every step of the way and there was nowhere we could go where He wasn't already. Through our doubts and fears, through any hardship or trial we might face He would be with us in it all.

We would read about the truth carriers of old in the New Testament and be encouraged when we came across books like James which said, *"Count it all joy my brothers, when you meet trials of various kinds because you know that the testing of your faith produces endurance."* We thought about the fact that God's Son Himself had to make the decision to leave the most perfect and comfortable of all places as He said goodbye to living with His own Father in order to come and minister to people like us. He faced the most gruesome trials and torture of all kinds and He knew that it was all going to happen to Him, but He came anyways. We came to the conclusion that because there was no turning back for Him, there could be no turning back for us. We knew deep down inside that we could never just stay here in America, the land of comfort and ease because we would be miserable if we did. The forgotten tribes were calling to us. The enchanting land of Indonesia had become like a set of gallows to us, but boy were they beautiful gallows. They were nearly irresistible.

We finally finished the course at the training center. Even if we hadn't done all that well in the survival type classes at least we had learned a lot about linguistics and how to write an alphabet for an unwritten language. Next came filling out the application for our Indonesian visas. Lordwilling, it was only a matter of time before we would be on a plane to the capital of Indonesia, Jakarta. We had a new outlook on leaving however. We began making preparations as if we would never be coming back. We began intentionally packing as if that was the last time we would see our families. The last time we would be in America. "Yes, our message was worth it," we had together decided. What else had we been created for if it wasn't for this purpose of making our Creator known to those who had not yet had a chance to know Him? If it was worth it for Jesus to leave the most perfect place in existence behind, would it not also be worth it for us?

We began talking through and mentally preparing ourselves for the worst of situations. Along that time came our one-year anniversary of marriage and we decided to go out on a date and eat a special dinner together to celebrate. There we sat in that little Chinese restaurant, reminiscing and telling stories to each other about our favorite memories together from the past couple of years since we had met back in Chattanooga. Jennie grew quiet for a moment and then looked into my eyes with a sad and serious look on her face. "What is wrong Jennie? We have been talking about good memories right? Why do you look so sad all the sudden?" I asked.

"Do you think the extremists would take our wedding rings if we are taken by them when we get to Indonesia?" she asked. "Well, I don't know. It seems like they would take our wedding rings. I mean, why wouldn't they take whatever is special to us? They could probably profit their cause by selling things like that, or perhaps they would use something like that for other purposes?" I replied.

Our wedding rings that we exchanged on the day we were married had an inscription written on them in Hebrew, the language of the Old Testament. The inscription was a quote from the book of Ruth, which reads "Wherever you go, there I will go". It was a lifelong pact in between Jennie and I that we would never leave each other. A pact that we were in this together no matter what situation we faced and no matter where in the world we ended up.

"Why don't we get our wedding bands tattooed on then? We could get the inscription tattooed on our wrists and then even if they separate us we will still know that at least we have that to identify with each other." she asked. It sounded like a great idea to me and just another way that we could prepare for the worst should we find ourselves caught in a situation like that. A few days later we were sporting new tattoos on our wrists and were all the closer in our relationship because of it. We loved each other, we knew deep down inside that we would even die for each other if need be. She wasn't just my wife. She was my best friend. We were one in spirit and we were ready to go through anything together. We felt inseparable.

It took a few months, but after a while we finally got the call that we had been waiting for! Our Indonesian visas had been granted and we had thirty days to get into the country before the visas were rendered invalid. To us, it was a miracle in itself that these visas had even been issued considering the paperwork for them had to be signed by various Muslim officials for us to even be able to enter the country of Indonesia. We thanked God for the news! It wasn't long before a few final purchases had been made, and we were saying our goodbyes and heading for the airport to catch our plane out of the country.

I don't think we had ever cried so hard as we did the day we had to leave our families standing there in the airport and get on that first airplane in a series of long planes flights. To us, this was very possibly the last time we would see their faces this side of eternity. The whole way to the airport neither of us could even talk for the lump that was in our throats. When we finally arrived at the airport and began checking in at the counter, we were informed that our baggage was overweight and were told that there were over a hundred dollars in extra charges we had to pay if we wanted our stuff on the plane. We didn't have much money to pay the overweight charges even if we wanted to.

My Dad knew we didn't have much money. He pulled out his wallet and without saying a word paid the charges for us. A few moments later they called out on the loudspeaker that our plane was leaving and that it was time to board. We all stood in a circle there in the airport, Jennie's family and mine and my Dad prayed for us, that God would watch over us on our journey and protect us from any harm that might be waiting for us. He committed us to the Lord and then finished his prayer looking up and saying to me "I am so proud of you, son." My mom was choked up even more than I was. She couldn't barely speak through the tears so she simply nodded in agreement and whispered "We love you, son". With tears blinding my eyes I was able to muster a shaky voiced "I love you too" and after one last round of embraces from all our family members present we turned and slowly headed for the plane, all the while glancing back over our shoulders every few steps to get one more glimpse of our families until we had rounded one last corner and they were completely out of sight.

As we boarded the plane I thought for a moment about all the disagreements I had with specifically my Dad over the years. I had always looked down on some of the career decisions he had made. Desicions which had taken such a toll on my brothers and our family. I had always felt like I had been robbed of knowing him the way I longed to because of his die-hard commitment to his work. Business meetings and long business trips had stolen my father from me and to that very day standing there in the airport I felt like I barely knew him at all. All growing up I had promised myself that if I ever found myself in his shoes, I would never do to my kids what he had done to my brothers and I. But on the day I had to tell him and my mom goodbye, I found myself thanking God that at least I had parents that sincerely loved my brothers and I. At least my parents were still together. And at least they believed the message that we were travelling across the world to share, were proud of me and supported Jennie and I in what we were doing. I thanked the Lord that He had given us parents such as these that cared enough about our message to let us go and to even stand behind us in this decision.

As we sat down in the plane, a verse from the book of Matthew that I had read the day before came to mind. Jesus said *"Every one that has forsaken houses or brothers or sisters or fathers or mothers or wives or children or lands for my names sake will receive in return a hundred fold both in this life and in the life to come."* What were we doing besides just taking Jesus at His word? Didn't we believe in the afterlife that Jesus had taught about? Didn't we believe that we would be reunited with all those that had trusted in the finished work of Jesus? Many of our family members had also placed their faith in the finished work of Jesus as we had. Would we not have all eternity to make up for lost time? I smiled at the thought of being reunited with my parents and brothers again someday. Whether it was in this life, or whether it was in the life to come.

We leaned back into our seats and looked out that tiny little oval shaped window taking in what would seemingly be our last view of the country we had grown up in. The plane engines roared as the plane thrust forward and rumbled down the runway. We grasped each others hand tightly as the plane made its way up into the sky. The coast got smaller and smaller below us and the thin golden brown line of sand, which separates our homeland from miles of endless ocean blue faded until it disappeared behind the clouds below us. It would take the rest of the day and the entire evening to travel the expanse of this great beast called the Pacific Ocean. Exhausted from the previous days of packing, anticipation and all of those emotional goodbyes, the slow deep humming of the jet plane engines lulled us to sleep in our seats. We would be waking up the following morning to see things we had only dreamed of and talked about. We would be setting foot in a country that we had studied on paper and in classrooms for a long, long time. We didn't know for sure what awaited us but at least we still had each other.

⟷

A forty-eight hour span of changing from plane to plane, first in Taipei, then in Hong Kong and then Singapore left us disoriented all together. The languages changed around us, as did the smells and the cultures we were engulfed in. We were carried along in a sea of world travellers rushing about from terminal to terminal. It was all so exciting but so confusing and surreal at the same time. Throw in some jet lag, some no-doze and the aftertaste of Asian airlines rice and fish and it felt like the morning after a party we had no business being at in the first place.

At last, we were on the final decent of our last plane. This time we were enroute from Singapore to Jakarta. With the changing of plane passengers the language had also once again morphed all around us from the Singlish, that's "Singapore-English" and the Chinese of Singapore to the short choppy sounds of Bahasa Indonesia. We took turns pressing our faces up against the tiny oval shaped window as the plane finally began to make its descent. "Look at all those islands!" I said to Jennie. It seemed like there were too many to count, each one decorated with a ring of bright white sand where the coast met the water, like a hundred splatters of green and white on a never-ending canvas of blue.

Then we neared what seemed like a significantly larger island than all the rest. Covered over with a carpet of green it stretched out long and slender like an ancient king of the sea to keep all the other little less significant islands in place. As we neared closer and closer we could see that there were thousands upon thousands of palm and banana trees and then finally the jungle was broken by the outer edges of a good sized bustling city below. The skyline was dominated by the minarets of hundreds of mosques poking their little dome shaped heads up from a chaotic sprawl of the rundown third world shacks of the lower class and the occasional concrete blockhouses of the wealthy. "This must be Jakarta!" Jennie exclaimed in an excited yet nervous voice.

The plane circled twice then slowly descended and leveled out before making an unusually hard landing. After the plane had finally and roughly bounced and screeched its way into a slow roll we began gathering up our things to disembark. The anticipation built as we stood in line in the little airplane aisle and brushed the crumbs of airplane peanuts and pretzels from our clothes. Then when the plane door popped opened and the line finally began to move, the Indonesian humidity rushed in and greeted us before we had even stepped out of the plane.

Inside the terminal we were met by a sea of four-foot tall Javanese men. They looked like escape convicts with their bright orange uniforms and stamped identification numbers on their chests. Each one was armed with a shiny, partially rusted porter cart that revealed their true intention. "I Hep yu meestir", "No...I hep yu, I hep yu!" they yelled, elbowing and fighting each other as they began encircling us and frantically grabbing for our bags. My first impulse reaction was to defend myself and our stuff and I started slapping hands like I was playing an arcade game at Chuckee Cheese. I knew however that I would have an extremely hard time carrying all our luggage myself and fighting them off at the same time. There was no reasonable choice except for to succumb to the pressure.

"Okay, you!" I frantically yelled out as I pointed at the unusually fat one that already had two of our four bags and was loading them on his cart anyways. To which the whole crowd of them replied "Me too meestir! Me too meestir!" Without our permission the fat one divided out our bags to three of his skinnier friends and we were off. We had no idea if we were going in the right direction or not, all we knew was that we needed to keep up. Lucky for us we gained some reassurance as we soon saw a few of the airport signs that had been written in both Bahasa Indonesia and also in English. They announced to us that we were headed towards customs.

Before we had even been able to stumble our way through the arrival terminal and make it to the customs line we were starting to get drenched with sweat. A couple sparrows zoomed by inside the terminal just a few feet above our heads looking as sporadic and confused as we probably did: Like creatures caught in a world not their own, flying at the speed of light though they also have no idea where they are going or how to get out.

Finally, we approached a long line of people standing at a little three by three foot wooden box. The box had a singular little glass hole for the man uncomfortably sitting in the box to speak through. The man looked like he had had a very long day in that little coffin of a box. He looked important and highly decorated though like he was a high ranking official with many years of experience, although the look of his baby face said he couldn't be older than twelve. Each person that wanted to pass had to first obtain permission from the important man in the little box. We all waited as the first person in line took his or her turn standing behind a red line about five feet in front of the box until he or she was motioned forward. While we were standing in the customs line waiting for our turn we studied the other people waiting.

I, for the first time realized that the majority of women standing in the room were covered from head to toe in the loose modest head covering and clothes of the Islamic religion. We heard the shy giggles of children coming up from a few feet behind us. They were whispering to each other long sentences in Indonesian as they pointed up at us and giggled. Finally one of them worked up the courage to say the only English that he probably knew. He looked up at Jennie and said "Halo meestir" in a thick accent and then ran back behind the long flowing traditional Muslim dress of his mother while all the other kids broke out into shy giggles with their hands over their mouths. Jennie smiled and replied "Well, hello!"

This seemed to give all the other kids and even some of the adults in the room a boost of confidence. From that point on all the other kids also began walking up and half yelling "Halo meestir. Halo meestir" and then running back behind their mothers again. They seemed friendly enough and at first we were happy to be greeted with smiles at all even if they were mostly from little children. We had anticipated nothing but scowls and anti-American sentiment in a city whose members had just recently tried to bomb the American Embassy, which was only a few miles from the airport we were standing in.

Finally we were at the front of the line after a series of "Halo meestir's" and "I luv yoo meestir's" from every kid in the room. The man in the little box seemed to have a routine he followed for each person. First he ignored us like neither we nor the many people behind us were really standing there. After about thirty seconds he would look to the right, take a deep breath, then give a disheartened and uninterested looking sigh before he waved his hand in a downward flap like motion towards us, giving us permission to step over the bold red line on the floor but still not making eye contact. He was armed with an arsenal of stampers laid out before him like a treasured coin collection. He first acted like he was bored and we were bothering him by coming to visit his private box but then as he took a look at our passports his face changed and he looked up with a new zeal. He carefully studied every line, crease and pimple on our faces and made sure we really and truly were the people in the passports we had handed him.

For a second we felt like deer caught in the headlights, awkward and nervous like we had perhaps done something wrong. Then after a series of uncomfortable smiles from us and penetrating looks from the very highly decorated baby-faced officer, he all of the sudden looked up with a big wide toothed grin. In broken English he pronounced "Tank yoo meestir", handed our passports back and we were good to go along with our fat friend and his three skinnier friends that still had our bags and who also affectionately still referred to both my wife and I as "Meestir".

As we walked out the front door of the airport we were met by a short stalky white man with the haircut of a Baptist preacher from my parents era. Despite the blistering heat he wore dress pants and a starched, collared button up shirt. He looked to be about in his early fifty's. He had the sun-kissed skin of a man that had perhaps been in this country a very, very long time.

"Well hello there! You must be Scott and Jennie! My name is Don" he said as we locked in to a firm handshake and then began walking out the main exit. Before we even had a chance to reply he had pulled out his wallet and paid our fat friend and his three skinnier friends the equivalent of twenty cents each and they walked away in an excited scuffle like they had just won the lottery.

Don had received word from the people affiliated with the training school we had attended that we were on our way and had agreed to meet us at the airport. He helped us get all our bags gathered and packed into his rickety mini van. Then, after a few moments we were off and speeding down the road towards a place that he had arranged for us to stay for the night. We were just glad someone had been there to meet us at all, let alone someone that knew English and had a place for us to stay!

We hadn't slept much at all for nearly 48 hours. I could feel the film on my teeth and our clothes smelt like sweat and airplane food, which anybody that has done a bit of airplane travel knows isn't a good mix. The unfamiliar streets of downtown Jakarta were crazier and more out of control than even the busiest eight lane freeways of Los Angeles. Horns were honking and hazard lights were blinking.

At about the same time that we realized that we, along with everybody else in an automobile were driving on the wrong side of the road, I began to wonder why everybody that passed us was honking as they drove by. "Is there something wrong with our car Don? Why is everybody honking at us?" I asked. "Oh, they are not honking at us, they are just being polite, letting us know that they are passing. That is Indonesian street etiquette. And as far as the hazard lights go, in this country you use your right blinker for a right turn and your left blinker for a left turn, but if you are going straight through an intersection you use both blinkers, also known as 'the hazards'." he explained as we swerved left to pass a horse drawn cart also using the freeway.

A little farther up, shortly after passing a car on the side of the road that was totally engulfed in flames, we were joined on the road by a whole circus of creations and modes of transportation as our speed slowed to a near crawl. The cars thinned out and we found ourselves in a sea of primarily small mopeds and motorcycles. The mopeds and "becak": small cab-like, bench seat rickshaws welded onto three-wheeled bicycles, competed for the road. We were mixed in with hundreds of mopeds, becaks, and some horse drawn carts and also other various wooden carts being pushed or pulled by traveling salesman and noodle cooks alike with their disc like pointed Javanese hats.

Most of the people pushing, pulling and driving the various carts wore a checkered wrap around skirt and sandals. Some of them were shirtless or sported an old ragged tee shirt and old shorts that looked to be left over from the seventies. Each cook and cart had its own unique sound that the salesman made to set him apart from the others. Everything from the clanging of a spoon on a bowl to a clown horn is used and could be heard. We were immersed in the fumes, smells and the unique sights and sounds of a third world country. After over an hour of going along overpopulated streets at a pace slower than my grandma in her walker, we finally turned down a back alley and came to the place that Don said we would be staying for the night. We took our bags in to a guest room and hit the showers to try to get all the grime of the last two days of travel washed off. Then we hit the bed hard and went into a near comatose state as the effects of jet lag set in.

It's was the middle of the night when we awoke to a very strange and eerie sound. Something we had never heard before. I pressed the little light button on my watch to see that it was later than I thought. It was actually 4:28 in the morning. At first I didn't remember where I was. "What was that sound? Who in the world would be out this early? Perhaps we are being robbed?" I thought as I lay silent and listened. I looked around the room as my heart began to beat faster. As I glanced to my right and then my left I suddenly remembered again where we were. Then the incredibly loud wail like sound set in again.

It sounded this time dark and drawn out, and so loud that it made me plug my ears. I jumped out of bed and stumbled to the window in the little tile floored room to pull the curtains aside and try to figure out what was going on but I couldn't see anything out the window except for a concrete wall. The sound stopped for a brief second again and then Jennie also sat up in bed and began looking around as the sound set in a third time. It was like someone had somehow gotten a hold of a mic and some loudspeakers and set them up right next to our bedroom window. Whoever it was, they were singing and wailing at the top of their lungs.

It wasn't in the Indonesian language. It sounded like it must be in some other language that I had never heard before. I walked out of my bedroom door groggily trying to figure out what in the world was going on and why on earth it was so loud. Looking out the front window of the house and towards the main road I could see people walking by the front gate one at a time all going in the same direction in a sort of slow procession. The men were dressed in long decorative shirts with a checkered sheet-like cloth wrapped around them from the waist down. The women were dressed completely in white from their head coverings down to their feet in what looked like robes. It looked almost spooky. I had never seen anything like it. Then I realized that the strange singing I was hearing was in Arabic.

It was the Muslim call to prayer. All of these people were walking to the local mosque at 4:30 in the morning to pray. Within minutes we could hear hundreds, maybe even thousands of loudspeakers ringing out from all over the city, one in every neighborhood calling their faithful followers to morning prayer. Each one of these thousands of people were responding to these Arabic calls before the sun was even up. It was something that they did nearly every day. I couldn't go back to sleep after seeing that. I just sat there and watched them walk by: men, women and children alike on their way to the mosque, one by one, each one entering, kneeling and rocking back and forth as they prayed until the first call of prayer for the day was over. This was such a strange and different place. So different from the world I had come from.

I felt burdened by these people and by what I was seeing. They also had their traditions, hopes, fears and questions. They had their prayers and rituals that they held onto and placed their hope in, just like I had grown up and held on to my prayers and rituals back in America. They also had their ways of trying to escape God's judgment, their special words that they repeated five times every day in hopes of being set free from their fear of hell.

As different as I was from these people, I realized that when it came down to spiritual things, we were the same, looking for the same thing. They were searchers. They needed Jesus just as much as I needed Him. They needed to be set free from their rituals and incantations and special words of religion, just as much as I had needed to be set free from the rituals and decoys I had been taught as a child. They needed to know that simple trust in the sacrifice of God's Son, Jesus was enough and that none of their special prayers, rituals or good works would compare to His finished work on the cross, just as I had needed to know. Maybe we were not that different after all.

Chapter 5

No Place for a Woman

Never doubt in the dark what God has shown you in the light.

V. Raymond Edman,
The Disciplines Of Life

We spent the next number of months in a small town called Salatiga located a few hours east of Jakarta yet still on the island of Java. This was at the recommendation of Don and some other older expats that we had met along the way in those first few weeks in Indonesia. Don and his wife had been here in this country a very long time and seemed to know this island like the back of their hands. Jennie and I being barely out of our teens and inexperienced, it seemed foolish not to trust Don's advice. They knew of a place we could stay in Salatiga and also knew of some Indonesian locals there that would be willing to teach us the Indonesian language and culture if we would hire them for the job. This sounded like a good plan to us. After all, how would we be able to function in Indonesia and find the tribe that we hoped to spend our future living among unless we knew the language well enough to get around?

We caught a plane to Salatiga and found a small Indonesian house there that would only cost us about four dollars a day to rent. One of the key pieces of advice that Don had given us before we left Jakarta was that we should keep a low profile. He said that it was in our own interest to try not to draw attention to ourselves. There was a lot of anti-American sentiment in this predominantly Muslim country and not everyone would appreciate seeing us around. Don said that it was for this very reason that we should "fly under the radar". We were instructed to try our best to "blend in" and "stay away from large crowds or demonstrations". "Low profile at all times. Got it!" I reassured Don as we packed up to catch our plane from Jakarta to Salatiga.

We had to first fly to a small city called Semarang and then from there, catch a taxi for another couple hours to get to another small town called Salatiga. After only a couple hours flying along the Javanese coast and watching the jungle and little third world towns blur by us outside the little oval window we were already coming in for a landing.

Jennie wanted to wash up a bit in the airport before we caught our taxi so after we got off of the plane, she headed for the closest restroom and I found a little area in a vacant corner a few feet from the bathrooms to sit down. I sat on our backpacks while I waited for Jennie. It seemed like Jennie wasn't the only woman fresh off an airplane with the idea to freshen up a bit. Due to the crowds of women from the multiple flights landing, she would have to wait in line for a while.

We learned soon enough that the process of using the bathroom in Indonesia is another thing about third world countries that is very different from our own. There is no toilet paper when you walk in an Indonesian stall. The floor is slippery and wet. Only a rusty faucet sticks out of the wall next to a squat style toilet, which is nearly level to the ground. There is usually a small cup or brightly colored ladle floating in a medium sized bucket underneath the rusty faucet. If you want your parts clean after you do your business, the Indonesian way is to pretty much strip down before you ever use the "squat pot" as we came to call it. You hang your clothes over the stall door then relieve yourself. Then before putting your clothes back on, using the ladle and small bucket of water you bathe from the waste down. You make sure to use only your left hand and the water from the ladle and bucket to get yourself clean. Then you re-dress and you are good to go.

We learned quickly to carry toilet paper with us at all times. That is, if we didn't want to take a ridiculous amount of half baths every day! We also learned very quickly why it is considered rude and impolite in Indonesia to ever hand anybody anything with or greet someone using your left hand. It made perfect sense! Being that I had to wait for about thirty different women to take baths with a ladle before Jennie was going to return, naturally I began to get bored. I had brought with me from America a small instrument that resembles a miniature backpack dulcimer with banjo strings. In my boredom I pulled out the instrument and began lightly picking away one of my favorite old tunes called "I'll Fly Away". This song always, even from when I was a little kid made me feel at home as I heard it.

A few moments later, as I was continuing to pick away on the little banjo strings I heard clapping in rhythm with the song and looked over to my right to see a couple of those escaped convict looking bag carriers walking my direction as they continued to clap to the music. They smiled big wide tooth smiles and jabbered away in Indonesian and Javanese as they watched me play. Then one of them ran back to the hallway he had come from, whistled real loud and looked as if he was calling some more people over.

Next thing I knew, although they had probably never heard the tune "I'll Fly Away" in their lives, there were about fifty or so black haired, four-foot tall Javanese men, locking arms, smoking cigarettes, and dancing in circles in the middle of the airport while I, blonde haired and six foot two stood in the middle of them all playing away on my little instrument. We were having a grand old time! We were coming to the end of the last chorus when Jennie came out of the restroom to see what all the commotion was about. The crowd was getting bigger and people were stopping to join in on the party. A drum had turned up from somewhere also so we had a sort of bluegrass, tribal, Javanese hoedown thing going on.

They wanted to keep dancing and carry on with our little bluegrass Javanese dance party but Jennie and I had to catch our taxi. To their dismay, the concert had to come to a close. We all shook hands, using the right hand of course, and patted each other on the backs as we parted ways. As we walked towards the exit of the airport and began looking for our taxi, Jennie looked over at me and said "Wow Scott, that was really 'low profile'. Way to 'fly under the radar'....Nice."

⟷

Salatiga is a beautiful contrast to the busy smog filled, overpopulated streets of Jakarta. A much smaller town than Jakarta, it is nestled in a cool valley that lies in between multiple towering volcanoes. "Gunung Merapi" the most famous and active volcano of this area has a name that can literally be translated "The Fire Mountain" and when we arrived there in Salatiga, it hadn't been long since the last eruption.

It was nice to be in a place a bit cooler and a little more laid back than the sprawling concrete jungle of the capital of Indonesia. After we had gotten settled in, we began walking around town and exploring our neighborhood a bit in hopes of getting a good start on learning the Indonesian language. Almost everywhere we walked we found that people were curiously looking out their doors and windows as we walked by. They all yelled the same greeting, "Halo meestir!" But they all yelled to us with smiles and a welcoming demeanor.

Then we turned a bend in one little alley a few blocks from the house we were renting to see a young man standing there wearing clothing a little different than all the rest of the locals. He looked to be in his early twenties, pants pulled up just high enough to make him look out of place. He sported a plaid collared shirt tucked in behind a polished leather belt and his hair was greased back and suave looking. He wore overly shined penny loafers and looked professional, almost like a businessman of some sort.

As soon as he spotted us he began confidently walking directly towards us, looking like he was on a mission. To our surprise he right off the bat said in near perfect English "What are you doing here in Salatiga?". I hesitated for a moment to answer his question. The words "low profile" came back to mind as I wondered whether I should tell him we are just tourists or whether we should tell him that we have actually moved here in hopes of learning their language and eventually in some way helping some of the people of his country. For all I knew he could be a government representative or some other type of official that might not want us there.

He continued to ask questions one after another. "Where are you from? How long have you been here? Why are you in my country?" After a few moments of short answers and uncomfortable silence, I hesitantly told him the truth. "Well we are here in Salatiga because we hope to learn to speak the Indonesian language but eventually we want to work with people in a more remote area that might need our help." I said trying to cautiously avoid giving him too much detail in case he was an extremist of some sort. It was very possible that he didn't like what we were there to do. With his hands crossed behind his back and an inquisitive look on his face he then asked, "Are you here to teach people about spiritual matters?" I didn't know what to say but I knew it wasn't right to lie to him so I just looked him right in the face and replied "Yes…I guess we are. We want to eventually share with people about Jesus in whatever remote area we end up in."

As soon as he heard this his whole demeanor changed. He broke out into a huge smile and said "Praise God! I also am a follower of Jesus and it was white-skin people like you from a country called Germany that came to my tribe and shared about Jesus with my grandparents!" He grabbed me by the shoulders and talked in an excited voice as he began explaining to us that he was a "Batak", originally from a tribe on the Indonesian island of Sumatra and was in Salatiga for the purpose of studying at the local university. Jennie and I breathed a sigh of relief as he continued.

"My name is Fernando....Fernando Hutajulu!" he continued and went on to tell us about how his people used to be cannibals and the very first group of Germans that had ever come to his tribe were murdered and then eaten by his grandparents and family. He continued, "More Germans came after we ate those first ones though! The people of my tribe were completely bewildered as to why more of these white skinned foreigners would continue coming to us even after some of them had been killed and eaten. So eventually we listened to the message that the foreigners brought and now most of my tribe are believers in Jesus. They remain followers of Jesus to this day despite the fact that much of Sumatra is predominantly Muslim." Fernando excitedly told us.

"Welcome! Welcome to my country. Welcome to Indonesia!" he told us over and over again. Fernando became like a brother to us during the following months as we studied the Indonesian language. He rode all over town with us in the local horse drawn carts that are referred to as *"dokar"* and he spent all his free time out of his university classes trying to teach us about Indonesian language and culture.

Before we knew it we were speaking out basic sentences in Indonesian though there were many times when we accidently said things that we didn't quite mean to say. There was one time that we walked by a stand with a bunch of handmade, bright and colorful hats. The Indonesian word for hat is *"topi"* and the word for head is *"kepala"*. I thought they were pretty cool looking hats so I walked over to the stand and confidently said in Indonesian "I would like one of those hats please, but I need a large one because I have a really big *kelapa*." Everyone there at the hat stand turned and began laughing at me while the man who ran the stand stood there looking confused. As it turned out, the word for head is *"kepala"* not *"kelapa"*. Everyone was laughing at me because I had used the wrong word and said I wanted one large hat for a very large coconut.

Another time Jennie went to the market to buy some fresh vegetables. She saw that they were selling soybeans, which in Indonesian is called *"kedelai"*. She walked over to the lady selling the vegetables and said, "I would like some *keledai* please.The lady looked at Jennie somewhat puzzled and confused and after thinking about it Jennie realized that she had asked for a donkey (*keledai*), not soybeans (*kedelai*). No wonder the lady was confused. We discovered pretty quickly that if we wanted to learn this new language, we needed to learn to be able to handle getting laughed at.

A few nights later, Fernando decided he wanted to treat us to a Batak culinary specialty from the tribe and island he had grown up in. When we arrived at his dorm room for dinner he had set out a specially made dish that looked pretty tasty. We had worked up quite an appetite from the long hours of wandering the streets practicing language so we sat down and with Fernando's permission dug right in. After swallowing a few bites I asked him what it was. It seemed like some sort of very tough stringy meat soaked in a sort of red spicy broth, I had never tasted anything quite like it. After a bit of deliberation he told us that it was dog, specially prepared in the Batak fashion and that Jennie was eating the heart!

"Usually we also make soup from the dog blood mixed with orange juice and special spices to go with the meat but I couldn't get a hold of a few of the specific spices needed. I will have to make it for you another time." he added, somewhat disappointed. Jennie and I didn't tell Fernando but we were relieved that he hadn't had those needed ingredients. The dog heart alone turned out to be almost more than our stomachs could handle.

A few days later Fernando announced, "I want you to see the real way that we Indonesians usually live. I want to get you out of this city and into one of the smaller villages outside of town and a ways up in the mountains. No hiring a private taxi this time, we will go by bus so you can really experience the way most of us live and travel!" He continued, "It is only here in the middle of town that people are wealthy enough to have these motorcycles and taxi's and live in these nice concrete houses. To me, this isn't real Indonesia and you need to see how most of us really live and eat if your really going to learn the language and culture of my people. Otherwise, you will never truly understand us."

He was right. The house that we were renting for four dollars a day was extraordinary even compared to many of the houses in our own neighborhood. It had running water, tile floors and a kitchen area for cooking. It had two bedrooms and even had plumbing for a squat toilet and a tile washbasin for showers. We stuck out like a sore thumb as possibly the richest people on our street. This wasn't the way the general Indonesian population lived. We were living by a completely different standard than the people we had dreams of ministering to. A couple days later Fernando had contacted some of his friends in a more remote village outside of town and we bought tickets to get on an old bus and go spend the weekend at his friend's village.

The farther we got from Salatiga the rougher the road got. The rougher the road got the less automobiles and motorcycles we saw. Eventually there weren't even power lines along the road anymore. After multiple hours of rough, pothole filled dirt roads in an old seventies model bus so packed we could barely move, we ended up dead ending on a muddy trail. It was the last stop on the road before the bus turned around to head back to the overly populated towns and cities. We gathered our things and Fernando led us up a thin dirt trail into a small, primarily bamboo constructed, mostly thatched roof and scrap metal walled group of houses.

Most of the men walked around in just the sarong checkered wrap around sheet that makes up the traditional

Javanese dress style. The women mostly had old ragged and plain looking skirts and t-shirts that looked like they were left over from the sixties. The kids ran around almost naked. But everyone was smiling and glad to see us.

Fernando showed us where we would be sleeping for the night. We were led to a small bamboo house that had a single five by five foot Javanese tikar mat in it and an old beat up couch partially held up by rocks and leaning against the wall. Fernando pointed at the old couch and said to Jennie, "This is the only padded place to sleep in the house so you can sleep there. Scott and I will sleep on the dirt floor. The place to use the bathroom is out back behind the house where there is a bucket of water you can also use for bathing."

We hadn't anticipated this at all. We hadn't brought sleeping bags or anything but it was warm enough to where no one in the house was even using blankets anyways. The locals of the small village began piling in the room all around us a few at a time until the little room was nearly full. Each person brought with them a little bit of food and some rice, which they would cook for the evening meal.

Fernando had brought along his guitar and the people gathered all began singing songs together in Indonesian. One of the songs sounded strangely familiar: *"Hari ini, hari ini, harinya Tuhan, harinya Tuhan...."* it went on and on everyone in the room joyfully singing and clapping with smiles on their faces. I leaned over and asked Fernando about the song and he sang the chorus in English: "This is the day, this is the day, that the Lord has made, that the Lord has made. I will rejoice, I will rejoice and be glad in it, and be glad in it....."

No wonder I had recognized the song. It was an old tune I had sung in Sunday School since I was a little kid. Somewhere along the way someone had translated it into Indonesian and it was one of Fernando's favorites as well. I was surprised to hear that specific song until Fernando explained to me that although most of the villages in this area were staunch Muslim villages, this specific one was one of the only predominantly Christian villages in the area.

A few moments later, we glanced behind us on the left to see a teenage girl with severely deformed legs using her hands to drag herself along. She was able to make it to the edge of the small group gathered and she began to join us in singing. Her mouth and the muscles in her face seemed contorted as she tried to sing along and the sounds coming from her mouth were strange and off pitch but she closed her eyes and half smiled as she continued to sing.

A few minutes later the meal was ready and they set out a few large bowls and dishes of rice and greens on the floor in the middle of us all. As the father of the house dealt out the rice into separate bowls and carefully made sure that everyone got at least a small portion, the crippled girl motioned to Fernando that she had something to say. Fernando leaned over and translated from Indonesian to English in a whisper so that we also could understand. The girl slurred her words as she struggled to speak.

"I have been looking forward to this ever since I heard you were coming. I do not have many things that I can enjoy in this life. But one thing that I can enjoy is singing to our God. I am just so, so happy to be gathered together with you all tonight. It brings me so much joy to get together and sing praises to our King. Thank you so much for visiting with us." she concluded as she looked over at Jennie and I with a sweet, contorted smile and tears in her eyes.

It is hard to explain how one feels in a moment like this. When you see someone with almost nothing materially. Her family and village had all gotten together just to come up with enough food to host us. They didn't even have running water or electricity in their house. We were all sitting on the floor under kerosene lit lamps. Most of these people didn't even have a proper bed to sleep on. And a girl that can't even barely talk and gets around by using her arms to drag the rest of her weak deformed body was telling us how happy she is, how the best part of her week is when she gets to sing to her God. It was humbling. I realized that compared to her, Jennie and I had everything and were extravagantly rich materially speaking, but that compared to her we were poor and had almost nothing, spiritually speaking. She had learned a level of deep contentment and joy in her poor physical state and lack of material wealth that we, in our excess might never fully know or understand in our lifetime.

A little while later and we had been in Java nearly nine months. We were getting near to fluent in the Indonesian language and so we asked Fernando and some of the other people we had met along the way what should be our next step. "Where should we go? Where are the greatest needs? Where in this country are there people with the least amount of spiritual truth? People that have even perhaps been waiting and asking for outsiders like us to come and live with them and teach them?" we asked.

According to Fernando, there were literally thousands of islands in Indonesia and many of them needed work. There was another man we met in brief however that told us about a specific area in Indonesia that had multiple people groups asking for outsiders to come and help them. Steve looked to be in his early forties with medium length salt and pepper speckled hair. Medium sized and clean-shaven, he had the look of a physically fit, high school gym class teacher. He was visiting briefly in Salatiga for some meetings with his sponsoring organization and a friend mentioned to us that he needed a place to stay during his short visit to Java.

Jennie and I invited him to stay with us for a few nights. During his stay he told us story after story about the extremely remote areas that still needed work in the Indonesian province where he lived: The farthest eastern island within the country of Indonesia, referred to by many as "Irian Barat" or "West Papua". Steve told us specifically of places a few days hike from the tribe he and his family had been working with. Groups of people that had still had almost no contact with the outside world. Some of them had still never had even their first outsiders come in and live among them and work with them.

"They are as backwoods as you can get" Steve said. "Still wearing nose bones and traditional dress. The men wear nothing but a small gourd over their privates and the women wear nothing but short, thigh length grass skirts. They are always carrying their bows and arrows and they even still use some stone tools. They follow the animistic ways of their forefathers, regularly killing each other in tribal warfare. They have scars all over their bodies because they believe that when they get a sickness, they need to drain out the bad blood. They make slices all over their bodies and literally try to pull the veins out of the gashed or sliced area trying to get the blood to flow. In fact, where we live they also follow these same practices and they seem to be killing each other off faster than we can even learn their language so that we can help them!" he continued.

His voice went from that of a lighthearted conversation to serious concern as he talked. He really did genuinely love the people that he was working with and it was exciting, yet at the same time very burdening to listen to him as he described where he had been and what he had seen. "These are mostly small tribes in West Papua. I realize that I am spending my life for a small group of people, probably only a few hundred at the most! But after getting to know these people and seeing the way they live and picturing their faces, I know that I would spend my life to bring them our message even if there was only one or two of them left!" he said as emotion filled his voice.

"There is plenty more work to be done on our island and plenty more tribes to be reached" he said with an inviting ring in his voice. The places that he described fit perfectly the description of what we were searching for! Finally we possibly had a good lead to find those types of remote people groups we had been hoping to come into contact with. So when those last couple months of Indonesian language learning were finally over and we had enough knowledge of the Indonesian language to get around without a problem, we made plans to head to the province of West Papua and check it out for ourselves. We figured this was as good a place as any to start looking for a tribe that might want people like us to come. Finally we were making headway.

Would we finally, in this place called Irian Barat get to see with our own eyes the most unreached of the unreached? Were there people far back in the jungles there that really had been waiting and longing for our message for literally thousands of years and had still not yet had an opportunity to hear it? We planned on finding out.

Our plane circled a medium sized, bustling city called Sentani. The old engines of the run down Indonesian airplane hummed and the propellers clicked away a few feet away outside the window. From the air, this had to be one of the most beautiful and topographically dramatic cities we had ever seen. We were just a few miles in from the coast but there were rolling hills and small islands nestled in a huge fresh water lake below. The lake was massive and spread out weaving its fingers down side passages all throughout the little town lining its borders.

A towering, pointy-topped giant, appropriately named "Cyclops", shadowed the airport. A huge, lone jungle mountain jutting up out of the jungle canopy the mountain looked to be over six thousand feet in height. A beautiful white waterfall spurted out of the center of its northern main face about a third of the way up and then trickled down through the center of the city and into the fresh water Lake Sentani. The mountain reminded me of something from Jurassic park. It stood tall and strong looking prehistoric, like an untamed beast poised and ready to devour the little city and its inhabitants in the shadows below.

The old rebuilt World War II airstrip we were about to land on was backed up to the edge of the lake. It seemed like we would plunge into the lake as we came in on the final approach. The belly of the plane was only a few feet above the waters surface as it neared the beginning of the old strip. We bounced and skidded to a stop only a couple hundred feet or so before the end of the runway, then the plane turned and taxied its way towards the exit ramp as we began to gather our bags to disembark.

Upon exiting the plane we were surprised by how different the people looked on this island as compared to the Javanese we had spent the previous nine months with. Their almost aboriginal dark skin and frizzy hair was a stark contrast to the lighter skin, silky haired, Asian people of Salatiga. As we entered an odd pinecone shaped, pointy roofed airport building, we looked to our left and right to see that the walls were spattered with red stains all around us. It looked like some sort of gruesome battle had recently taken place right there in the airport and fresh blood was spattered all over everything. As we carried our backpacks into the terminal, I tried to take a closer look at the red stains all over the walls. Then as another red line of thick liquid hit the wall right next to me. I looked up to see an afro headed local man smiling. Thick, bright red liquid was all over his mouth and dripping off his lower lip. He looked like he had just bitten in to a bloody, raw steak.

As it turned out he was chewing a local plant that we would soon find out is called betel nut. A plant which the locals mix with a powdery, cocaine-looking lime powder: it is like the chewing gum of West Papua. The man smiling at me was chewing it the same way I had seen some of those good ole Tennessee boys back down South working their chewing tobacco. Purely in the interest of learning about the local culture of the Papuan people, Jennie and found out later on that betel nut has a slight narcotic affect if you keep it in your mouth for a while. It turns that blood red color as it mixes with the lime powder in one's mouth.

As we listened to the sounds of that new place we quickly noticed that when the local Papuan people spoke Indonesian it seemed like it was almost a different dialect of language all together because they're pronunciation was so different. This place even smelled different. The airport reeked of sweaty bodies and diesel fuel mixed with betel nut. Most of the Papuan people have a stout muscular build and the rough sandpaper type skin on their arms and legs is covered with thick curly hair unlike the smooth skinned almost hairless people of the other islands. We might have been intimidated by their rippling muscles and blood red teeth if it weren't for those beautiful welcoming smiles and friendly eyes.

The Papuans were helpful to say the least and it seemed we couldn't take a single step without someone offering to carry our belongings for us. Also, The Papuan men walked around the airport holding hands and thinking nothing of it. It seemed like in their culture this wasn't a sign of homosexuality, it was just a way to show friendship. And there were no escaped convict looking types here armed with rusty baggage carts either. Just a bunch of smiley, frizzy headed, cuddly bear like people with blood red teeth that looked like they just wanted to help.

After we had gathered all our belongings, we walked out the door to find a friend of Steve, the man we had met a few months before in Salatiga, waiting to greet us there at the airport. A shaved headed, blue eyed Canadian, Tim was smallish with the stout frame of an average middle-aged man. He took us to a place that he said we could stay for the time being until we figured out what our next step would be. Tim and his wife, Kathy, had also spent time in the jungles in the past and they would prove to be not only extremely hospitable but also very helpful in their advice as time progressed. Tim advised us that if we wanted to get to know the island and find out where the people were with the least amount of contact with the outside world we should be talking to the veteran pilots. There was no one that had seen more of the terrain and mountains here than those old weathered pilots and Tim knew it.

We hadn't even completely finished unpacking and getting settled in before we were excitedly going around to the different flight organizations based in Sentani, trying to track down good leads on old veteran pilots we could talk to. We asked for copies of their maps so that we could see where there were already airstrips in progress on the island and where there weren't. Seeing those maps was our first major clue as to where we should start looking as the first thing that usually happens in an area when it is opened up to the outside world, is than an airstrip is built. Then shortly after the airstrip usually comes schools, medical clinics and government outposts as the area is developed. We could look at a pilot's map outlining the airstrip locations of the island and see clearly where there had not yet been any airstrips built.

After only a few weeks we had gathered as much information as we could from the fixed wing flight organizations that use only airplanes. It seemed like we had nearly hit the end of our information gathering rope so one weekend we caught a short plane ride up into the mountains to visit a small town called Wamena. It was here that there was said to be a base for an organization called Helimission: An organization that specialized in flying helicopters into areas where there were no airstrips available. Helimission had done medical evacuations and various emergency flights to areas all over these islands and specifically in some of the most remote places. So their pilots would very possibly be a great wealth of information to us, considering the type of places we were looking for.

Upon entering the Helimission office in Wamena, we heard the air above us rumbling with the "chop,chop,chop,chop" of heli blades as one of their helicopters was just returning from a med-evac flight. One of their veteran pilots was just landing, having come in from a remote area to the east. A tall, slow-spoken man, Tom looked strong and sturdy for his age. He was nearly six foot four with wiry veins running all up and down his forearms. He sported the clean, standard button-down pilots shirt with black and gold bars on the shoulders. "Well, welcome to Indonesia!" he said with a slow steady voice after we introduced ourselves.

He had years of experience under his belt and we knew it. If there was anyone that could steer us in the right direction it would be this man. We told him our story and why we were coming to him for advice. "Surely if there is anyone that knows this island like the back of their hand it would be you! Can you recommend to us a good place to start looking?" I asked. The sides of his mouth curled up into a smile as he slowly got up from his creaky office chair and walked over across the room to a big map on the wall. It was easily the biggest map I had ever seen, about eight by ten feet in size. It outlined the entire island and had a little red pushpin on most of the places that they had landed in the past or regularly fly to.

"I can tell you right off the bat that there are two main places that I would recommend to you guys considering what you are looking for," he said. "One of the places is called '*Gobog Dua*'" he continued. "This place has had contact from the outside world and has even had some work done in it. They are called the *Kimyal* tribe. We fly in and out of there once in a while doing med-evacs and I can tell you that this is one of the most hopeless places I have seen" he continued. "They desperately need someone to come work with them," he concluded.

"The other place that I would recommend you look into is waaaaay over here toward the western side of the island" he said as he took a step to the left and reached his arm way over to the other side of the map. His finger stopped where there were no names or even topography lines printed on the map, only a small text saying over and over again in small print "Relief Data Incomplete". "Some people say they are called the *'Jaya Dua'* people. Others say they are part of the *'Maniwo'* people or can also be called part of the *'Wodani'* tribe. I don't know exactly what you would call them or who they are a part of but I do know that in this area right here, most of the valleys and hamlets have virtually no signs of the outside world. Rarely, if ever, have most of the people here come into contact with outsiders." I tried to keep calm and cool on the outside but my heart raced with excitement as I listened to Tom talk of the places he had seen.

He had to get back to work so after he wrote down some exact map coordinates on a piece of scrap paper for the places he was talking about, we concluded the conversation and thanked him for his time. As soon as we had gotten out of the door I could have screamed out loud and ran down the street in my excitement! "Did you hear that Jennie?! Almost no contact with the outside world! No hospitals, no missions, no schools, no government presence...no anything! We have got to get in there!" I said out loud as we walked down the street twice as fast as usual in our excitement.

We went back to the house that we were temporarily staying in and began calling around to different airplane organizations and trying to schedule a time that we could get a flight to go and see these places for ourselves from the air. We would be able to gather more information on this extremely remote area by taking GPS waypoints from the air. Not to mention that for the first time, we would be able to see with our own eyes that remote area that had been described as "nearly untouched by the outside world."

We began renting a house there in that highland town of Wamena to base out of and continued researching the remote areas Tom had talked about. It was along that time also that we met and began to spend time with a couple guys named Jonny and Derek. They were there in the province of West Papua on assignment from a local non-profit organization to do a year of survey work. They were gathering information about the areas and people groups that might still possibly have a need for outsiders to come in and work with them.

Jonny, a tall, lanky, sandy-haired, blue-eyed guy was engaged to be married. He was love-struck to say the least and seemed to spend all his time talking about how he couldn't wait to be reunited with his fiancé. He was on his last couple months in Indonesia before he would head back to the United States to get married and he had all but checked out already mentally. Derek was an ex-military man that had served in the Canadian army. He wore old worn in combat boots twenty-four-seven and still kept the high and tight military style haircut of the army and carried a military issue backpack.

They had been spending the last few months taking trips up and down various jungle rivers, doing language surveys and gathering information from areas all over the island. Many of these groups they had been visiting had sent representatives out to the cities and towns asking and pleading for teachers and humanitarian aid workers to come and help their people. We listened intently as they told us about the different places they had been. They described in detail about a tribe they had just returned from called the *Muyu* that was asking for people to come work with them and teach them. "Have these areas already had church or government work done in them though?" I asked, wondering if they were perhaps places that we might want to consider going to. "Well most of these places do have church buildings, and they have even heard of Jesus as well, but they are no better off than before," Derek replied.

Jonny continued, "Yeah, you have to consider that even where there has been work done, missionaries and church workers haven't had the best strategy in the past. In most of these places the missionaries just built church buildings for the purpose of claiming the territory for their denomination and then left. They didn't do almost anything at all to actually help the people or even necessarily teach them anything! On this island just because they may have something they call a church building doesn't mean they are any less animistic than they have always been. They are just as hopeless as their ancestors were and they know it. That is one of the main reasons they keep sending out representatives asking outsiders to come and help them and teach them!"

With all the experience that Jonny and Derek had hiking around in these jungles, these guys had knowledge about the terrain, the people and the culture of this island that Jennie and I didn't. Even though we concluded that we wanted to first check out uncontacted areas in our search for a tribe to move into since it was those areas that seemed to have the least of the least, we knew that Jonny and Derek would be extremely helpful on a foot survey. I began mentioning to them that we were hoping to do some survey ourselves sometime soon into the area that Tom had told us about and asked them if they would perhaps be interested in joining us. They agreed to come along providing it coincided with Jonny's very tight plans to soon leave Indonesia to get married. "Well, priorities are priorities I suppose," I thought to myself as I remembered my own engagement time with Jennie and the weeks leading up to our marriage not too long ago.

It wasn't long after that we were contacted by a local fixed winged flight organization that said our flight request to do an aerial survey by small plane was approved and that they had our flight on the schedule for October 5th. We met with the pilot assigned to our aerial survey a few days before the flight and explained to him in detail that this would just be the first step in what we hoped would be our first face to face contact with the people of this remote area. We then gave him the coordinates that had been written down and given to us by Tom. We could hardly sleep those last few nights leading up to the flight we were so excited for what we might finally get to see with our own eyes!

Finally, the day of our first aerial survey flight arrived. We went down to the hangar bright and early before the sun had even poked its head up from beneath the horizon. This was an area way farther out than the pilots usual flights and we would need to get an early start if we wanted to beat the afternoon rain clouds that were so common in these jungle mountains. As the designated pilot looked over the coordinates we gave him and then looked at his maps he realized that this area was so far back in the jungles that no one had yet even completed the aerial maps that usually outlined the rivers and valley systems. Even the most dependable maps available couldn't give him good information on the area. There was simply not much information for him to go by.

The only single thing that he had was an old, incomplete map made up of information gathered by pilots during the allied occupation of the island during World War II. On the map, once again there was "Relief Data Incomplete" written over the entire area that we wanted to survey and that specific part of the map was blank. "Well, we can just fly that general direction anyways and see where we end up but I can't guarantee you will see anything." the pilot said as we climbed into the little white Cessna airplane. "Well it's better than nothing! At least then we will be able to see whether there really are people living back there or not," I replied. Jennie and I buckled in and got ready for takeoff. After a few moments the little plane was rumbling down the runway and we were off!

It would take well over an hour to even get close to the place marked out by our coordinates. As we flew towards our destination mountain range after mountain range lay sprawled out below us covered over with a shaggy carpet of deep green. Villages of thatched roof houses dotted the ridge tops and stretched out in the areas along the twisting jungle rivers below. Most of the little villages we saw seemed to have one large building in the center that stood out from the rest, a building with a corrugated tin roof and a perfectly manicured yard. Usually a government built school, medical outpost or church building, to us these represented the influence of the outside world. Not far from most of these types of villages there was always an airstrip for bringing in knickknacks, foods, medicines and government officials from the larger towns and cities. But as we continued to move farther and farther out, the shiny tin roofs of government schools, hospitals and church buildings became less and less common and the signs of human population become sparse and nearly non-existent.

Finally after ridge after ridge and mile upon mile of jungle forest the pilot announced that we were drawing close to the area referred to as *Jaya Dua*. As we crossed the final ridge of mapped territory and entered the beginning of the area that says "Relief Data Incomplete" on the old charts, the pilot set his maps aside and focused his attention on the jungle canopy surface and ancient tree tops below us. At first we saw two separate valleys that both dead-ended into a massive group of mountains. The huge jungle mountains jutted up into the sky and looked like prehistoric giants standing nearly ten thousand feet high. Below the peaks on the sides of the mountains we saw only extremely steep cliff-like walls nearly unfit for human habitation.

The cool scattered clouds of the morning were still huddled up along the ridges and cliffs as the rising sun attempted to burn them off. Steam and fog lazily floated up from the emerald canopy below distorting our vision of many of the mountainsides and crevices. We could only see patches of green through the occasional breaks in the clouds and for a moment I found myself more concerned that the pilot knew what he was doing in uncharted territory with ten thousand foot mountains like that than I was about anything else.

As the little plane buzzed along, dwarfed by the surrounding mountains and cliffs, the clouds finally began to rise and evaporate and we began to get a clearer view. We couldn't see any signs of human life, just ridge after ridge of tangled vines, mossy prehistoric looking trees and muddy rivers. The occasional waterfall spurted out from the side of one of the mountain faces and plunged a few hundred feet down below to disappear into the jungle again before it joined into a larger river at the bottom of the valley. This place looked so wild, so untamed, so pristine and cut off from the rest of the world. It was like nothing Jennie or I had ever seen. As we continued to fly along wandering and circling up one small valley after another we still did not see a single sign of life beyond the occasional bright white cockatoo or flock of birds sporadically darting from tree to tree.

I could feel my stomach drop in disappointment as I started to wonder if we had flown all the way out there for nothing. At the pilot's recommendation, we circled down towards the less extreme and less dramatic mountains of the lower elevations in hopes of getting a closer look. Still, a few minutes of circling up different dead-end valleys and then back out again and....nothing. Once again only jungle canopy, tangled vines and no sign of human existence.

We circled back and went up another small nameless valley a little farther to the southwest. This time however, as we popped over the ridge I glanced downward to see an unusual looking bald spot on the side of one of the smaller mountains below. It could only be one of two things: it was either a small landslide, which are common in these mountains of heavy jungle rains and moist conditions, or it could be a small garden sight were someone had possibly cleared some brush for the purpose of planting or gardening.

As we came in for a closer look we saw a small plume of smoke coming up from the clearing. Behind the smoke, a single, lone standing thatched roof house on the ridge! In a small clearing in front of the lone house stood a few dark skinned figures frozen in fear. They turned and began running from the plane and darted into the little thatched roof house as if we were some sort of large metal bird swopping down to snatch them up! It seemed that we had unintentionally scared them half to death by coming in so close!

"Did you see that Jennie! Did you see it? There are people back here after all!" I laughed out loud as we buzzed on past the hamlet, the belly of the plane only a few hundred feet above the little thatched rooftop. "There is another house over there I think," Jennie shouted out a few seconds later as we went farther up the little unnamed valley. The pilot directed the nose of the plane towards where Jennie pointed and there wasn't only one but three more small thatch roofed huts and another garden clearing! "In all my years of flying here in Indonesia I have never seen people running from the airplane before, this surely is strange to see," the pilot remarked. "Perhaps these people have never seen planes fly in this close," I replied as we flew over the second hamlet.

From that point on we kept on seeing hamlet after hamlet, each one comprised of one to four approximately ten by ten foot houses. All of the little houses were made up of what looked like hand-hewn boards and then tied together with split jungle vine. The roofs were made of layered tree bark and palm fronds. From the plane, we took photographs, notes and waypoints of as many of these hamlets and small villages as we could. We would need as much information as we could get if we were going to come back and hike in here so that we could establish a first face-to-face contact with them.

As they ran into the jungles and houses, none of the people that we caught a glimpse of were wearing western clothes. Every single one of them had on traditional tribal dress and they looked nearly naked altogether. There were also no signs of the outside world, no corrugated tin roofed buildings, no government outposts, schools, hospitals and not a single airstrip. We had taken GPS waypoints of thirteen different small villages and seen approximately thirty-five separate thatched roof houses when the storm clouds began to move in. "We had better call it quits and start heading back if we want to make it back safely. Those storm clouds are moving in fast and they don't make for good flying!" the pilot announced as he banked the plane into a sharp right turn and pointed the nose back in the direction we had come from.

After about forty-five minutes or so the storm had gotten too bad for us to continue on. The rain was pounding down on the little airplane and the sound of the raindrops on the little tin wings was almost deafening. The conditions had gotten to the point where we could not continue any further. We circled above a small town called Mulia. We landed with only a few skids and bounces despite the harsh blowing winds and wet runway and thankfully the plane remained intact and we were able to make it down on the ground. We bedded down for the night in an old expat house there that the pilot knew of and were able to scavenge some old canned food from the kitchen cupboards for an evening meal as we hadn't brought any food of our own.

The following morning we awoke to skies of blue and a warm sun burning all the puddles off the runway from the day before. The little plane once again rumbled down the strip as the steam and humidity rose and evaporated on either side of us. A quick twenty-minute flight and we would be able to make it the rest of the way back to Wamena safe and sound where we could plan our next step.

Over the following weeks we staged two more aerial surveys and tried to the best of our ability to take good notes on the rivers, placement of the hamlets and the elevations of the various mountains so that we would know what to expect when we made our first journey into the area by foot.

During that time we also figured out who was working the closest to this extremely remote area and tried to meet up with them as well to glean information about the nature of the people and their language. Months had past since we had seen him the last time in Salatiga, Java but we were able to once again talk to Steve who was working about a weeks hike to the east of this area in a tribe called the *Moi*. We also met a tall, slender, middle-aged man named Mike who was working about a weeks hike to the southwest and had been working there for some time with a group called the *Biduu* people. Both Mike and Steve had heard many stories from the tribal groups that they worked with about the area we were looking into and were able to confirm through the local people in their areas that the tribe we had seen from the air were in fact known as the *Dao* people.

This was mainly because according to the neighboring tribes, the central river that runs through their territory is called the Dao or Dago River according to which dialect was being spoken. Also, Dao women had in the past intermarried into both the Biduu and Moi people groups on either side of them and so we had a very good source of information about the culture of the Dao people through talking to Mike and Steve.

As it turned out, Mike also knew a local man from the more advanced *Dani* tribe, farther east on the island who had hiked through and spent some time in part of the Dao territory in the past. Apparently the Papuan Dani man had hiked around there in hopes of finding a flat area he could use to open up an airstrip sight. He had plans of profiting off of opening up this remote area and its resources to the outside world. The terrain was too extreme however and eventually the man had given up and headed back to his own people, the more modernized Dani tribe.

"I would very strongly recommend that you don't try to make an initial contact with the Dao people alone or try to hike through these mountains by yourselves." Mike told us with a tone of caution. "The terrain there is incredibly extreme. I have seen it by both plane and helicopter as I have gone back and forth from the area I work in and I have heard stories about it from the people I work with." he continued as he thumbed through and showed us some of the pictures he had taken of the Dao area. "Beyond that, I think the people there will react much more positively if you are with someone they are already familiar with" Mike concluded.

He provided us with the information we needed to contact the man from the Dani tribe and also wrote down for us a list of basic phrases and friendly greetings from his tribe that we could memorize and try to use in our initial contact with the Dao people. Even though the Dao were far back in the jungles they had regular contact with the neighboring people groups along their borders for the purpose of trading and obtaining new and valuable goods from the outside world like axe heads and machetes. For this reason, they would probably understand some of the language from the neighboring people. We spent the next few weeks trying to memorize these basic greetings so that should we come face to face with the Dao people for the first time we would have some familiar phrases we could say in hopes of showing friendship.

One afternoon Derek, Jonny, Jennie and I went over to the house where the Dani man whom Mike had recommended to us as a guide was said to be living. We worked our way up a rocky dirt road to a small group of old tin roofed houses on the edge of town. There were a few kids with tattered clothes running around and playing out front in the midst of sporadic chickens and swaying banana trees. As we neared the houses an older dark skinned Papuan man that looked to be about in his fifties came slowly walking out to greet us. He had a bright colored Indonesian style dress shirt on and wore a frizzy afro that stood about five inches tall off of his head. The lines and crows feet all over his weathered face gave testimony to his age and he walked stiff-legged as he worked his way towards us. *"Selamat sore"* we greeted him in Indonesian.

"We were told that a man lives here that has spent time in the Dao territory. We were sent here by Mr. Mike." Jonny explained to the old afro-headed man. "Mike said that the mountains in the Dao territory are very rough. We are planning on hiking into that area in the near future and need a guide so we have come here looking for that man, do you know where we can find him?" Derek asked. "It's me, I am the man you are looking for. I have been to Dao, and I can show you the trails by which you can get into their territory" he responded with a slurred accent. He was missing so many teeth that it was hard to even understand him when he spoke.

At first I didn't even know what to say-surely this was a joke! This couldn't be the man Mike had told us about. We hadn't even responded yet when the man began talking again "I need food for my family and I need you to pay me if I am going to go with you." he replied. "This can't be the guy, he doesn't look like he could even make it halfway up one of those mountains if he wanted to...he's old!" I leaned over and whispered to Jennie in English just to make sure the old, afro-headed man wouldn't understand what I was saying.

I was sure there must be a mistake but as we continued to listen to him and ask questions about his experience in the Dao territory we realized that he was telling the truth. Quite a few years had passed since he had hiked last but he really was the only outsider that had been through that territory and on those trails. This was the only man that could help us. There was no one else that could be our guide. "Well, at least we will have Derek and Jonny with us, and we can always leave him in a village along the way and then come back for him if he is to old to keep up." I thought to myself as we reluctantly agreed to hire him for the job.

After we agreed to pay the old Dani man to lead us into Dao territory and after we had paid him half of the agreed upon price, we began putting down the final details of our plan on paper. We set the date for Friday, November 19th for the start of our journey. According to the old Dani guide we would need to plan for at least three weeks to get all the way into Dao territory and then back out again.

First we would need to catch a boat from the capital city, Jayapura to another coastal city much further down the coast called Nabire. Then we would need to hire another smaller longboat to take us along the coast and into the lowlands river system. After that we would travel all the way up to the twisting, muddy Taane River until we made it up into the beginning of the foothills. We would have to take the river up into the foothills until the rapids were too high for us to go any farther. Then from there we would hike at least two days through 4-9,000 foot mountains to get to the first Dao village. After we had made it up to the first village, we would look at our coordinates and figure out which village we were at according to the waypoints and information we had gathered from the plane during the previous aerial surveys.

We planned for three weeks hiking around the Dao territory at the least. All together the trip may even take as long as one and a half to two months. It looked like everything was coming together and we began bracing ourselves both mentally and physically for our first foot survey into the Dao territory.

Jennie and I had spent every morning for months now trying to prepare for the day that we would be walking jungle trails and hiking those extreme jungle mountains for the first time. Every morning we had been running, exercising, and trying to prepare our bodies for life on the trail. Most weekends we would spend our time climbing local hills and mountains with our backpacks purposely stuffed full with filled water containers so that we could get an idea of what it would be like to hike with three weeks worth of food supplies pressing down on our backs. We had also already been cutting unnecessary foods out of our diet and had been trying to get into the best physical shape possible for our first foot survey.

The way we saw it, we had crossed the earth and left behind family friends and everything we had known just to have this opportunity. We had gotten married with this goal in mind. There probably hadn't been a week go by in our marriage where we hadn't talked about the day we would finally get to establish contact with our tribe for the first time and now, it was almost surreal. We would finally get the opportunity! We would perhaps be some of the first outsiders that had ever hiked up into this territory, some of the first white skinned people that some of these uncontacted villages had ever laid eyes on!

It was late afternoon and we had just finished running around from little run down store to store trying to get everything together that we would need for the trip. The light afternoon rains of the tropics had set in and everything was drenched with precipitation but the sky was finally starting to clear again as the sun burnt all the moisture up off the streets. Only a few more days and we would be on a boat and headed for the base camp in Nabire from which we would stage our foot first survey!

Word of our plans had spread around the little expat community there in that town pretty fast and we soon found out that some people held very strong opinions as to the way Jennie and I were going about things. One specific expat that had been there for many years told us he had some important last minute tips for us concerning traveling, hiking and surviving in the jungle terrain of this island and he wanted to talk through our survey plans with us. We wanted all the advice we could get and this man was said to have a lot of experience as he had been working on the island for nearly ten years before our arrival so we agreed to meet with him one evening. We dropped off our supplies at the house we had been staying in and raced up a pothole filled gravel road on an old rickety Honda motorbike we had borrowed for a few weeks to get around town. We would just barely make it up to his house at the agreed upon time.

On arrival at his office we saw that he had also invited a few other older expat men to join in on the meeting. After shaking hands with the different men in the room we sat down in his little concrete office as the man sat down behind his polished wooden desk. I reached into my backpack and got out some paper and a pen to write down anything pertinent to our trip that the men might have to share. We were grateful that these men had invited us to get together with them and glean from their experience. After all, this was our first foot survey, we had never ever done anything like this before.

We felt a bit out of place sitting there in that little office with the older gentlemen as they looked like they had gathered for a high-dollar business meeting with their starched collared shirts, dress pants and shiny dress shoes. Jennie and I wore mud splattered cargo shorts, worn in boots and old t-shirts and were sweaty from the days events. The men reminded me of my father and his friends gathering for their business meetings as I watched them complimenting each other on their dress shirts and nice dress pants as they walked in and sat down. They were however the veterans on this island and even though I didn't necessarily understand how they could dress like that in the constantly ninety and one hundred degree weather of this humid city on the edge of the equator, I respected the fact that they had been here much longer than we had.

We assumed that they had probably thought of many things that we hadn't considering all of their past experience. So after we had shared with them our plans and route for the survey, we asked them their thoughts and if they had any information or advice they thought might help us. One of the men had barely started to talk when a statement came out of his mouth that blindsided us all together. "These jungle trails and mountains are no place for a woman when it comes to surveys!" he said in a slightly raised and extremely serious tone while glancing at Jennie and then looking back and forth at the other men in the room. "I have seen places like these and hiked trails like this. It would be nearly crazy to take Jennie along don't you see?" he continued.

Jennie glanced over at me with a slightly perplexed look on her face as the other men in the room "Hmmm"-ed and grunted in approval to the man's statement. "I don't think you should go Jennie!" another one of the old missionaries added in. "You could be putting the whole survey team in danger! Besides, the guys will be sleeping on the ground, using the bathroom in the jungle and probably changing clothes and bathing right out in the open in the creeks and rivers! What are you going to do then?" another one added in.

"Even beyond that, what if you have your monthly cycle right there in the middle of the survey, huh? Then you will be weak, and the whole survey will have to come to a complete stop and be turned around just for you! Do you really want that?" one of the men asked in a sharp and somewhat demeaning voice.

I felt paralyzed as I watched the expression on Jennie's face. Her eyes widened and her jaw dropped as she slowly looked over at me and then back at the other men in the room again. When we agreed to this meeting we hadn't in the least expected to hear anything like this. Had we known this was what this was all about, we might not have agreed to come at all! I could tell by the look on her face, that Jennie was beginning to boil inside after hearing the opinion of the well meaning yet extremely biased old missionaries. I felt anger rising up in my chest as the men continued on with their comments. I began breathing heavier and could feel the blood leaving my hands as I clenched my fist tightly around the pen with which I was supposed to be taking notes.

As they went on and on and I watched the expression in Jennie's eyes I wanted to stand up and lash out in defense of my wife but I held myself back. Neither of us had seen this coming. We had heard a lot of different things from missionaries and old expats over the past few months, some good and some bad. Many expats seemed to look down on us because we were so young. Others had rolled their eyes at us because we didn't have any kids yet. We had constantly heard the phrase "You don't understand, maybe someday you will when you have children of your own." But we had never heard anything like the demeaning comments made towards Jennie that day just because she was a woman.

I had always planned on Jennie and I being side by side in the jungles, hiking these trails and doing everything together. After all, isn't that why we had even gotten married, to do this together? Even if we had never been married at all wouldn't she have been over here anyways, even without me? Even if she was alone and there was no one else at all to go with her, I knew that she would be hiking the jungle trails by herself if she had to! Jennie could see the whites of my knuckles and the hardened look on my face as I squirmed and sat forward on the edge of my seat. Before I could get a word off though she lightly touched me on the arm and then started in to her soft-spoken yet very sincere reply.

"I have trained and waited for a long time now to go on this survey. I know I will struggle! You don't have to tell me that I will be the slowest one on the trail! Don't you think I know these things?" she continued. "But don't you think that when the people and specifically the Dao women see me struggling on the trail and they see the sweat pouring from my face and perhaps even see me in pain from the journey to get to them, then they will understand all the more in the future what our message is worth to me? I want the women of the Dao tribe both young and old also to know that this is a message for them, not just the men of the tribe. I want them to see in my life that the message we bring is for everyone, man or woman! That is why I am going on this survey, the hardship is worth it to me!" she concluded.

I could have stood up and yelled out a "That's right!" in that little room. Jennie was right on! And whether the old veteran missionaries backed us up or not, this was a non-negotiable point to us. We had come here to do this thing together. The way we saw it, on the day we said "I do" we decided that we would work as one. We always had been together and we had no intention of splitting up now! There were a few more moments of uncomfortable silence in the room. I reached over and grabbed on to Jennie's hand and gave it a squeeze of approval as she looked over at me. Neither of us said a word in that moment but our eyes said it all. We knew we had each other's back. She knew I was proud to be sitting there by her side and that I agreed with every word.

One of the men looked at me and said in an obnoxious tone, "Well, what do you think Scott? She is your wife!" "I think she is right. I don't see any reason she shouldn't go just because she is a woman! Just because she lacks a certain reproductive organ! She has just as much a right to be there as any of us do. I agree with every word she said and as far as I'm concerned she is going!" I responded probably in a much harsher tone than I should have.

The man let out a big breath as if to say, "Well, I tried". "I just wanted to make sure you realize how serious this is. Some of us are much older and more experienced than you. We have been here for a long time. We have hiked in these mountains and I have hiked these jungle trails before. More than once I found myself on my knees thinking I would never make it out! You guys just need to realize what your getting yourselves into and you, Scott, need to realize what you are taking your wife into" he said in conclusion.

As the days counted down we continued to think about those old missionaries and their advice even though we didn't much care for what they had said. Deep down inside we knew that some of what those men were saying was probably exactly right. This probably would be one of the hardest and most physically challenging times in our life. We had never felt more inadequate as the date set for our survey drew closer.

One thing we did know however was that God is faithful. He had seen us through up to this point and He would be faithful to see us through to the end. We were immortal till our work was done and we weren't about to start doubting in the dark what God had shown us in the light. Ultimately, our message was worth whatever we would find on those jungle mountain trails and we wanted the Dao people to know it.

Chapter 6

A Welcome We Wouldn't Soon Forget

God, give me the grace to do your will and I will do it until the end.

St. Augustine,
The Confessions of Saint Augustine

The words of those old expat men echoed in our heads over and over again. What was it that made them so incredibly insistent and bold in their conclusion that Jennie shouldn't be allowed to take part in this survey? It seemed there was more to this than what we could see on the surface. An issue that was possibly even steeped in years and generations of western tradition that define a man's and a woman's respective roles in society. Perhaps to their knowledge, no woman had ever done what Jennie was about to attempt. We had certainly never heard of a woman attempting such a trip. It was always the big strong, heroic men that stepped forward while the "weaker" women were left in the city safe and sound to cook and clean and do laundry. This was just the way it was.

Whether we liked it or not these were the patterns that had always been followed and left unquestioned in our "Christian" society and had even been carried all the way over here to the other side of the world by people from our own culture and homeland. Perhaps these old experienced veterans were just afraid of the unknown. Or perhaps they felt that because of her gender, Jennie was out of line and about to try to be a part of something she had no business being a part of.

Maybe they just thought we were plain crazy for trying something that they had never seen done in all of their years of being in Indonesia. What they didn't know with all of their years of experience though was that the worst thing they could have done was to imply to us that it couldn't be done because that only made us want to do it all the more!

A few days later, Jonny, Derek, Jennie, myself and our old Dani guide had gathered our final supplies and caught an ocean liner up the coast to a small coastal town on the North side of the island. Our guide said we should base out of that specific town because he knew boat drivers there that might be able to take us up into the lowlands and towards the Dao territory in their long dugout canoes.

We were well into the first leg of our survey and had made it to that small coastal town with no problem at all but it wasn't long before progress began slowing and we found that we had hit a brick wall already. Three days and three nights in that little run down seaside town and we still couldn't find a single longboat driver willing to take us up the lowland rivers and into the highlands. "What is the problem? Are they scared? Scared for themselves? Scared for us?" Question after question flooded my mind as we walked up and down the streets and beaches of that town coming up with one dead end after another.

Even though there had to be a hundred long boats, dugout canoes and other motorized boats lining that single stretch of beach not a single driver seemed to even consider our request. "There's no fuel available" many of them would reply, but then these same men would get in their boat, armed with a gas guzzling outboard motor and three or four extra jerry cans of fuel and race back and forth along the coast all day long. We sat there watching them zooming around fishing and transporting goods for other people from sunrise to sunset. Something that we thought would be fairly simple had turned out to be a much more complicated task than we had anticipated. Why didn't anybody want to drive us? I decided to try to get down to the bottom of it.

During lunch the following afternoon I struck up a conversation with one of the local frizzy headed coastal Papuans that looked to be in his sixties or so. After a series of "Halo meestir's" and standoffish smiles he was surprised to find that we were fluent in the national Indonesian language. "We don't see a whole lot of foreigners like you in our town! Why are you here?" he eventually inquired. This seemed a good opportunity to get some information so I explained to the old man our intentions of going up the lowland rivers and into the highlands to try to establish contact with the remote tribes in that area. His facial demeanor changed from that of an inquisitive smile to a sour looking scowl.

"The people that live up in those foothills and mountains are wild!" the man replied. "Just a couple years ago is when the Kehu were discovered on the very river you want to go up! When they were found they were completely naked, no clothing at all! It is said that they still use stone tools for building their small dwellings. Their little lean-to shelters lay hidden under the cover of the jungle trees, which makes them nearly impossible to find. They cover themselves with mud and lay in the jungle completely silent and still when they hunt. They wait for a cassowary or wild pig to come along and using the element of surprise jump up from the mud and beat it to death with a large rock grasped in their bare hands! Some say they still don't even know how to make fire!" the man excitedly went on as he used gestures with his hands to demonstrate.

"When the military found out about them and discovered that the Kehu were still cannibals, eating their own people, it was all over. They went up into the jungles in search of those evil cannibalistic people and next thing we knew there were rumors of hundreds dead. It is even said that a full boatload of human skulls was brought down to town to prove that the job had been done. Is it true or not? I don't know! But I wouldn't want to go up those rivers to find out" he concluded.

Maybe this was why none of the boat drivers would take us? Maybe they knew these same stories and thought we were crazy for going up there in the first place? Whatever the case, finally, on the fourth day of waiting and searching our old Dani guide came to the little run down hotel we had been staying in for a few dollars a night and announced he had found a man that would do the job "for the right price".

We had already lost almost a week of our time in between the two days on a large transport ship that we took to get to this little coastal town and the additional three days it had taken us to even find a boat driver that was willing to take us up into the lowland rivers. So when we finally found this boat driver, even though he was asking way more than we had anticipated paying, we agreed to his price pretty quickly! He seemed to be our only choice anyways. We set the time for 7:00 a.m. the following morning to depart.

We met on the beach close by the small room we had been renting for the past few nights. The sky above us was exceptionally clear and it was a beautiful day to travel. The sea seemed calm enough and we were happy to finally be making some progress! While walking a few hundred feet down the thick sandy beach to where we where we were told the boat and driver would be waiting, we could already see our little afro headed Dani friend conversing with the boat driver.

When he saw us coming he began motioning to us to come on over to where the boat was tied up a few feet off shore in the shallows. We dropped our backpacks there in the sand and greeted the boat driver while inspecting his little dugout canoe. It looked to be around twenty five foot or so in length, a gas powered outboard motor was fastened to the back and there were two skids, one attached to either side of the boat to keep it cutting through the water smooth and straight. It seemed very small for the amount of people and gear that we had to fit into it but the driver insisted that it wasn't a problem and that there would be plenty of room. The driver and his assistant worked on getting the multiple jerry cans of extra fuel loaded into the boat while we did an inventory of our supplies and made sure we had brought everything necessary for the trip.

Jennie and I opened our bags and made sure that everything was there that needed to be there: light weight ramen noodles, a few small bags of uncooked rice, a change of clothes, a few pots and pans for cooking, flashlight, video camera, lightweight sleeping bag, journal, some nuts and other high protein snacks for the trail, malaria medicines and bandaging for gashes, satellite phone for any emergencies, our notes and coordinates from the previous aerial surveys, drinking water.....check. We had everything we planned on bringing and were ready to board.

One at a time we waded through the thigh high salt water with our backpacks over our heads, climbed up in the dugout canoe and then tried to get comfortable in the small boat. It had a few wooden crossbeams about two inches wide each but no real seating. The boat halfway submerged under the weight of the fuel, all our gear and our survey team along with the driver and his assistant.

Before we knew it we were off and screaming down the coast with the cool, salty wind whipping through our hair. The warm sun beat on our faces and reflected off of the glassy water all around us. Finally! We were headed towards the Taane River, the beginning of the trail that was said to lead up to the mountain tribes! I leaned back using my backpack for a backrest and closed my eyes as the ocean breeze hit my face and the water occasionally sprayed up from the front of the boat as it moved through the water. Despite its small size, the twenty-five foot dugout canoe seemed to have no problem at all lazily cutting a path through the ocean as it bobbed up and down from the ocean currents. The thin white coastline was to our right and we would occasionally pass a small palm tree covered island or two on the left.

The smell of the salt water in the air and the sound of the waves lapping up against the shore were nostalgic. They brought back childhood memories of those after school trips down to the Southern California coast with my mom and brothers. I closed my eyes and breathed deeply, taking the moment to pretend I was a kid again. I day dreamt about Corona Del Mar and wiggling my toes in the golden brown

California sand while my mom made my brothers and I hotdogs and s'mores on the open fire. At times it was hard to believe that I was so incredibly far from home.

As we made our way up the coast an occasional flying fish sprang up out of the water and glided a few inches above the surface next to the boat. Then a few hours later, after nearly half a day of going along the coast we could feel the long dugout canoe make a slight right turn and hear the sound of the engine change as the boat slowed a bit. We neared a muddy brown inlet lined with riverweeds and thick jungle trees and vine and began to make our way up through a few rippling waves then coasted up into the beginning of a muddy lowlands river. Thousands of gallons of chocolate brown water emptied itself from the lowland jungles into the salty, Asia Pacific Ocean. As the muddy brown mixed with the ocean green we began scanning the surface of the river looking for the crocodiles that are said to live in the lowland rivers and in those brackish waters.

At first, the river was quite smooth and steady flowing. After a few hours of winding our way up through the twists and turns of the thick jungle however, we found ourselves surrounded by faster moving light rapids. Every few hundred feet some brush or an old log would poke its knobby antler looking branches up out of the water as if to warn us not to come and closer. The driver frantically tried his best to quickly steer the boat to the right or left to avoid a collision. Then as the water got rougher, the driver's assistant moved up and positioned himself in the front of the boat. He held a long bamboo pole, probably a good twenty feet in length. Every fifty feet or so he used the bamboo pole to check how close the boat was to the bottom of the river as we went along. He yelled an occasional *"Kanan!"* or *"Kiri!"* back to our boat driver in Indonesian meaning "Left!" or "Right!" so that the driver knew if there were any obstacles coming that he couldn't see from the back of the boat.

For hour after hour we zigzagged our way up that muddy winding river until it was too dark to go any further. Then just as the sun was going down behind the horizon we finally pulled up to a small village on the riverbank. The first village that we had seen all day in fact, although we had seen occasional clearings and small lean-to's that looked to be uninhabited and abandoned. "This is where we will be staying for the night. We will continue on in the morning." the driver announced. I asked our Dani friend where we were and to my dismay he said a word that I had hoped not to hear at all on this journey. *"Kehu"* he replied and the stories of that old man back in the coastal town we had stayed in the previous night came back to mind. We were going to be sleeping the night in a tribe that was said to be cannibalistic.

A couple of Papuan men that seemed friendly enough and that looked just as city-like as the boat driver and his assistant who had brought us to this place came out and greeted the boat driver as if he was an old long-lost friend. It turned out that our driver had been here before and was more experienced with this river than we previously thought. To our surprise, the men of the village were also fluent enough in Indonesian to have a basic conversation and didn't seem the least bit bothered that we had come to their village. That is, until they saw Derek get out of the boat.

Derek seemed to make them nervous and we at first didn't know why, until one of them asked if he was a soldier. Of course Derek was wearing the same Canadian army style jungle boots that he always wore and was sporting the high and tight hairstyle of the army as well. Not to mention that his backpack was army issue. Derek had been out of the army for some time at that point and so of course he tried to play it off and told them that he wasn't in fact a soldier at all. From that point on however the women and children of the village seemed to keep their distance. It was only a few of the men that took it upon themselves to keep us company.

After a while the man that seemed to be in charge of the village motioned for us to follow him. We followed him to a room where we were told we could bed down for the night. The room was small but to our pleasant surprise, very comfortable and well-built. Most of the houses in this village were the same type of wood plank and corrugated tin roofed housing that we had seen back in the coastal town where we spent the last few nights. After talking to the village leader a bit throughout the evening we learned that the Indonesian government had a well funded project going to integrate the Kehu tribe into society and they not only built these beautiful buildings free of charge for the people to use as a school, but also provided them with teachers for the school. The government also generously built a number of small houses for the people as well which made up this village.

A few of the Kehu men cooked us a nice meal of rice and fish on new shiny pots and pans which they had also seemingly received from the government. They made us feel plenty welcome and fed us rice and potatoes until we couldn't eat anymore. Then we bedded down for the night in that little government built school as the evening rains let loose and began pounding away on the tin roof.

The sound of the heavy rains on the corrugated tin roof was deafening which needless to say made it very hard to sleep. I will have to admit though that neither Jennie or I would have slept much that night anyways. One, because even in addition to the sound of the rain hitting the tin above our heads, the mosquitos were so bad in those lowland jungles that we could hear the little blood sucking varmints buzzing a continual high pitched scream in our ears all night long. Two, simply because we were said to be sleeping in a village of cannibals. I couldn't help but wonder if a big, taller than usual, meaty guy like me might have been tastier looking than the average. I didn't want to be anybody's meal, that's for sure!

To our relief, before we knew it, it was morning again, none of us had been eaten and we found ourselves once again packing and boarding the little dugout canoe. We thanked the Kehu men for their hospitality and as we were pulling away even the standoffish women and children came out to wave goodbye. Again we were winding our way up the rapids and maneuvering through fallen branches and brush. That second day in the boat, the sun seemed to beat down on us even hotter and harder. The rapids and waves of the muddy lowlands river also seemed a bit higher.

All of us had sore backs from sitting in that little boat for the entire previous day and the fact that none of us slept too well the night before didn't help either. We rounded one bend after another in that muddy jungle river until it seemed we lost our sense of direction all together. Also, we had been passing little groups of one to three thatched roof houses for a couple hours. They all seemed vacant and nobody was in them. When I leaned back and asked our driver if he knew who the huts belonged to, he replied that they belonged to a part of the *Burate* tribe: a group of hunters and gatherers that traditionally lived out on the coast but whom had recently been moving up river to find better sources of food and places to garden. The Burate had come up the river looking for natural resources such as sandalwood and other rare trees, which they could gather and take down to the coastal towns to try to sell. The uninhabited thatched roof lean-to type houses we had seen the day before also belonged to these people.

We continued on hour after hour after hour, sitting on hard, hand hewn wooden crossbeams. The hours began to blend together and seem like an eternity. But then as we rounded one more bend on that seemingly endless river, we finally saw something that broke the monotony of the trip. Something that caught us all by surprise! There was a group of little Burate thatched roof houses that looked newly constructed with fresh thatch on the roofs. This time, there were people on the river bank in front of them jumping up and down and frantically yelling at us as if their lives depended on it!

We had just begun to see the small hills of the lowlands peaking up from behind the river at this point on the river. The rapids had grown even larger and our speed had slowed down considerably because of the faster flowing water and the amount of dead trees and branches that we had to steer through and around. The river was louder and wilder than it had been earlier and so the outboard motor on the back of our boat was also much noisier as the driver worked it harder so that we could continue making progress up the fast flowing river rapids. We couldn't make out any of what the Burate people on the riverbank were yelling at us because of all the noise, but we knew by their frantic gestures that whatever it was, it must be important.

Perhaps they had a sick villager that needed medical attention or some other medical emergency with which they needed help? None of them were armed our acting like they had any intention of harming us and so our driver maneuvered the boat as close as he could to the riverbank, under the trees and quickly cut the engine so that we could try to hear them.

"They will shoot! The really will shoot you!" they yelled at us in Indonesian. "Who? Who is going to shoot at us!" our boat driver yelled back at them while he hurriedly glanced back over his shoulder towards the other riverbank. We all began scanning the patches of jungle that surrounded us for any movement. As far as any of us could see there was nobody there. We also knew though that these dense jungles are so thick that they could have been hiding anyone or anything, even an entire army of tribesmen.

One of the Burate continued yelling to our boat driver and frantically explained that just seconds before we rounded that corner they had seen something on the other side of the river that they were deathly afraid of. They continued frantically yelling at us "*Orang Maniwo*! They are the ones that will shoot you! There are *orang Maniwo* hiding in the jungle! Be careful because they are right over there! We just saw them! Don't get any closer to the other side of the river, they will shoot! They have got bows and arrows and are waiting for you!" they frantically yelled.

A look of fear swept over our boat driver's face. Our Dani guide also seemed confused as if he also was frozen in fear. None of us knew exactly what we should do. All of us were still scanning the trees up and down the muddy jungle riverbank trying to get a glimpse of these "Orang Maniwo" and then it struck me. One of the phrases that Mike and Steve had both used to describe these mountain people in and around the Dao territory was "Maniwo people". These were very possibly the people we had come here to find. This was our first contact with the mountain tribes. It had begun!

A few more seconds and I spotted one! "Look, there he is! Over there by that log on the edge of the jungle!" I excitedly whispered over to the others in the boat. There, just along the edge of the tree cover we could see one lone man standing with his bows and arrows. He was muscular and proud looking standing there on the riverbank, completely naked except for a traditional small gourd covering of his people. The arrows he grasped with his right fist were so long and the bamboo shafts of the arrows so thick that when we first saw the man I thought he was holding a fistful of spears. He wasn't the slightest bit scared and didn't look to have any intention of running from us or retreating into the thick jungle behind him.

Just then the old Dani guide stood up in the boat and yelled to the lone man standing on the riverbank. "*Kayoo bagee?*" he yelled over to the man. There was no response at first. The man just stared at us with what looked like a scowl on his face. We weren't sure if he was happy to see us there or not. The fact that he still had his bow and arrows in hand didn't seem to be a good sign though.

Another time, *"Kayoo bagee?"* our old Dani guide yelled over to the riverbank but this time there was a response. *"Maniwo!"* the man replied. The Dani looked over at us and said to us in Indonesian "I asked the man in the local language where he is from. He says he is from Maniwo." Then he turned back towards the bank and yelled out another line of the little bit of mountain language that he knew from his previous time hiking around in the Dao territory.

"Aa too ye?" Again there was no response. *"Aa too ye?"* he yelled a second time and then as the lone tribesmen turned and motioned towards the jungle two more younger muscle covered, wirey young men popped out of the jungle and onto the river bank both of them also armed with bows and arrows. Our guide had been asking how many of them there were and this was their response. If there were more than three of them they didn't have any plans of telling us so.

We could see them conversing in their own language towards each other for a few seconds while still watching us out of the corner of their eye. They were still clenching their bows and arrows and holding them close. "What are they talking about? Why aren't they putting down their bows and arrows? What will they do next?" I wondered out loud as I looked over at Jennie sitting in the boat right behind me. At that range we couldn't have gotten away from them in time to not be shot even if we had wanted too. They were probably only thirty feet or so away. And so there we were, sitting ducks in the middle of that muddy jungle river, wondering what would happen next.

We sat for a few moments in nervous anticipation and then all at once we saw that first tribesman set his bow and arrows on the ground and motion for the other two to do the same. They set their weapons down and then began walking down the riverbank and closer towards us. They weren't more than twenty feet from the place where they had set down their bows and arrows when one of them stuck out his arm towards our boat and motioned with his hand like he wanted us to come over to where they were.

We knew that this was the time that we had been waiting for; this was our opportunity to show friendship. This was our first face-to-face contact with the remote mountain people of these once seemingly impenetrable jungles. Our Dani guide assured our driver that if we would slowly work our way over to the bank where they were standing, they were not likely to try and shoot at us. The driver nervously started the engine and we began slowly working our way towards the other side of the river where they had cautiously positioned themselves.

As we drew closer to the men we continually scanned the jungle to see if there were more of them. Needless to say, our hearts began beating faster as we slowly drew closer and closer to the bank they were standing on. We all recognized that every foot closer we got to these people made us an easier target for those long thick arrows. It wouldn't have been difficult for them to dash over to their bows and still have plenty of time to open fire on us if they so desired. With every foot closer we got to these men the less our chances of survival would be if they opened fire on us. We purposely had not brought any weapons with which to retaliate should we be attacked. We were there for one purpose: to show friendship. We had left friends and family behind and traveled all this way to communicate a message of life, not death. We were willing to die for our message if that was what God would ask of us.

In that moment Jennie and I were hit head on with the fact that we very well may have been breathing our very last lungful's of air but at that very same moment we experienced an incredible peace that everything was going to be absolutely fine whether those were our last breaths or not. I felt absolute excitement, remarkable peace and nervous anticipation all at the same time!

The Burate people, still standing on the other side of the river behind us watched in astonishment as we pulled up to the side of the river not far from these *orang Maniwo* and one at a time got out of the boat and started walking up the riverbank towards these seemingly dangerous remote people that they were so deathly afraid of. Then as we got within a few feet of the three men one of them reached out his hand with a big grin on his face as if to say "Don't worry, we will not be trying out our arrows on you today!"

We took turns, one at a time reaching forward and grasping their hands to greet them. We had learned from Mike a good friendly greeting that he said most of the mountain tribes in this area were familiar with. *"Epaoo"* I said to one of the men as I reached forward and grabbed on to his hand in an effort to show friendship. After we had all greeted each other, the head tribesman opened a net bag which was draped over his shoulder and removed a small black bird which I assumed that he had shot and killed earlier that day. It seemed that he was presenting us with the bird as a sort of token of friendship and we responded by giving each of them a pack of dry ramen as our return gesture of friendship. Our boat driver had a pack of cigarettes that he had carried up from home so he gave them each a cigarette as well and we all sat down on the riverbank there together as they smoked and excitedly chattered back and forth to each other in their own language. It seemed they were excited with what they had received in return for the small bird.

I can only imagine what must have been going through the minds of the Burate people on the other side of the river as they watched all of this take place from a safe distance. They must have thought we were crazy for getting anywhere close to such people. But then again, there were many of our friends and relatives back in the United States that felt the same way. We knew many people in our homeland that felt as if risks like these should not be taken and that people such as these are not worth such a price. It seemed to be the same on this side of the world.

After the men had finished their cigarettes one of them walked over to the boat and put his hand on it. He pointed up river and spoke another long line of mountain language. Our Dani guide said to us in Indonesian "It seems that if we are going up river, they want to go with us." We still had not made it to our final stopping point on the river and we needed to work the dugout canoe as far up river as possible before we started hiking by foot. The boat driver said that it was fine if the three *orang Maniwo* joined us and that the small boat could handle their weight so we all climbed into the long boat and then motioned to our three new friends to join us.

They cautiously climbed into the boat still tightly grasping their bows and arrows as the driver started up the engine. As we started up stream again, it was obvious that it was the three tribesman's first time in a boat because as the driver revved up the engine their eyes got wide as saucers and they looked as if they began to panic for a split second. Then as the boat got back out into the middle of the river and was rocking because of the rapids they seemed to make their bows and arrows a little less of a priority and they began holding on for dear life as they let all their weapons fall down into the bottom of the boat. The driver announced that it shouldn't be long now before we would hit the farthest up point possible that we could continue by boat.

The rapids were getting wilder and we were already working our way up through the foothills.

From that point it wasn't more than an hour before the rapids were too rough to go any further and I began to get a bit nervous as we continued up stream. More than a few times I glanced back at the three tribesmen behind us as they chattered back and forth in their own language. They were covered with muscle from head to toe. They probably knew exactly where they were though we didn't. "Would they continue to be friendly or would they turn on us once we had taken them as far as we could go?" I thought to myself as the water violently lapped up against the side of the boat and we rounded another muddy bend in that jungle river.

A few moments later we could hear the three men talking faster and more excitedly as we rounded what seemed like it had to be our last turn. The strong fast moving current and the rough waters seemed to be getting more dangerous by the second. The water had now changed from a dark muddy brown into more of a swirling greyish color and we began seeing pointed boulders also sticking their ugly heads up from beneath the churning waters surface.

Then all of the sudden the three tribesmen began to excitedly point up river. As we looked up ahead to where they were pointing we could see off in the distance three more men standing on the river bank right out in the open, all nearly naked and wearing the traditional dress of the mountain tribes. In addition to those men there were also a few more groups of two to three people a little farther up and there was even a small shelter on the riverside!

"I think we made it Jennie! That must be the first small village!" I excitedly announced. "Those might be Dao people!" she replied back with a huge smile on her face. As we drew closer and closer to the riverbank the three tribesmen in our boat and the people on the bank began yelling back and forth and smiles swept over the faces of those on the riverbank.

We still didn't know exactly how the rest of the people would react to us coming into their territory completely uninvited and unexpected but it seemed by the looks on their faces that we were going to be just fine. Perhaps the three tribesmen we had picked up farther down river were a blessing in disguise, our ticket into this first village. No one was putting arrows in their bows strings even though they were all holding their bows and arrows close. We breathed a sigh of relief as we neared the riverbank and heard *"Epaoo! Epaoo!"* said back to us as we greeted them with the only little bit of mountain language we knew.

The people here looked much different than any of Burate, Kehu, Dani or people of the cities and towns we had encountered up to this point. They had huge gleaming white decorative bones or long bird beak looking pieces stuck through their septums and decorative hand-woven arm bands on right around the bicep or just above the elbow. Every single one of them was covered in muscle from head to toe. They seemed to have about zero percent body fat for the most part.

A young Dao man walked up next to me as we got out of the boat and made our way through knee-deep water pulling the boat up as close to the shore as we could get it. He was trying to help us pull and guide the boat and he laughed as he looked at my funny clothes and pale skin. "He must think I look strange!" I thought to myself as we tugged on the boat together pulling it until the boat driver yelled out that we had pulled it up on the riverbank far enough.

We grabbed our bags and one of the Dao men showed us to the small shelter beside the river where we pulled a few more packs of those lightweight packs of ramen noodles from our backpacks. We shared the packs of dry noodles once again with the Dao people that were gathered there on that riverbank in an attempt to show friendship and then we cooked some more noodles up for dinner a little while later. The Dao men scarfed the noodles down almost immediately, as if they were some rare, long awaited delicacy, but then again, back in these remote jungles they probably were.

Some of the Dao people also seemed to recognize our Dani guide from his previous time in their territory. We sat around the glowing fire in that little shelter on the riverbank the rest of the afternoon until the sun slowly began to descend behind the ravine walls and the sky changed from a bright blue to a deep orange. One of the Dao men had a small hand carved bamboo instrument about the length of a ballpoint pen with him. It seemed to be the equivalent of a mouth harp or what some people call a juice harp. He played different interesting patterns and songs on it and then passed it around to others so that they also could take turns playing. The little bamboo instrument was passed around for a while, each person playing their own unique pattern or song.

It struck me from our first few hours in their territory that these were a people that loved to laugh. The air was constantly filled with laughter as we sat around eating, smiling and making gestures of friendship toward each other. It wasn't long before all we could see was the dancing light of the fire on the silhouettes of ancient jungle trees. The Dao people that were gathered in the small shelter with us started lying down next to the fire and one at a time we all drifted off to sleep on that stiff wooden floor to a soundtrack of crackling fire and jungle insects and birds.

I fell asleep thinking about how the next morning would kick off our first day of hiking. This was the part that Jennie and I suspected would be more challenging than any other part of this journey and possibly of our lives. We needed to get as much sleep as possible if we were going to be able to make it up those jungle mountains. Little did we know just how much of a challenge it would be.

The next morning we awoke early to stiff backs and achy necks from those hard floors. A few of the tribal guys already had a small fire going and the warmth of it on our feet felt good. I listened to the rapids racing down through the mountains a few hundred feet away. Jungle birds and unusual bugs were perched and hidden somewhere up in the trees, adding into the jungle background noise with their screeches, squawks and songs. Jungle vines dripped with the cool morning mist of the moist jungle.

The men sitting across the shelter looked over at us with smiles on their faces and then over at our backpacks and back at us again. I knew what they wanted. They liked those Ramen noodles we had shared with them the day before. I pulled out a couple more packs of noodles and one of the men ran and got some water and a small container we could boil them in.

It wasn't long before the rest of the men in the hut had also woken up and we were all smiling and laughing again. They were chattering away in their own language as they slurped up spoonful after spoonful of noodles.

Our knees were stiff from multiple days sitting in a dugout canoe and we hadn't even started hiking yet. I stood and tried to stretch a bit as we began getting our backpacks back in order and prepared to begin our long trek up into the mountains. We stood on the riverbank after we had packed our bags and waited for our old Dani guide to get his things together. He insisted that he had been to this place before and that it would be no problem for him along with a couple of the Dao guys to lead us the appropriate direction, that is, to the main population and villages of the Dao tribe.

Even though I was still nervous that our old, Dani guide might not be able to cut it on the trail, I sure was glad that we had him with us. Mike was right, it might have been somewhat foolish to come here alone. After the events of the previous day and the way that our Dani friend had been able to use the little bit of mountain language that he knew to get us through that standoff in between the Burate and the Orang Maniwo, I was convinced that he had already played a key part in this first survey which no one else could have played. When the sun was up past the tree line a few of the Dao men started up a small trail behind the little shelter we had stayed in the night before and our Dani guide said in Indonesian "Okay, it's time. Let's go" as he started up the trail after them.

It seemed like those two Dao men in the front were nearly running up the trail. Every couple hundred feet they would begin to disappear down the trail in front of us and we would try to go faster so that we could keep up with their pace. All they carried with them was a small string bag about the size of a small purse and their bows and arrows. They went barefoot and almost completely naked. We could barely hear them at all on the trail they were so stealth and smooth in their movements.

As we worked our way farther up into the mountains the brush got thicker and the trail seemed thinner. Prickly vines, and strands of thin creeper and razor grass stretched along the trail and would dig into our skin if we weren't careful to watch for them. Then within an hour we had given up as far as trying to keep up with the Dao people went and we just tried our best to stay on what seemed like the trail they had gone up before us. We occasionally wouldn't see some of the bushes and vines that had thorns and spurs on them and they would dig into our ankles or arms making long scrape marks across our skin.

The trail wasn't completely on solid ground either. It seemed like half the time we would find ourselves walking along slippery fallen trees or mossy underbrush. Sometimes the trees would give way under our weight and we would fall a few feet down into the wet soggy jungle floor. Legs tangled in the jungle roots and vines we would scramble to climb back up onto the trail out of a healthy fear of what might lie below the surface of the thick underbrush.

Poisonous centipedes, some close to a foot long with poison strong enough to kill a small child are seen frequently in those jungles and we occasionally saw them scurrying across the trail in front of us. Not to mention the "two-stepper": a poisonous death adder also common on the island that is so deadly it is said you have approximately two steps you can walk before you will die from the snake's poison once bitten.

More than once we sank into the mud and moss of the jungle up to our knees or even our thighs and we had to help each other back up and onto what seemed to be the trail because we were too tangled to get out ourselves. After a while the scrapes and cuts from our falls and the thorns began to swell out and sting when we would touch them. Occasionally a hornbill or white cockatoo flew overhead above the trees and screeched at us as we tried to work our way up through the mountains. We also often heard things rustling in the jungle a few feet away, perhaps a wild pig or tree kangaroo.

After we had hiked a few hours we hadn't even made it to the top of the first ridge and I began to feel nauseous from the heat. I tried to drink some water but it just made me want to throw up. I stopped and looked down at my leg as I felt a pinching sensation and realized that there was a huge black leech that had been sucking blood out of my leg. By the size of the thing it had been drawing blood for some time. I yanked it of and threw it in the jungle as the blood started trickling down my leg and into my sock.

"Jennie, check yourself for leeches, there are leeches here!" I said in disgust. She realized she had two more on her as she looked down and shrieked in dismay. "I don't know if I can do this Scott," she said to me as she sat down on the side of the trail, the weight of her backpack almost toppling her over. I couldn't blame her though, I felt the same way. Even after all the training we had done to get ready for this we were nowhere close to adequate for these trails. Here we were, only a few hours into our first day of hiking and we were already feeling ready to give up. I couldn't believe it. "Drink some water. Let's just keep on going," I told Jennie while trying not to let her see on my face that I also was wondering what we had gotten ourselves into. Lucky for us however, after nearly four hours of hiking we finally cleared the first ridge and found a small two hut village with a few more people in it.

We slid our backpacks off and let them fall to the ground as we sat down in the sun. "These huge, backpacks are killing us!" I thought to myself. I began sorting through my pack and trying to find stuff I could leave behind and also went through Jennie's pack trying to redistribute some of the weightier objects to other bags so that hers was lighter and easier to carry. Anything metal and all the cookware and small pots and pans were removed from my pack and placed in one of the two tribal houses in that small jungle clearing in order to lighten the load. We then rested for just a few minutes but our guide said that if we wanted to make it to the next place with shelter where we needed to sleep that night, we had to keep moving.

We stumbled back up onto our feet again and headed down the other side of the ridge where things began to finally seem a little bit easier for a while. It was nice to go down hill instead of up hill, but those jungle logs we had to walk across over and over again seemed twice as slippery as we hiked downwards. Time after time we fell and struggled to keep ourselves from tumbling down the mountainside. I could tell by how sore and bruised my legs and back were getting from the falls that I was in for an even harder day tomorrow if we were able to find the strength to continue at all.

It only took us half as long to get down the other side of the mountain as it had taken us to get up it earlier that day though. Then as we got closer and closer to the bottom of the mountain we could once again hear a river and jungle rapids winding and crashing down through the valley. When we finally made it down to the bottom of the ravine we walked out on to a rocky river bank to see the first Dao style vine bridge that we had ever seen. "Are you kidding me?" Jennie said out loud. "Do we have to cross that?" I yelled over to our Dani guide in Indonesian.

"There is no other way!" He yelled back trying to be heard over top of the rapids, "Don't worry! I will go and get new vines and tie them across the bridge so that it will be able to hold your weight!" he added in. "Wow, that's reassuring" I sarcastically mumbled to myself. I had never been good with things like this and now I had to cross a one sided vine bridge over a bunch of rapids and jagged rocks with a nearly forty pound backpack strapped to my back. Even worse, my wife had to do it too!

"Do you want to go first or should I?" Jonny asked me as we stood there gawking at the swinging vine bridge. Even despite all of their previous jungle survey trips Derek and Jonny both admitted they hadn't yet encountered terrain this extreme or bridges this sketchy. The bridge stretching out across the jagged rocks and class four rapids of a roaring jungle river reminded us of something out of an old Indiana Jones movie. We all knew that this brittle, vine bridge wasn't made for six foot two inch, two hundred pound foreigners like Jonny and myself.

As our Dani guide worked his way across, his feet slow and steady, his arms locked around the upper vines just in case the foot vines were to snap on him, we could tell that he had encountered bridges like this before. We watched in amazement as even at his age, he crossed the bridge smoothly and confidently the way that only a Papuan could. When he got to the other side, he shook his head in disagreement and motioned to us to wait. Then he disappeared into the jungles on the other side of the river. A few minutes later he reappeared with some pieces of fresh green vine in his hand. He then began to work his way back across the vines bridge, retying and replacing old rotted vines that had snapped because of their age. He had found and cut fresh green rattan vines from the thick jungle, which he used to strengthen the different sections which seemed the weakest, then it was our turn.

Second in line was Derek, the member of our group with the most experience in situations like these. Because he had served a few years in the Canadian army in addition to all the survey work he had done in the past, we knew that he was probably the best person to go first after our guide. In general Derek seemed like the type of person that lived for adventures like this! But we could tell that even he was a bit nervous about what might happen in the next few moments. We would be the first white outsiders in the world to ever cross this bridge even though tribal people had probably been using it and rebuilding it for centuries. Derek strapped on his forty-five pound army style pack and began inching his way across the vines, one small sidestep at a time.

We all watched in nervous anticipation as he slowly worked his way to the halfway point where he would be hanging right over the center of the roaring river. The river was so incredibly powerful and loud that those of us watching from the riverbank had to yell to each other even though we were standing no more than a couple feet apart. Derek took another couple steps passed the halfway point and then "SNAP!" One of the medium sized vines that held the two main sections of the bridge together broke under the pressure of his body weight!

He looked back at us for a split second as if to say "Did you hear that?!" and then turned back with determination towards the other end of the bridge. We continued to nervously watch as he took a couple more steps towards the other side. Just a few more steps and he would be the first of us to make it. Three more steps, two more steps, one more step, he made it! We all gave a big sigh of relief but it wasn't over yet, we still had three to go.

A quick discussion took place in between the three of us that had yet to cross. We had to decide who would go next. We quickly came to the conclusion that it would only make sense if Jennie was next seeing as how she was the lightest of our group. The bridge had done its job now for both our guide and also for Derek. Not to mention that Derek had just crossed the bridge with a backpack almost half the weight of Jennie herself! Besides, if any of us were going to weaken the bridge or make it worse, it would be Jonny or myself: the weightiest and tallest of the team.

Jennie looked at me with a nervous smile on her face and said "I love you Scottie" presumably just in case it would be her last opportunity to let me know, then she proceeded to climb up onto the vines. I knew from the moment that we saw the bridge that this would be no easy task for Jennie. One of the first things out of her mouth when she herself saw the dangling vines was "Oh man Scott, I'm afraid of heights". If she was going to get across that bridge, something would have to drive her that was greater than her fear of heights and falling. She would have to set her eyes on the other side and step by step, move forward by faith.

I will never forget watching her cross the jungle vine bridge that day. The determination on her face, the emotions running through my chest as I watched my young, wife, barely out of her teens climb up on the vines and utter her "last words" just in case the bridge didn't hold. As she began to inch her way across those vines one little sidestep at a time, it became a reality to me that I was no longer in control of my wife's safety. It was God that was in control, and He would do with her as He saw fit. All I could do was yell words of affirmation and encouragement from the side of the river and watch her step out in faith.

She moved slowly but steadily, determined the whole way. I watched her every move in nervous anticipation. In what seemed like no time at all, she was passed the halfway mark and getting closer and closer to the other side. She didn't even flinch when she was over the worst part and not a single vine broke. A couple more steps and she would be there! I prayed under my breath that God would help her and give her the strength both physically and mentally to make it the rest of the way.

"You can do it Jennie! You're almost there!" I shouted out as loud as I could. She only had a little ways to go, and then before we knew it, she was climbing up onto the other side and giving a victory yell with one fist up in the air, while looking back at us with a huge smile on her face! I whooped back at her in approval even though I knew she probably couldn't hear me over the roaring of the river. Three down and two to go. So far so good!

Jonny and I stood there looking at each other, knowing that if the bridge was going to snap, it would most likely snap on one of us. "Well Scott, one of us is next. Do you want to go first or should I?" Jonny asked. I thought about it for a second and it came to mind that Jonny was looking forward to a long awaited and anticipated event in his life. He was engaged and was to fly back to the States to be married only one week after our return from this survey trip. I looked across the river at my wife and remembered what it was like to be in his place, so close to something I had looked forward to for so incredibly long. "Well bro, your about to get married and I have already enjoyed marriage for a couple years now, so I'll go first." I said with a nervous laugh. He smiled and nodded in agreement.

After nervously strapping on my gear, I began to climb up onto the vines. As I shifted my full body weight onto the vine bridge it felt anything but promising and it began to sag under my weight. It seemed as if the vines beneath my feet were flexing twice as much on me as they had on the people before me. I was only about five sidesteps into my crossing and "SNAP!" one of the vines had broken already. Fear flooded my chest and I started second guessing myself. Nonetheless I kept on going one step at a time. I could see the halfway mark, the place where I would be hanging directly above the center of roaring river below. It was drawing closer and closer with every slow step. I had a death grip on those vines as I knew that the majority of my weight was on the few creaking vines beneath my feet. If the vines under my feet were to give way, I would have only my arms to keep me from falling into the rapids below. As I approached the center I intensely focused on every step, trying not to unnecessarily bounce or swing the bridge any more than I had to.

"SNAP!" another vine broke under the pressure of my weight and I still had a full half the bridge to go! I began subconsciously praying with every step, "God help me get to the other side. God help me get to the other side." It became very clear that not only had my wife's life and safety been in God's hands in these past moments, but so was mine. If I was to make it across, it would be by the grace of God. I pressed on, trusting that my Creator would not let anything happen to me that He had not planned to happen before I had ever entered these jungles. The other side was slowly coming within reach and I was almost three quarters the way across and "Creeeek…SNAP!" Another vine broke and fear shot through my chest once again. I was so close to the other side…just a few more steps!

Stepping up the pace to try to get off the bridge as soon as possible I tried to take bigger, quicker strides towards the end of the bridge. I could hear Jennie cheering me on from the other side…two more steps, one more step, I made it! Letting out a big sigh of relief I also let out a big "Thank you Lord!" and gave Jennie a big bear hug. I felt as if my very life had flashed before my eyes in those few moments.

One more to go, and we would all be across. Jonny climbed up on the vines on the other side and started taking his first steps across. You could once again see the bridge flexing under two hundred pounds of weight as he began. I was all the more nervous watching him cross as three of the vines had snapped on me alone as I was crossing only minutes before. I thought for sure another few vines would break under Jonny but the remaining vines seemed to be doing their job well as he slowly approached the halfway mark. Once again, we were all yelling our encouragement. "You can do it Jonny! You're doing great! Keep on going!"

He was past the halfway mark now and working his way up towards our end and still, not a single vine had broken on him! He only had a little more to go and our whole survey team would be across. A couple seconds later and we were welcoming him to the other side and praising God that we had all made it across safely. This would be a moment in our lives that we would reminisce over for years to come.

We sat down beside the river and celebrated the victory with a few strips of beef jerky and half a power bar each that we had gotten in a care package from the States a few weeks before: we had been saving it for a special occasion. We snacked on our western foods for a few minutes and rejoiced together that God had seen fit to bring us all across safely.

Being in a ravine after crossing the vine bridge, we were once again at the bottom of another towering jungle mountain. Now we would begin the accent of our second mountain for the day. The second mountain seemed like it was almost twice as steep as the first. Now we were also doing quite a bit of hand over hand hiking and the jungle seemed to get cooler and wetter as we eventually began nearing higher elevations. We had been trekking for close to eight hours total when I began to get dizzy and even more nauseous than I had been earlier in the day.

Hugging closer to the mountain, I tried to hold even more tightly to the roots and rocks that I was using for handholds. I didn't say a word to anybody else in our party but they could tell I was wearing down fast as I began lagging behind the rest of the group. "Scott, are you sure you are drinking enough, you need to keep drinking!"

Jennie said from a few yards in front of me. She knew me better than anyone else. She could tell that something was wrong. I stopped and took a swig of water from my water bottle, then kept moving.

A little while later I got even dizzier than before. Dropping to my knees when I came to a flat part on the trail, I started dry heaving. "Your dehydrated man, you need to get your electrolytes back up!" Derek yelled down from in front of me on the trail as he looked back and saw me beginning to wretch fluid all over the jungle floor.

Lucky for me, Derek had a small packet of rehydration powder with him that he said might help. He mixed the powder into my water bottle and we stopped there for a good fifteen minutes or so as I tried to get down as much of the rehydration powder tinted water as I could. "We don't have time to sit any longer. We have to get moving and make it to the place we are headed to before sundown or we will be spending the night in the jungle" our Dani guide interjected after I had rested only a few minutes. We didn't have time to waste. We had to keep moving.

A little while later I ran out of water and thought as if I would lose hope altogether. We had been hiking over ten hours and it seemed like we would not make it before sundown but then finally, as we rounded one last bend in that seemingly endless trail we could see one small lean-to and a few banana trees in a tiny clearing. It wasn't even a village, and there were no Dao people there at all but the Dani insisted that this was our destination for the night.

None of us could believe how far the Dao hamlets were apart. "Is all of the Dao territory like this? Is this what we will be facing for nearly two and a half more weeks?" I wondered as I let my backpack fall to the ground and nearly collapsed in exhaustion there by the small thatched roof lean-to. I didn't want anything except a place that I could lie down. This was obviously just a temporary garden house someone had thrown up as it didn't even have walls.

Throughout the day, the two Dao men that started with us earlier had eventually grown impatient of waiting for us on the trail. They went up ahead to the next village because we were too slow to keep up with them. It looked like it was once again just our survey team and we would all be huddling under this small shelter for the evening. At least there was a small stream close by though where we could get some water as we had all run out completely. The small shelter had a dirt floor and a place where we could tell people had made small fires for the purpose of cooking recently so we got out some food rations and cooked them over the fire to try to get up our strength a bit. We had hiked over ten hours that day and still hadn't even come to the main population of the Dao people.

"I don't know that I can keep doing this Scott, and by the looks of things you can't either," Jennie said to me later on that evening. "We'll see how we feel in the morning" I replied. But I knew that unless our guide was planning on spending the next day recuperating in that small clearing with a single lean-to, we wouldn't be going too much farther up into these mountains. Not to mention the fact that our guide himself had been complaining for the last three hours as well. He had rambled on and on in Indonesian about how his knees hurt and he was too old to hike these trails anymore. At his age, I was surprised he had even made it this far. His strength was wearing thin.

That was a hard evening as we realized just how inadequate we were to be in a place like this. We were learning fast about the Indonesian jungles and just how treacherous it would be should we ever end up stranded in a place like this alone. After we ate a little bit and felt a little more rested Jonny looked over at me and said "I think we should just turn around and go back tomorrow. There is no way that you guys can keep going at this pace even if you wanted to, and the farther interior we get, the harder it will be to make it out." He had said the words that we were all thinking. I had not wanted to admit it but Jonny was right and we all knew it.

Then Derek piped up, "It can't be any one person's decision to turn back! Jonny can't decide for the rest of us. If we are going to turn back, we all have to decide that together and I for one did not come all this way just to give up and turn around." he said in a strong voice. Jennie and I didn't want to turn back anymore than Derek did. "Let's just rest and talk about it again in the morning. Perhaps we will all feel a little better after we have had some time to recuperate" I said and tried to close my eyes as my head throbbed with a migraine brought on by the dehydration.

The next morning we woke up to cloudy overcast skies and the screeching of cockatoos and hornbills amongst all the other jungle sounds. It was much colder in these mountains than we had expected but it wasn't long before the sun was burning the clouds off the mountains and everything began to warm up to a nice comfortable temperature. We knew that we had to make a decision as to whether we would press on or not.

The day before, every time we had asked our Dani guide how much further it was to our destination he had replied either "Just a little ways farther up the trail" or "Another half-hour". He had done this since we got to the bridge and for nearly four more hours afterwards and so we learned pretty quickly that we couldn't completely trust his answers. It was the Dani however that was the only one in our group that knew where we were going, so there was no one else we could trust. "Today's hike will not be as long as yesterdays" he assured us but none of us knew whether we could take him at his word or not. We were all feeling much better after some rest however and after a quick breakfast of left over rice, dry noodles and a little bit of instant oatmeal that we had backpacked in with us we were all feeling a bit more positive.

"You have got to make sure you drink today Scott or we are not going to make it." Derek said. "Yeah, you cannot get to the point you did yesterday where you were on your hands and knees throwing up or that's it. We will have to turn around, we won't be able to go any further" Jonny added in. I was a step ahead of them. I had been drinking water since I had opened my eyes a few hours earlier in hopes that I could get ahead of the game. Jennie was feeling better as well besides the fact that all of us had sore knees and thighs from all of the previous days hiking. We decided to give it another shot! A few minutes later we started out on the trail once again and off we went up the spongy mossy ground of the jungle trail.

This mountain terrain sure was different from the sandy beaches of the coast! We were once again making our way across fallen trees and jungle roots trying not to make any bad choices in our footing lest we fall through. Our skills for walking on this type of terrain had slightly improved though as we had learned from the many long hours of hiking the day before what we could and couldn't step on. We were still occasionally making bad choices and falling through but not nearly as much as the day before.

About two hours into the hike it felt like the ground suddenly began to shake underneath us. We had seen on the other side of the valley the day before a few places where there were landslides on the sides of the steep mountains. These mountains were so steep in places that when the trees grew too tall the top soil would let loose of the side of the mountain and whole huge sections of jungle nearly a mile long and a mile wide would let go and come crashing down into the valley.

There was a huge jolt one way and then the other underneath our feet and I was sure that we were caught in one of these landslides. *"Ada gempa bumi!"* the Dani guide yelled out. It was an earthquake! "Hurry everybody run for flat ground" Derek yelled out but there was nowhere to run! We were at a very steep part of the trail, which once again involved hand over hand climbing. We were literally holding onto the side of the mountain by tree roots with our hands while the ground jolted back and forth beneath us. We couldn't do anything except for just wait and hold on for dear life.

As soon as the earthquake subsided enough to where we could move a little Jennie and I worked our way over to the root of a big tree where we had a little more of a spot to hold onto. We waited in complete silence as we listened to the jungle trees cracking and popping around us as if the whole jungle floor would let loose. Finally, the mountainside quit jolting underneath us but we were still frozen in fear. We sat still and watched the leaves of small jungle plants continue to quiver from aftershocks as though they themselves were still frightened.

The small tremors and aftershocks carried on for quite a few minutes and we would later find out that one of the biggest fault lines in Indonesia runs right through the center of the Dao territory. The small coastal town where we had based our survey out of and slept those first few nights had been nearly leveled in that earthquake. Most of the main buildings in that town had collapsed, many Indonesians had died and many of the surviving Indonesian families would sleep in the streets for the following weeks because they had nowhere else to go.

I had been in earthquakes before having grown up in California but never had I been caught in one as I was doing hand over hand climbing on the side of a jungle mountain. Jennie being from Tennessee, she didn't know what was going on! This was the first earthquake she had ever experienced. "Wow, isn't it insane that I would experience my first earthquake on our first foot survey? That was intense! I felt the whole mountain moving underneath me!"

she said as we slowly stood up and brushed ourselves off. Hopefully this would be the only earthquake during our journey. It was not something that we wanted to experience again, especially while hiking such extreme terrain!

A few hours later we were once again starting to feel exhausted. Our knees throbbed, our water supply was low and I once again started to grow weary and a little nervous that we were going to find ourselves in the same situation as the day before. Again, our Dani guide was saying "Just another hour... Just another half hour" over and over again. This time however the Dani had been honest, after only four or so hours of hiking we found ourselves walking into another small village, this time with a couple men and two older women in it. It was only mid afternoon and we had already made it to the village where we would seemingly be staying for the night. "Thank you, Lord" I said under my breath as I tried to smile at the few Dao men that were there waiting for us and watching our every move with eyes as wide as they could be.

The people in that village had heard from the two other Dao men that went up the trail before us the day before that we were coming and they were smiling at our arrival though they held their bows and arrows close. *"Epaoo"* I said as I stretched my hand forward trying to greet them. Instead of grabbing my hand however one of the men just stuck forward the knuckles of his middle and index finger and wrapped them around the knuckle of my single index finger. *"Aba, aba, aba"* he said as he quickly pulled his two fingers back off of mine making a loud snapping type noise. He then repeated this action two more times.

"This must be the greeting that they usually use in this area when they meet others" I thought and repeated back to him *"Aba, aba, aba"* as we snapped each others fingers. We spent the rest of the afternoon laughing around the fire and sharing food back and forth. We gave them noodles and they gave us sweet potatoes then we cooked both over the fire and ate them together as we tried as much as possible to communicate through hand gestures and also through our Dani guide's limited knowledge of the Dao language.

We were still incredibly tired and Jennie was really worn out so I motioned to the men that my wife was tired and asked our guide if there was a place she could sleep a little while. She was doing great so far but I knew that especially she needed to keep her strength up if we were going to continue on like this. The two older women in the village had still not ventured over to greet us but had instead stayed in their own separate thatch roofed house peering out at us from the inside. The men pointed over to the women's house and motioned that Jennie could go over there with the other women if she wanted to.

She slowly walked over and into the little smoky hut. It had a dirt floor unlike the tree bark floored men's house. There were a couple domesticated pigs sharing the house as well as she walked in and spotted a place she could lay down. Looking over to her left she realized that two older ladies were over in the corner looking up at her with their eyes as wide as they could get. Jennie calmly smiled at them. They nervously smiled back so she sat down on the dirt floor across the hut and motioned to them that she wanted to lie down. They motioned back with their hands that she could rest there and rambled off a few short unintelligible phrases in the Dao language. Jennie lay down there by the fire and within minutes had fallen asleep on the dirt floor in the women's house, completely exhausted from the hours upon hours of hiking.

A little while later as the sun was working it's way down towards the tree line we heard the voices of women and children coming up the trail. Jennie was still resting in the women's hut as the voices grew closer and louder. In a moment all the voices suddenly stopped and when I turned and looked behind us there were three women and a few children that looked like a bunch of deer frozen still in the headlights of an oncoming vehicle.

Their jaws were hanging open and their eyes were opened as wide as could be with terror. One of the children screamed out loud in fear and started crying as he held onto his mother's leg, then they all began running towards the woman's house and right into it as if they had seen a ghost. Some of the children jumped into the jungle behind the houses. We looked all around confused at what they were so scared of but there was no one there except for us. That is when we realized that it was us they were scared of. They had never seen white skinned people before in this village. As far as they were concerned, they didn't know whether we were people or not!

The women were all clothed in nothing but thigh length grass skirts and all the children were completely naked. The women also wore decorative white nose bones through their septums just like the men. They carried large net bags of garden foods on their backs, which hung from a single strap tied just above the hairline on their foreheads. They had just returned from their garden and to their surprise, we were sitting right in the middle of their village waiting for them.

We didn't know what to do. Should we get up and greet them or just stay where we were? We didn't want to scare them but it was obvious from the panic stricken looks on their faces that they didn't know what to do or how to react to us. Just then one of the Dao men poked his head out of the door of the little thatched roof men's hut and yelled something to them and they seemed to calm down a little bit. Nonetheless they stayed close together and well away from us at first as they all made for the door of the women's hut as quickly as they could!

Jennie, still sleeping next to the fire inside the women's house, awoke to all the commotion to find about five tribal woman and multiple tribal kids looking down at her in shock, all of them with huge nosebones and some with eyes as wide as saucers. The other two older women that had motioned her into the house earlier began rattling of long lines of Dao language that seemed to calm all the other nervous women and children down a bit. Then one of the old toothless ladies reached out and handed Jennie a small potato type root that she had cooked on the fire for Jennie as she was sleeping. Jennie sat up and slowly reached out taking the sweet potato in her hand. She took a bite of it and swallowed and the other Dao women began laughing and once again excitedly chattering back and forth in their own language as if to say "Look! She eats too, just like us! Perhaps she is human after all!"

After a few hours they had warmed up to Jennie and before you knew it they were all sitting around the fire laughing and having a good time together continuing to try to communicate basic things through simple hand gestures. Eventually some of the children had even worked up enough courage to stop hiding in the jungle or behind their mothers and they began taking turns sitting next to Jennie. They crowded all around her feeling her arms and smiling as they gawked at her yellow body hair and white skin. They giggled and laughed as they talked back and forth amongst each other and looked back and forth at Jennie and then at each other again. They must have been talking about how different and funny she looked compared to them. They had warmed up to each other in what seemed like no time at all.

I watched Jennie as she picked up one of the children and held it in her arms, cuddling it on her lap as if it were her own. With mud smudges on her beautiful face and little bits of ash and thatch grass hanging from her long, curly yellow hair, she sat there in the middle of the small crowd of Dao women and children and laughed. In that moment as I watched my young wife and best friend sitting in that little thatched roof house, a sense of pride hit me. In the midst of all the negative comments that had been made about her coming on this survey, in spite of all the odds that were stacked against her, she had made it. She had been waiting for this experience for years. These women of this tribe had perhaps been waiting for this for centuries.

When the sun began to go down the Dao men made it clear by their gestures however that Jennie would have to stay with us in the men's huts. They didn't yet trust us or her enough to let her bed down for the night with their women and the children. The Dao men and women have separate sleeping houses. This is Dao culture and if Jennie was going to sleep in a house at all, she would have to sleep in the men's hut with all the men. I found a spot in the corner of the little bark floored hut and there was just enough space for us to sleep side by side. The room was very small though and with all of the men that were in the hut and a few more Dao stragglers that came into the village at the end of the day, our quarters would be very tight.

As we lay down for the night I looked up and around at the little tribal structure we were in. This was our first time spending the night inside a proper Dao house and not just a makeshift lean-to. Their building style was very interesting. It was a rectangular house with a raised floor. It looked as if there had been tree bark stretched and layered over the floor. A fire pit was located directly in the center of the room. There was only one doorway and no windows.

The smoke filled the room and burnt my eyes as it billowed up into the rafters. I could see that the poles and rafters of the house were all tied together with jungle vine. The four walls seemed like they had been made from hand-hewn planks and were once again tied together with jungle vine in a neat decorative w-like pattern. All of the inside of the thatched leaf roof as well as the rafters were covered thick with shiny black soot from the continual cooking fires.

I leaned over and told Jennie that I loved her and that I was glad that we had made it. We drifted off to sleep watching the shadows from the fire dance on the black, shiny soot covered rafters and thanking God that we had at least made it this far. Even if we didn't make it even a single step farther we had already at least accomplished the first of our objectives: a peaceful and friendly first contact with the remote people of these jungle mountains.

Early the next morning we woke up to the sudden jolting and cracking sound of wood and then what sounded like the whooping war cries of Dao men. I opened my eyes thinking we were under some sort of attack. As I looked over to see if Jennie was alright, then looked back to my right again I could see all the Dao men and also our Dani guide jumping through the door with their bows and arrows.

They seemed to all be scurrying outside as quickly as they could. The whole house seemed to move back and forth as the chanting grew louder and louder. "Are we under attack? What is going on!" I thought as I hurriedly jumped up and grabbed on to Jennie's hand. Jennie trailing closely behind me, we began scrambling towards the door of the hut frantically trying to see what all the commotion was about as we braced ourselves for the worst.

Chapter 7

The Great Snake

Even the strongest current of water cannot add a drop to a cup that is already full. Likewise, the most difficult subjects can be explained to the most slow-witted man if he has not formed any idea of them already; but the simplest thing cannot be made clear to the most intelligent man if he is firmly persuaded that he knows already, without a shadow of a doubt, what is laid before him.

Leo Tolstoy,
The Kingdom Of Heaven Is Within You

We jumped out the little entrance opening of the thatched roof hut to see something that left us standing speechless and perplexed. All the men and a few of the women and children were running in big circles hooting, whooping and hollering as they ran. It almost looked like a strange dance but it was too frantic and sporadic to be planned or follow any type of rhythm. They ran and jumped in a circular pattern stomping as hard as they could as they went, kicking up bits of dust and debris as they ran.

Some of the men held their bows and arrows high above their heads with one hand while firmly striking the bamboo shafts of their arrows with the other hand. The arrows and bows would make a loud rattle sound as they were struck over and over and over again. At that moment we realized that it wasn't just the house shaking and jostling back and forth, everything outside was also violently jolting! We could once again here cracking and popping noises coming from the towering jungle trees all around us. It was another earthquake and it was just as big as the day before!

"Aa too otoogiyoo! Aa too otoogiyoo!" one of the men yelled frantically as he ran circles. We hurried towards the clearing in the middle of the small thatch roofed houses in case one of the small huts was to topple over or one of those huge prehistoric trees was to come crashing down around us. They continued hooting and hollering making their "Whoop! Whoop! Whoop!" noises as they ran in circles and stomped until the earthquake one again subsided. "What is going on? Why do they run circles and whoop like that? Is it because they are scared?" I asked our Dani guide a few moments after the earthquake had finally stopped. "They think there is a giant snake," he replied. "What? A giant snake? What are you talking about?" I asked.

"That is what they think causes the earthquakes: a giant snake with a body the size of a tree trunk. It is said to be a demon snake that goes around underneath the ground causing everything to move and jolt as it slithers along under the surface. That is why they run in circles hollering and stomping! They are trying to get the snake to go away!" he continued.

We would find out later that their word for snake is *otoogiyoo* and the men that had been yelling *"Aa too otoogiyoo!"* were calling out to the snake to leave as they ran. We would also find out later on that the Dao link earthquakes and unusual natural phenomena with significant events and omens. To them, the fact that these huge earthquakes were taking place during our arrival to their territory was no mere coincidence.

The earthquakes came again and again over the following few days until we eventually lost count as to how many had taken place. Every time there was an earthquake we would see the Dao people doing this same thing. They would run and whoop and hoot and holler and stomp until they were out of breath. To top it all off, that very afternoon after we spent our first night in that specific village a huge tropical storm settled in. The clouds let loose and a torrential downpour unmatched by any I had seen fell down on us with fury. The lighting strobes continually froze our movements in flashes of white as we sat in the little leak filled thatched roof house waiting out the storm. The deafening cracks of lightning struck up and down the mountain tops all around us and the deep guttural sounds of thunder rumbled across the sky all night and into the following morning.

By the time the storm finally slowed into a light sprinkle, the rain had continued on for two days almost without stopping. We had lost two more valuable days of our survey time as a result as we didn't have the option of hiking whether we wanted to or not in weather like that. If the weather was bad in these jungles then the trails became slippery and treacherous. It could take hours to go only a short distance and the logs that have to be crossed over various ravines and jungle holes would turn into slippery deathtraps. We could fall and break a bone or ankle much easier were we to continue hiking despite these heavy rains and harsh conditions.

There was also a positive side to getting stuck in this little village though. Our bodies were thankful, as was our old Dani guide, for some recovery time. We were also able to do a bit of language survey there in that little village and find out some more important information about the Dao people and their culture and language. We found out during that time waiting out the storms that the village we were staying in was called *Pewok*.

In that village, occasionally the putrid smell of feces would drift up over the hill from behind the houses. It was almost unbearable at times and the smell was strong enough to send us reeling. We discovered a little while later that this was the community bathroom, located only a few feet from the small circle of thatched roof houses. It was what from that point on we would refer to as "the poop trail". The women had one and the men had one. When someone had to use the bathroom they would follow the appropriate trail and squat over a stump or old fallen tree that was conveniently placed and do their business right there within a few feet of the houses. We also saw the community dogs and pigs going down the trails and scavenging through the human waste looking for a meal and eating whatever they found. After seeing that, we made it a point to quit petting the community dogs no matter how friendly they were.

We also observed that for the most part the Dao people didn't bathe at all. We would find out later that water is closely associated with many of their traditional beliefs in evil spirits. When they got sick water was the first thing they usually cut from their diet. They had many taboos set up around water. When they caught certain sicknesses they were often forbidden to even cross a stream or any body of water. It surprised us though that even though they didn't bathe they usually didn't smell that bad like we would of expected them to. They had a natural form of deodorant in the way that they spent a lot of their day and every night in a smoke filled hut. They smelt of smoke and jungle for the most part. Although when we would get to hiking and the sweat began to pour off their bodies, those were the times when they would start smelling pretty ripe.

Then again, even with bathing regularly we smelt pretty ripe ourselves after we had been on the trail for a while! More than once the locals commented that us white people had a funny smell to us. Most of the people and especially the children had a lot of soot and dirt caked on their faces from not bathing but this was again a part of their complex belief system. They had reasons for everything that they did. We would continually find out that their social and cultural structure was just as intricate as ours even if it was fairly hard for us to understand.

While we were there in Pewok we tried to scribble down in our little notebooks every little word and sound that we heard. We had brought with us a few papers that Mike and Steve had given to us which laid out some of the language features and expressions of the neighboring tribes on either side of the Dao. We used the information from Mike and Steve to try and determine if the Dao language was related to the languages of these other groups a weeks hike away on either side of them.

We also found out during those couple days that the Dao language was tonal. It almost sounded like they were singing when they said certain groups of words together. For instance, if they were talking about the cannibalistic tribes in the lowlands and said the sentence "That person eats people" they would say in the Dao language *"Mee mée mee mée nugi"*. We would find out later that three of the four of these *"mee"* words had different meaning according to the context and also the pitch at which you spoke them. This would not by any means be an easy language to learn! It was possibly the only language of the eight hundred plus languages on the island with both tone and accent.

We found out later that there were close to twenty different distinct forms of even just the word "go". Their language was more intricate than any we had ever heard before and if we wanted to eventually work here with these people we would need to not only become fluent in this language but we would have to actually form an alphabet for their language as this specific dialect had not yet been broken down and figured out. Without first breaking down the sounds that the Dao language used and making a custom tailored phonetic alphabet for this language, nothing could be accurately written in their language.

As we continued to gather as much information as possible there in Pewok, Jennie grew closer and closer in her relationship with the Dao women. She began trying to learn their names and even though they didn't have a "J" in their language they also tried their best to learn hers. One of the women even let Jennie hold and take care of her baby for a good part of the day which showed that they had already built up a significant amount of trust towards her. Jennie noticed during that time as did we that the majority of Dao people had large scars all over their bodies and backs where it almost looked like they had been tortured in some way.

One younger woman had fresh wounds on her back and shoulder blades. Deep gashes three to five inches in length that were oozing blood and puss and had been infected. Jennie removed some gauze and medicine that she had in her backpack and offered to treat her wounds but the women's husband refused to consent to letting Jennie treat the women. Why did all these people have so many scars? Why wouldn't they let us treat their wounds? We wondered.

On our third day in Pewok, the rain had finally slowed enough to where we could get back on the trail and continue on up the mountain to get to the next village. We looked at the waypoints we had taken from the aerial surveys and tried to get our bearings and figure out exactly where we were. It seemed we were only half a day's hike or so from the top of the ridge. We had to watch our schedule very closely though as we had agreed with the boat driver to meet down at the river again on a certain day. If we missed that boat, we were stranded.

There were at least two more villages that we needed to make it to. One was a possible airstrip sight that our Dani guide had seen years before and told us of. If there really was a good airstrip sight there, it would be a good place to move should we decide Dao was the tribe we needed to work with. Especially considering that there wasn't much flat land in the extremely mountainous Dao territory to begin with. We needed to see if there really was suitable airstrip sight land there or not.

The other village we needed to make it to was said to be the home of the most influential man in Dao. He was said to be the head of this area: what we might refer to as the tribal chief. Our Dani guide and even the other Dao people seemed to talk a little quieter whenever they even mentioned his name. He was a man that had great respect and we would need to win his approval if we ever planned on returning. For that reason we had to make it to this other village also and we had to try to gain his friendship in order to keep a good peaceful relationship with the tribe. After losing another two days of our survey to the torrential downpours of the Indonesian rainforest however, we were beginning to question if we really had enough time.

⟷

After packing up our belonging once again we headed up the mountain, desperately trying to make it to the top before sundown. The rain had stopped later in the morning and so we were getting a later start than what we would have wanted but we all felt great. Our packs were a little bit lighter because we had used a lot of our food rations during the few days leading up to this point. Not to mention that the two days of letting our bodies heal and recuperate while we were waiting for the storm to pass did us a lot of good.

Even though we got a late start our guide assured us we could make it if we moved quickly. He also told us that should we find no one in the small hamlet at the top of the ridge, he was almost sure there was still a shelter there that he had set up a number of years before the first time he had come through. We could spend the night in that shelter if we needed too and we would also be able to see whether or not the ridge was a suitable place for an airstrip should we gain the people's approval and decide to come back to Dao in the future.

We were making good time and moving up the mountain pretty quickly. A short, stalky, Dao teenager named Adis had been appointed by the village men in Pewok to join us for the journey and to make sure that we were following the right trails. He had seemingly somehow come across a pair of scissors and given himself a flat top that made him look like a character from an eighties sitcom. He had tried to learn a little bit of the Indonesian language of the cities from our Dani guide and so Adis enjoyed trying out on us the few little Indonesian words and phrases that he knew. I was glad to have him along and we tried to communicate all the way up the side of the mountain. As we hiked, we took turns pointing at birds and trees and occasional butterflies or bugs and trying to pronounce whatever they were called first in Indonesian and then in the Dao language.

The water was also more abundant as we neared the higher elevations and our surroundings got colder and wetter. It probably also helped immensely that it had rained for two days straight leading up to this point and we were glad to have an abundance of water once again so that we didn't have to worry about dehydration as we had the first couple days of hiking. Although the trails were still grueling and incredibly steep and they were more muddy and slippery than they had been the days before, we were well rested for a change and this made all the difference.

After about four hours the trail started getting less steep and leveling out a bit. The huge jungle trees and vines as thick as a man's wrist we had seen in the foothills and lowlands were looking a bit thinner and more spread out as we climbed higher and higher. The clouds were settling down in between the trees all around us so that the jungle vines and moss even looked a little spooky and dripped with moisture as we worked our way through them.

Then finally, after about four and a half hours of hiking, just about the time our thighs were starting to burn as if we had been on a never ending stair-stepper machine, we popped out of the jungle and into a clearing on top of the ridge. The ground that stretched out in front of us was swampy and the air was cold and wet. The grass here grew in small round clumps on ponds of ankle deep mud in many places and we had to watch our step as we began making our way across the ridge top to where the guide said there would be some more solid ground.

After about a hundred feet of walking along the top of the ridge, we spotted the shelter that our Dani guide had referred to earlier. It was positioned right across from two tribal style huts both of which were unoccupied. Then a few minutes after we had made it into the shelter the heavy rains of the Indonesian rainforest let lose once again. We would find out over the next few days that it rains a lot more in these jungles the higher you go into the mountains. There were fewer hours of sunlight than there are in the lowlands because mid-afternoon the clouds usually move in and settle around the scraggly mountaintops everyday. We would have to once again wait out the storm and until the next morning to look around the area and decide what was our next step.

The shelter had a nice wood floor though and we wouldn't have to sleep on the cold dirt so we were happy about that. We opened our backpacks and each changed into whatever dry clothes we had and then after a fire had been started, made some more of the lightweight ramen noodles we had brought along. I shared some of my food with my new smiley Dao friend Adis as I continued on picking his brain for more Dao words I could try to learn.

He would say something and I would repeat it as he pointed to what it was and laughed at my sorry attempts to mimic the words he spoke. Then I would say something in Indonesian and he would repeat it with a big smile on his face. Jennie, Derek and Jonny joined in also and we laughed and traded words and phrases for a couple hours as I frantically tried to keep up with the game and scribble down every new word that I heard.

A couple more Dao teenagers heard from the previous village of people about us and that we had hiked up to the top of the mountain so they came up in the rain and joined us for the night also. We were all packed into the little shelter and continued on trading words and laughing at each other and eating dry instant noodles late into the evening. I would point at my big toe and say *"Apa ini*?" in the Indonesian language meaning *"What is this?"* Then one of the Dao teens replied in the local Dao language *"Mpeagiyoo?...Kepoo da"* which I assumed meant "What is this? This is a toe." I then pointed to my hand and repeated one of the phrases I had just heard them say in the Dao language.

"Mpeagiyoo?" I said, assuming that in the Dao language I had asked "What is that?" Then they all laughed and one of them gave me the Dao word for hand as he put his hand out and touched mine. *"Yagaa da"* he replied. Then I told him the Indonesian word for hand. *"Tangan"* I said as I reached forward and touched him on the hand. The game went on

and on until finally we had all grown bored of it and bedded down for the night.

As we lay sprawled out next to the fire I took a deep breath and thought about the day. It was so good to finally be here. We had been waiting for and training for this opportunity for so, so long. We had wondered if the day would ever come that we would actually be laying down to sleep in the middle of a remote tribal area like this alongside nearly forgotten people like these: people that had no idea who Jesus Christ was or what their Creator had done for them, people that desperately needed our message but had no one to tell it to them.

We had even wondered ourselves if we would ever make it here or if we would just give up or even die trying, but we were here. Despite being tired from hiking and trying nearly in vain to make our achy bodies comfortable on that hard wood floor, words couldn't describe how happy we were that night. We wouldn't have wanted to be anywhere else.

⟷

The next day we were up bright and early. It was significantly colder up there than the previous nights we had spent at lower elevations. Jennie and I were both shivering from the cold moist air of the highlands! One of the Dao guys must have seen the looks on our faces and our shivering from the cold when we woke up because he got up and almost immediately walked over to a small pile of charred firewood that was left over from the day before. I couldn't understand how the locals could even stand it in these cold elevations wearing nothing but a gourd. Being nearly naked they had to be much colder than we were! I would have nearly frozen in what they were wearing but they barely acted like the cold bothered them at all.

He pulled a bamboo tube from his string bag and then reached inside the tube and pulled out what looked like a small piece of glass or quartz crystal and a little piece of dry moss. He pinned the moss to the piece of glass in between his thumb and index finger and then struck it against the bamboo three times. The moss started smoking then he pulled what looked like some sort of dry seed husk from his bag as he lightly blew on the moss and it grew bright orange. Then tucking the glowing moss inside the dry husk he continued to lightly blow on it. As he blew on it he placed it in between the pieces of charred black firewood from the day before and threw a few twigs on it. In just a few seconds "Poof!" you could hear the fire catch and he had a big heap of firewood burning in no time.

This was amazing to me when I thought about the world we came from. With all our modern inventions and all our knowledge, I couldn't have effortlessly started a fire like that from a rock, some moss and a piece of bamboo even if I wanted too. He smiled at us and rattled off a long string of Dao words that we couldn't understand as if to say "Bada bing...there you have it...fire!" then motioned to us to come closer by the fire so we could get warm.

As the sun came up we ate a breakfast of the last of our instant oatmeal and a few sweet potatoes then we all went outside to walk around a bit and see what the area was like. While we were here, we needed to see whether this ridge top really was suitable for a possible airstrip sight or not. I pulled a small camera from my backpack to take some pictures of the area. I knew that we would need to get the opinion of pilots when we got back to the city on whether or not they thought this would be a good place for an airstrip were we to move here.

The Dao people up in these mountains had apparently never seen a camera before, so needless to say this really sparked their interest. They watched with curiosity as I held the camera out in front of me and snapped pictures while looking at the fold out screen on the side of the camera body. They walked close behind me looking at the screen and eventually figured out that I was looking in the screen at the same thing that the camera was pointed towards.

"I wonder what they will do if they see another person on this screen" I thought so I pointed the camera lens at Jennie and let them look at the screen as Jennie smiled and waved at the camera. The look on their faces was priceless. They didn't seem to know whether this was something to laugh at or be scared by. "How could she be in two places at once? How can she fit into that little box?" they must have wondered.

The screen on the camera could be flipped out and turned around so I positioned it in a way that we could all look at the screen while I pointed the camera at myself. In the screen we could see not only me, but also the Dao guys standing to my right and left. They stared at the screen for a second and then I lifted up my hand and waved just as Jennie had earlier. At that moment I heard a big "Waaaaaaaaoooooooooo" and saw all the Dao guys disappear from the screen as they ran a few feet away towards the jungle behind me.

All of a sudden it hit them: "That's us in that box!" and they really didn't know what to think! None of them had grabbed for their bows and arrows though and when they saw me laughing they started nervously laughing too, though they had an expression on their faces like "This guy must be crazy!" We repeated all of this a couple more times until one of the Dao guys seemed like he was no longer afraid of the camera. He started making faces at it as he looked into the screen and shortly after began laughing at himself in the screen making funny faces. Eventually the other Dao men there were also laughing at him and then they began taking turns making faces into the screen and laughing at each other.

It was hard to get anything at all done throughout the remainder of the day because they kept on pointing to my camera again and again. They wanted to continue this game of watching themselves make faces and laughing at each other. The camera could record as well so we recorded some of them saying things or singing and then played it back to them. They would hoot and laugh as they listened to and watched themselves talking or singing on the little camera screen. Word spread quickly through the Dao valley about this interesting contraption carried by the white man. Everywhere we went from that point on people asked about this strange device.

After we walked all around and tried to get a good idea of the area and the layout of the land on top of the ridge we went back to the shelter and began talking about our plans for the following day as we ate a late lunch. It would take a few days of hiking to get all the way back to the area where the boat had dropped us off and we had to make sure to be there on time.

The problem was that we didn't know whether or not we had enough time to make it up valley to where that influential Dao leader named Totopwi was said to live. So what should we do?

Only a few moments after we began to plan our course of action we began to hear more voices outside and then the door was pushed open. There was a skinny, smiley, almost toothless man standing there with his bows and arrows in hand. He had no clothes on except for the traditional gourd of the Dao people but he also was wearing a big, ridiculous looking, western style safari hat. "*Epaoooooooo*" he said in a big long drawn out sort of way. Our Dani guide leaned over and excitedly whispered to us "This is Totopwi!"

The man started confidently walking around the room and talking full paragraphs in the Dao language as if we understood everything he was saying. It looked like we wouldn't have to hike all the way to his village to meet him after all! He continued jabbering away in the Dao language for a few moments and then all the sudden he stopped and looked around the room at all of our backpacks and belongings. Stretching out his arm and pointing one at a time at the various bags, *"Kaa! Kaa! Kaa! Kaa! Kaa! Kaa!"* he exclaimed over and over again. He pointed to each one of us as if to say "Man! You guys sure do carry a lot of stuff!" Then he sat down on the wood floor and continued babbling on in his language.

"Well what should we do? This is the man we have been waiting to meet!" I leaned over and asked Derek. "Let's share some food with him and maybe in a little while we can get our Dani guide to try to convey to him what we are here for" he replied. We dished him out a good sized portion of the food and Totopwi laughed with delight as Derek stretched out both his hands and set the food in front of him. Another long line of Dao language came out of his mouth and then Totopwi began shoveling the food into his mouth using the upper portion of a long hornbill bird beak, which he had pulled out of his small string bag.

The other Dao men in the room were excitedly chattering back and forth with Totopwi in between bites as he ate. I could only assume they were talking about the interesting things that they saw us pull from our bags that afternoon because when he was done eating they began once again pointing at my camera. It seemed they were asking for another demonstration. I turned the camera on and pointed the screen towards Totopwi and *"Waaooooooooooo!"* he said as he nodded his head and then thumped the end of his gourd with the nail of his index finger while making click noises in the back of his throat as a show of astonishment. About an hour later, when he finally began to seem a little less interested in the camera and my batteries were almost dead, we finally got the opportunity we had been waiting for.

The Dani barely spoke the Dao language at all but he did know a bit of the related dialect that Mike worked in nearly a week's hike away so we asked him if he would ask Totopwi a few important questions for us using that neighboring dialect. The Dao people in this area seemed to have a good knowledge of related and bordering dialects up to this point. We assumed this was because they often traded with people from other areas.

"We are here to bring you a message" we said at first as our Dani guide began to translate. The old chief got quiet and looked at us with interest. "We are from a land very far away but we have hiked into your territory because we want to tell you a story about the Creator of all things" we continued. At this point all the other Dao people in the room were also completely silent. You could have heard a pin drop if it wasn't for the crackling and popping of the fire.

"We don't come to bring you material wealth or things of this earth. We come with a message about the trail to eternal life. We come with a message primarily for your spirit" our Dani friend continued to translate as we spoke one phrase at a time. "We want to tell you of these things and give you this important message that we carry but in order to do so we must first learn your language so that we can tell you well in a way that you will understand. In order to do that we would need to move here and live among your people. We would need to spend time learning your language and your ways," we continued and then waited again as the Dani continued translating.

"We want to come and tell your people of their Creator and His great message but we will not move here and live among your people unless you want us to come. We will not build houses here unless we have your permission and you want us to come live among you and tell you about this message that we carry. We wait to hear what you have to say." we concluded.

When all of these words had been translated for the old chief his demeanor had completely changed from earlier. He had a penetrating and serious look in his eyes as he listened. Then a huge hopeful smile had swept over his face. He began speaking in his language fast and excited and our guide tried his best to translate as Totopwi spoke.

"We have been waiting for your message. Come! We want you to come and live among us! You can have trees for your houses and land to build them on. Come here and live among us and we will help you learn our language. We will help you so that we can hear your message. Thank you! Thank you! Yes, come!" he excitedly replied as the other Dao people in the room also nodded in agreement.

We could have jumped up and shouted for joy at hearing the words of that old nearly toothless chief. It seemed God had prepared these people before we had ever hiked into their territory. We hadn't hiked all this way in vain. They wanted us to come. They wanted us to live among them and learn their language. They wanted us to bring them the greatest message of all time. They wanted to learn about their Creator!

The next day we headed down the mountain and back towards our pick up point with smiles on our faces and laughter in our voices. The hiking had been incredibly hard and we had seen, learned and experienced things that we wouldn't soon forget. We did still have two to three full days hike ahead of us just to get back to the boat. If the weather held out though and we could keep on moving it seemed we had enough time to make it back and the driver wouldn't leave without us.

Our packs were lighter because our food was almost all gone and this also made it a lot easier on our knees. We were following the same trail to get back as we had used to hike up into the mountains so we knew where the water sources were and didn't have to carry quite as much water weight most the time unless we knew for sure there was a long stretch coming up with no streams.

We had accomplished our main purpose for being there and were encouraged at the words of Totopwi and the general favorable response of the Dao people to our being there. We had shown love and friendship to the Dao people, men, women and children during our first contact despite all of our inadequacies and the many times that we had nearly given up and turned around. Now we had just one final task lying before us: to make it back to the boat in time and out of the jungle alive and without serious injury!

Chapter 8

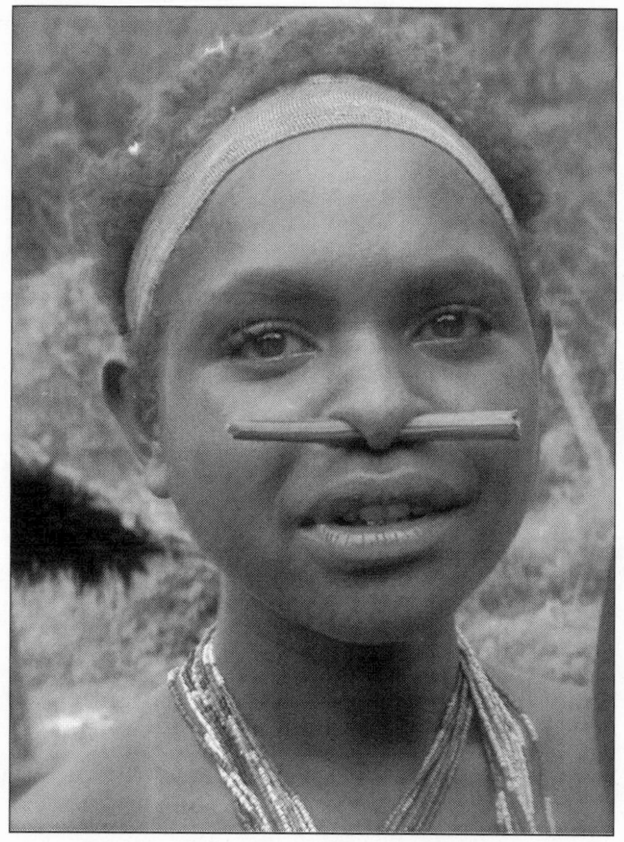

Prophecies of Pale Skin

It will change your life dramatically if you believe that you deserve nothing but wrath and God gives you nothing but mercy. Not many of us realize just how undeserving we are yet how loved we are.

John Piper,
Desiring God

By the time we were headed down the last mountain our knees were so weak that they rapidly and involuntarily shook with every downward step. At times they would buckle and we nearly fell down as we grasped for limbs or rocks along the side of the trail to hold ourselves steady. We were on a tight schedule though and we couldn't even consider stopping now no matter how tired we were. We had to keep going! The boat was supposed to leave first thing in the morning. Our very well being and whether or not we would make it out of the jungle depended on it.

It had taken longer than we expected to get back to our starting point despite our lighter backpacks and fortunate good weather. As it turned out, the places where we had done hand over hand climbing going up into those mountains were incredibly hard to get back down. We fell and uncontrollably slid down small segments of the trail over and over again. Derek and Jonny were more sure-footed hikers and climbers than Jennie and I were because of their experience from past survey work but even they fell at times.

Jennie and I on the other hand had so many bruises and scrapes on the backs of our legs from slipping and then sliding down various parts of the mountainside that our legs were beginning to resemble raw meat. Our hands and arms swelled out in various places where we had been scraped by jungle thorns and creepers. We had been bitten and sucked on by leeches so many times that we lost count. We could see by the blood stains on our socks and muddy pants that those leeches had sucked way more than their fair share. Our bodies bore the crisscrossed cuts, whelps and swollen red marks of the Indonesian jungles.

Finally, we came around the last corner to a medium sized stream just a thousand feet or so from our original starting point. I dropped my backpack on the riverbank and lay down in the water for a minute as it rushed over my worn and tired body. The cool water felt so good on my throbbing swollen knees and seemed to take away some of the sting of the various cuts and leech bites that dotted my legs and arms.

A few moments later, as we came into the clearing by that small shelter where we had spent the first night of the survey many days before, we could see the boat driver off in the distance already testing and revving the outboard motor on his long dugout canoe. He looked as if he was already departing! His helper had already completely loaded the boat and was hopping in. "Wait, wait! Your not leaving without us are you?" our Dani guide yelled as he sped up his pace and stumbled off of the jungle trail towards the boat.

"You don't understand! My whole entire family lives down on the coast in those city houses! Last time there was an earthquake as big as that one that hit last week close friends and family of mine died in the falling rubble! I fear that I have family and friends that have been killed in those earthquakes!" he said with a grief stricken panic on his face. "I need to get to my family but I knew I had promised you we would not leave before the agreed upon date so I stayed as long as I could" he continued. "Well we are all here now! Don't leave yet! Just let us rest the night here and we will leave at first light. Both of us know it's not good to leave this late in the day. Besides, if we leave early enough in the morning and the conditions are favorable we can probably make it back in one day since we are going downstream" the Dani replied.

To our relief the boat driver reluctantly agreed. Jennie and I thudded down on the ground in exhaustion but at the same time with a sigh of relief that we hadn't been left behind. Who knows what would have happened if we would have ended up stranded there with no food or supplies left at all? We began unloading our backpacks in the shelter and bedding down for the evening. We would spend one last night on the Taane River before sitting in that uncomfortable hard wood boat all day long beginning the following morning.

It would be so good to get back into civilization! Hot showers and good hearty meals. We had eaten almost nothing but potatoes and roots for the past three days. Even before we had run out of food though, dried noodles and instant oatmeal that we backpacked in had made up most of our daily diet for a number of weeks. It would be nice to have something different for a change. Not to mention these hard dirt and roughly planked wood floors were killing our backs!

Jennie talked on and on about how she couldn't wait to sleep on a nice fluffy mattress again. It had been weeks now since we had experienced a comfortable night's sleep. As tired as we were from the long hours of hiking, we could barely sleep that night we were so excited to get out of the jungle. At the same time however we continued to talk nonstop about how God had gone before us.

It couldn't have been clearer that God had given us just enough strength to accomplish our task though we in and of ourselves had felt completely inadequate. He didn't give any more than we needed or any less, He gave us exactly what we needed. And most important of all He had given us favor in the eyes of the Dao people. It would have only taken one man and one of those many bows and arrows we had seen and the survey could have gone bad, not to mention one or all of us could have ended up dead. As I lay there that night drifting in and out of sleep on that hard floor an old saying once again came to mind: "We are immortal until our work is done."

⟷

Our return back down the Taane River, back into the lowlands and then down to the coastal town we had started out in went smooth and effortless. We just got as comfortable as possible in that old dugout canoe and enjoyed the novelty of downstream movement without effort for a while. The current was on our side this time as opposed to the trip up into the Dao territory and we were able to make it back downriver and into the salty breezy ocean in half the time it had taken us to get up those muddy swirling waters.

Within a few days after that we had caught a bigger ocean liner from that small coastal town back up the coast to the capital city, Jayapura. Then within a week we had caught a small plane back to Wamena and were getting ready for our next journey into Dao. God had confirmed in our hearts and more specifically by His word in Romans chapter fifteen that the Dao tribe was the place we needed to be.

It seemed to us that when the Apostle Paul himself had penned the words in Romans: *"I make it my goal to preach where the name of Jesus Christ has never been named, and where there has not yet been a single church established or any foundation laid."* he might as well have been talking about the Dao tribe. There couldn't have been a better description of the Dao people than this! After all, the Dao territory was a place that had not a single outside worker or religious group of any denomination working with them. Most of their territory was nearly untouched by the outside world. They had not the slightest idea who in the world the God of the Bible was, let alone that He had a Son whose name was Jesus.

Besides that they had extended to us an open invitation to come and live among them! And if that strategy was good enough for Paul, it seemed like it should be good enough for us! The words of Totopwi echoed in my head over and over again: *"We will help you learn our language so that you can teach us of your message."* Jennie and I couldn't stop talking about it. It was so obvious to us that God had prepared them for our arrival and that He had given them a desire to know about the message that we wanted to share with them. It was nearly too good to be true!

A few weeks later Jonny was off to the States to get married and it seemed we wouldn't see him again for quite a few years. Derek however had no immediate plans. He told us that he also would love to be a help in any way he could as we moved into Dao and started learning the language. He even made plans to go back into the Dao territory with us and help us build a house for the next few months before he was due for his next furlough. We were delighted at the thought of having his help as he had become a good friend to us and had proven himself to be a very valuable team member on those foot surveys. He had always pulled more than his fair share of the weight and it seemed he would be very valuable in the house building process as well!

With the decision finalized that Dao was where we wanted to serve, we went down to the Helimission base to tell the Helicopter pilots and mechanics of our plans. We asked them for air support for our food and medical supplies during the house building process and in the future and they agreed to support our work and also to get us and our building supplies into the Dao territory so that we could begin living among them and learning their language. Everything was coming together perfectly!

It seemed that it wouldn't be long and we would be back in the jungle where we knew beyond the slightest doubt, God wanted us to be. The helicopter schedule was pretty full though due to the fact that there were many areas on the island that had no airstrips and were helicopter access only. We weren't the only ones on the island that needed air support. This being the case we had a number of weeks to wait before the helicopter could get us back into Dao so we used the time to make final purchases and preparations for house building.

Things were wrapping up as we excitedly bought our last few supplies and checked them off the list. We could barely believe it was all finally happening! Then one afternoon a few days before our helicopter flight I got an extremely bad headache. At first, it seemed like a migraine. I had experienced these before when I got dehydrated or stressed out.

"I'll be okay. I'll just take a few Tylenol and drink some extra water." I told Jennie. But after a few hours the pain got so bad my head felt like it would burst. My body broke out in a cold sweat and I suddenly felt weak and even nauseous. "I think I should go lay down." I told Jennie and went into our bedroom so that I could rest. "This has got to be the worst headache I have ever had!" I said out loud. I could barely think my head was throbbing so bad and then for some reason my feet got ice cold and I felt like I was going to throw up everywhere.

I ran to the bathroom a few steps away and emptied everything in my stomach into the toilet. I heaved and heaved until there was nothing left but still I couldn't stop. I kept involuntarily dry heaving until I doubled over on my knees in the bathroom and fell down onto the cold tile floor. Jennie had heard everything as my heaving echoed of the bathroom walls and she hurried in to see if I was alright. Then when the dry heaving had finally stopped she helped me back on to my feet and back to the bed.

I lay there continuing to sweat profusely though my feet were still as cold as ice. My head continued to throb and every thirty minutes or so I would begin dry heaving again. Jennie tried to get me to drink water but everything kept coming back up. Then whenever I looked at a window or light my head seemed to throb even worse. I asked Jennie to shut all the windows and turn off the lights. She didn't know what to do and there was no other doctors or westerners around so she got on a phone and called a missionary doctor that she had met in the capital city, Jayapura a few months before.

After a few tries she was finally able to get a hold of the doctor and describe to him what was going on. "There is no doubt in my mind! If he has got ice cold feet and is at the same time sweating profusely and his eyes are sensitive to light then he has contracted malaria. You need to get him on malaria meds right away." the doctor replied.

Jennie ran to the closest small store where they sold medicines and bought some of a medication referred to as *kina* then rushed the medication back to me. I was barely able to choke the two large white pills down. I tried with everything in me to keep them down at least long enough to where they might have had the chance to dissolve into my stomach lining but moments later I was again throwing up and then dry heaving the medication all over the floor.

A few hours later my ears began ringing with a high pitch noise and I felt even worse than before. I rocked back and forth in the bed in the fetal position trying to get my mind off of my throbbing head until late, late into the night. I had never experienced a sickness anything like this! Eventually I came to the conclusion that for sure I was going to die. Just the month before we had heard about an American translator a few hours west from us that had contracted cerebral malaria and it had gone into his brain and killed him. He had gone to bed complaining of a headache and the next morning his wife had found him dead.

I decided it would be good to say goodbye to Jennie and tell her that I loved her one last time just in case I was headed for the same fate as the missionary we had heard about. She hadn't left my side since I had taken the first kina pills. "I love you Jennie" I said to her as I looked up at her face. She looked angelic to me the way those golden ringlets of hair framed her face. Her bright white-blue eyes were so beautiful. I had never met anyone with eyes as bright as hers.

She looked down at me and began to cry. "I love you too Scottie" she said in a soft voice. "If for some reason I don't make it through tonight you keep on going forward okay? Keep on going towards those Dao people and don't give up until they have had their chance to finally hear about their Creator and what He has done for them for the first time alright?" she nodded in agreement as she looked down at her hand in mine and the tears ran down her face.

I don't remember anything after that except for waking up the next morning to blinding rays of light coming through the cracks under the doors and the small creases in the drapes. To my surprise I had made it through the night. I still had a headache but it wasn't near as bad as the day before. My ears were still ringing and the bed was drenched with sweat but I had enough strength to get up and wasn't as nauseated either.

I continued taking the kina for three more days and eventually stopped feeling nauseous and began to regain my strength but I would go on to get that same strand of malaria every four weeks for the next six months in a row. We eventually figured out it was a specific strand of malaria that lay dormant in my liver and came out over and over again every month. I could only rid myself of it by taking a special blood cleansing treatment that would go into the liver and kill the malaria but which could also have very bad side effects on my liver if I was to use too much of it or use the medication too frequently.

By the time we had finally gotten that strand of malaria out of my system I had lost nearly thirty pounds from those reoccurring bouts with it. Nonetheless I was just happy that God had seen fit to spare me. He had drawn me closer to Him through it. Jennie and I also were closer than ever before as we had been reminded of the brevity of life and that we may not always have each other. I was just happy to still be alive as was Jennie happy that she still had her husband.

It was during those six months of bout after bout with malaria that we made our initial move into the Dao territory. They were some of the hardest and most challenging months of our lives because of the constant bouts of sickness. Just about the time I was recovering and starting to feel strong again and putting on a little bit of weight I would get hit by malaria again. Nonetheless we were able to make our helicopter date as it fell in between two of the malaria bouts and it seemed we had gathered enough supplies and tools to get a good start on house building.

We had saved all of our spare money for a number of years in anticipation of having to buy all the supplies to build a house in the jungle. Even after we had bought all of our supplies and paid for the helicopter flights though we still had nearly ten thousand dollars in our account in leftover funds. It turned out that building a house in a third world country was much cheaper than building one back in America! So a couple days before moving in to the jungle permanently we took all the rest of our savings that we hadn't spent on food and house building supplies and gave it away. We transferred our savings to a local non-profit organization that had been a huge help to us over the years and left it also behind. We had nothing left.

The way we saw it there were no returns and no retreats. This was a one way road and we didn't want anything in our lives that we could fall back on or that could possibly become an excuse for giving up. To us, giving up the last of our reserves was symbolism, like the cutting of an anchor from a ship: it was the cutting loose of any remaining dead weight that might keep us from running our course well. It was all or nothing.

The last purchase we made before giving our savings away was a small black dog. We purchased it from some locals there in the city of Wamena where the helicopter was stationed and where we had bought most of our house building supplies. The dog was small and jet black except for a small white patch on its chest. The local Dani people said that the word for black or dark in their language was *"mili"* so we named our dog Mili and took her into Dao with us to keep us company.

⟵⟶

The primitive people tucked back in those deep jungles must have heard the loud "Thud! Thud! Thud! Thud!" of the whirling helicopter roter blades from miles away when the day finally came that we returned to the Dao territory. It took nearly two hours of gliding along above the mile upon mile of mountain ridges before we finally neared the little bare spot on a ridge where our meeting with Totopwi had occurred a few months earlier. The heli was crammed to the max with as much food and basic building supplies as we could stuff into it and still get our bodies in as well.

The jungle looked so lifeless and tamed from the air, a sea of green with the occasional line of white water dashing down through the mountains and making its way toward the swamplands. By this time however, we knew better. We had experienced first hand the extreme jungle terrain that was hidden beneath that seemingly endless deep green layer of trees.

A small granite speckled brown hole in the jungle was what we had marked for our landing pad a few months earlier. I sat in the front passengers seat to the right of the helicopter pilot: our friend and veteran pilot Tom, who had first pointed us towards this area on the map and told us about this place. Jennie along with our newly acquired faithful pup Mili, were in the back. Derek along with an Indonesian couple that would join us for a short time would also catch the heli in and meet us there along with the rest of the supplies.

Within a few hours of landing and unloading on that little ridge top hole in the jungle people had begun curiously gathering and hiking to us from hours and hours away. By nightfall they had come from every direction, many of them having set out on the trails within minutes of hearing the helicopter and seeing us fly overhead. Most of the people: men, women and children had stopped in the middle of their garden work and hiked up to see and greet us. They had work to do as well but they took time out to help us get started and also appointed certain young men to stay and help us build our house and get settled in.

We learned from our previous time in their territory that the largest Dao villages were usually only about three to four houses. The tribe was semi-nomadic and most families had multiple gardens and garden houses spread out over miles of jungle trails and ridges. That being the case they were constantly moving and traveling from place to place according to which gardens had the most food. So while we were working to build our house the individual small villages and clans took turns coming up and helping us chop down trees and carry the wood back to our house site as others worked on their gardens. Then they would switch off and a few new families would come and help us for a few weeks while the others went back to tend to their gardens again.

Our Dani guide was not with us any longer after that initial survey and none of the Dao people knew Indonesian so we primarily communicated through hand motions at first. We were however learning little words and phrases one at a time. We would together with a few Dao guys go and get a piece of wood out of the jungle and discover from listening to them communicate with each other as they picked up a new load of wood to carry that the word for *wood* seemed to be *piyaa*. So we would try out the new word as we pointed to the piece of wood they were picking up to carry back to the house site. They smiled and agreed with head nods if we had guessed right but on the other hand seemed to laugh and correct us if we had guessed wrong.

We then together carried the piece of wood back to the house site and heard again and again another new word which seemed from the context that it might be the word for *carry*. So we again tried the new word out and through trial and error figured out that the word for carry in the Dao language was *doga*. Both Jennie and I made sure to always carry a little pocket size pad of paper and a pen and write these new words down as we heard them. Then we studied them in the evening and the next day when we went to carry another piece of wood I would say *piyaa doga* hoping that they understood that I wanted to carry another piece of wood.

They laughed and then corrected me saying *"piyaa dogaanaka"* from which we were able to assume that there were multiple tenses and that the future tense of the word *carry* was *dogaanaka*. I had just said "I am carrying wood" and because I didn't yet have any wood in my hands they had corrected me and said "No, that's not right. Say 'I'm going to carry wood'." We made mistake after mistake and nearly always learned primarily through trial and error but nonetheless we were little by little learning words and phrases one at a time and it wasn't too long before we could communicate many basic things.

It took only a couple weeks to gather enough wood to make a basic twenty by twenty foot jungle house. While we were gathering the wood for the house, malaria only knocked me out one time for a few days but Jennie and I had both contracted giardia from drinking the local water. A couple weeks after the helicopter had dropped us off we were both having regular, re-occurring, sharp stomach pains. I even started regularly passing blood when I used the bathroom and this went on for a good week. We prayed about it and eventually it stopped however so we just continued on working and took charcoal pills to help ease the symptoms.

We went ahead and began to build on that mountain ridge where the initial talk had taken place with Totopwi because this was where he said we could build and also because there was a good sized flat piece of land here, which was very rare in the extremely mountainous Dao territory. We worked together with the Dao people in the entire process of building the house and only used the resources from their jungles that they gave us permission to use. We purposely decided before we ever started building that we wanted to go as simple as possible in the house building process. This was so that we could model with our lives as well as our words that we were there for only one reason, which was to get them the most important message they would ever hear as quickly as we could learn their language and get it to them.

We felt it was contrary to our message to spend months upon months building nice fancy houses instead of learning their language. We wanted our lives to match our message from the beginning. We wanted them to not only hear in our words but more importantly to see in our lives that our message and learning their language so that we could share it with them was the most important thing to us, even more important than having a nice extravagant house.

The local people kept good on their promise to provide us with land and wood and they were already helping us learn their language so that we could tell them about their Creator. We could tell however that they were still very curious as to whether we were there for the reasons we said we were. They watched our every move. They continually kept their bows and arrows within a few feet reach at all times and they always followed us wherever we went curiously staring at us and jabbering back and forth to each other in the Dao language about whatever it was that we were doing at the moment.

Finally, after about three weeks of fourteen hour workdays we had completed a small, simple house. It was a plain, all wood, twenty by twenty foot mixture in between a tribal style house and western style house. We did this so that our house was comparable to the Dao houses close by yet still efficient for living healthily. We placed large barrels underneath the edges of our roof that would gather rainwater during the daily tropical storms and connected a simple pipe and faucet to those barrels that ran into the house. It was a simple gravity fed water system with no electric pumps at all. This way we had the ability to wash our dishes with uncontaminated water and take cold water showers when we needed to also.

We also dug a hole in the backyard and covered it over with logs after running a pipe into it from a small Indonesian style squat toilet. After nearly a month of using the bathroom in the jungle we finally had a way to do our business in peace and in private when we needed to! Our house had no interior walls except for some bark around the bathroom and shower area. We had a cooking area in one corner and a loft style bed up above the cooking area and put a small table made from left over wood in another corner. Then we left the last corner as a place to sit and visit with the Dao people.

Last of all we put a couple solar panels out which we had brought in on the Helicopter. We did this so that we could have a few hours each evening with lights and also a way to power a computer so that we could record and learn the Dao language on more than just paper and eventually translate also. It wasn't much to look at, but it was our first official home as a family. We had only been married a short time and we were still only barely out of our teens, but it was the first home we had built with our own hands and we were proud of it. It was perfect for us and we loved it.

Derek also kept true to his word to help us build but then it was time for his furlough and so he called the helicopter to pick him up and got together his belongings to get ready to head back to Canada. Then the day came that the helicopter came in to pick up Derek. As the heli slowly rumbled in closer and closer our hearts pounded with excitement. It had only been a couple of months since we had seen it last but it had become the symbol of the outside world to us. Our only link to the world from which we had come, manned by a pilot from our country that even spoke our language.

After it touched down, Derek climbed inside the heli with his military issue backpack and the helicopter once again smoothly lifted off again, hovering for a few seconds about fifty feet above us as it turned and then banked to the southwest into the direction it had come from. Then as the helicopter got smaller and smaller in the distance and finally disappeared into the clouds we suddenly realized that for the first time in our lives Jennie and I were the only foreigners within miles upon miles. The closest expats to our location were Mike and his family, a full weeks hike to the southwest or Steve and his family, a full week's hike to the east.

The closest hospital was literally weeks of hiking away on treacherous mountain trails through the jungle. There was no regular dependable electricity besides a little bit of power we were able to gather each day from a couple solar panels and which we had to use sparingly. There was no running water besides what we could gather from the rain off the roof of our tiny jungle house. There were no streets, streetlights or cars. No big fancy malls and not a single restaurant or store. No televisions or intranet. No family or childhood friends.

There was only Jennie, myself, our faithful pup Mili and some of the most remote people in the world. It was just us, our little house and a hole cut out of the jungle. Whether we liked it or not it seemed that this would be our life for some time and possibly for even years to come.

I will never forget seeing that heli lift off the day that it carried off Derek and left us standing in its wake. Jennie and I stood there immersed in a feeling we had never experienced before. The air was thick with silence. It was so quiet that it was disturbing. An eerie, empty feeling engulfed us as we watched our only link to the outside world lift off without us. Derek told us the day he left that he planned to be back in a number of months but not long after he left we got word that he met a girl back in Canada. He was going to stay in Canada and get married. Only time would tell if he would ever return to Dao or not.

⟵⟶

When the helicopter took Derek out that was the last time we saw white skinned people for a very long time. Being that there were no other English speakers around Jennie and I grew closer than we had ever been before. We were the only ones that each other had to talk to and know that we were being understood because we didn't yet know enough of the Dao language to have very deep relationships with any of them.

This culture was so different from what we were used to. The Dao people didn't live by the clock as we westerners do. Not a single one of them even had a watch, they simply got up when the sun came up and went back inside their houses and closed the doors again when the sun went down. Life was simple in that respect. At the same time however, this way of living made the Dao people very unique from the people in the world we had been raised in. They obviously knew the concept of days and even the concept of a month from watching the moon follow the same pattern as it moved back and forth along the mountain ridge across the valley. They didn't however have any concept of weeks or years. Not a single person here knew what day it was or how old they were because they had no way of keeping track of weeks or years.

Because their concept of time was a bit different from what we were used to, we learned quickly to live by their schedule instead of our own. We could pretty much bet on the fact that within a few minutes of the sun popping up above the mountain ridges we would have curious Dao children on our porch peeking in the cracks of our walls and trying to look in our windows. This being the case we daily got up a good couple hours before the sun was even up in order to have time to read and study our language notes as we sipped our morning coffee. Then when the people were up we were ready for them.

In addition to that we began eating both breakfast and lunch with the people around the fires in their houses every day. We would eat sweet potatoes, which they call *dugi* and another potato type root they call *sibigi,* which are the main staples in their diet. We ate most of our meals communally with them and tried to listen to what was being said at each meal so that we could more quickly learn their language. When we weren't around their fires or hiking to their gardens to do garden work with them we were looking for other opportunities to get involved in cultural events around the area and hiking to visit other villages.

One such opportunity that arose, during which we gained a lot of insight into the culture of the Dao people, presented itself in the form of a feast. The feast was talked about for months leading up to the actual event and was to be hosted by the clan of Totopwi. They referred to it as a *yoo* in their language and everyone within days of Totopwi's village seemed to be preparing to attend. The men all spent most of their time hunting tree kangaroo, cuscus, birds and wild pig. The women and children were spending sun up to sun down doing garden work and digging up the various root type foods and potatoes needed for all the people that would be gathered.

The older teenagers worked together to build a special type of house with a raised floor and demonstrated to us as it was nearing completion that the houses use was meant specifically for dancing. They crisscrossed hundreds of small, thin, flexible sticks and weaved them into a sort of tribal trampoline with walls and a thatched roof around it. As they practiced jumping and dancing on it, the flexible trampoline type weaved floor would bounce them up into the air and they would hoot and laugh with excitement.

Finally, after weeks of preparation everyone started gathering and the dancing began. We hiked nearly a day from our own village along with a few other Dao families to get to the event. Then as we joined in on the feasting we for the first time observed the dancing styles and specially prepared foods of the Dao people. One such food that they saved for the event was a type of blood red, cone shaped fruit that we had never seen outside of this island. After gathering all the pulp from the fruit they had crammed it down into bamboo tubes and then placed the bamboo tubes in caves for a number of years. When they pulled the bamboo tubes back out of the cold musty caves for the feast, the fruit was so old that it had fermented into a thick paste.

They then heated the fermented pulp filled bamboo tubes over the open fire. Upon cracking open the tubes the whole village filled with the overpowering smell of the thick, fermented red contents. Some of the red paste was eaten, with bird beaks used as spoons, just the way it was straight out of the tube. Other parts of the paste were mixed with sweet potatoes to make a blood colored mashed potato mix. Upon trying the mix, both Jennie and I were surprised at how much the mixture tasted like a finely aged cheese. It was delicious!

The people that were hiking from farther away areas to get in on the feast had also brought with them wild pig meat from pigs which they had shot many months earlier. They had taken the pig meat, wrapped it in banana leaves and then buried it a few inches underground for preservation. When they dug it back up for the feast the meat had a thick white layer of mold all over it. After carrying it to the feast location, they unwrapped the leaves and cooked the white, fuzz covered moldy meat over the fire and the mold burnt off. The people would then distribute the meat and feast on it together. We tried some of the many month's old meat as they gave it to us but it was so rancid we could hardly swallow it. We tried to the best of our ability to choke down some of it and smile with appreciation.

As it turned out, we learned through our observations that the primary function of the *yoo* feast was to handle any ongoing disputes in between different clans and villages. During the mornings and afternoons the big men of the various clans would discuss debts, payments and unsettled disputes while the women continually cooked and distributed food. When the sun went down the dancing would commence and as many people as could fit into the small dancing house crammed in that little hotbox of a hut and began energetically dancing and singing in unison as they jumped in a sort of circular fashion. The men would bring their bows and arrows also into the dancing circle with them and hold them high above their heads hitting them continually like an off beat tambourine. The singing and dancing continued from sundown to sunrise the following morning each night of the feast. The *yoo* lasted nearly a week and we gained a lot of interesting knowledge about the social structure and governmental system of the Dao culture by attending.

⟷

Back in our own village, if we were at home for the day and not hiking anywhere, we followed the Dao example in opening our front door when the sun came up and keeping it open until the sun went down in the evening just like they did. The people came and went from our house as they pleased just as they did with each others houses and they would constantly and curiously watch everything we did. This helped to break down a lot of the curiosity that they had about us and why we were there because our house had no interior walls and they could see everything we owned or did right out in the open.

People came in and watched us for literally hours at first and there were almost always kids hanging around giggling and playing in our house. If we sat down, within seconds kids would be huddled up all around us petting our pale white arms and tugging on our strange yellow hair as if we were their new favorite village pet. They seemed to love our house because it was just a little bit different than theirs in style, not to mention the fact that there were two strange looking alien-like people in it. Those first few months word spread all over the Dao territory about our being there and people would hike from three days away to see what we looked like because they had never seen white skinned people before.

There was almost always someone around that wanted to feel the hair on our arms or legs and study our skin to see if it felt the same as theirs. There was constant traffic in our house from sunrise to sundown every single day of the week. Often times we would purposely wait to have our last meal of the day until after sundown when all the Dao people had gone in their houses and shut their doors as this was the only way Jennie and I could get a chance to talk about the day's events and finally get a little bit of quality time together of our own.

With the exception of a few people that we met on our first foot survey into the area, for the most part the Dao people seemed very reluctant to tell us their names. If we were meeting a new person for the first time and asked them directly what their name was they would act uncomfortable and awkwardly look at the person to their right or left as if we had said something wrong. Then the person standing next to them would think for a moment and then say something like "Oh, his name is Peter."

The person we had asked for their name would then nervously smile and nod in agreement. This would happen day after day until we had to come to the conclusion that either half the tribe was named Peter or the people were giving us false names for some cultural reason. On top of that, they never seemed to call each other by the names that they had given us.

Eventually Jennie and I just began making up nicknames for them so that we could tell them apart in the course of conversation. One had unusually large lips so we began calling him "Lips". Another was missing all his teeth and had an unusual high and raspy voice so we referred to him as "Smeagol". One teenager always had a partially dreaded afro and seemed to have a bit of a groove to his walk so we called him "Jimmy" short for Jimmy Hendrix. There was a man that would come up every day asking for random stuff so we named him "Mr. Gimme" Then there was the oldest man and women in the tribe with grey hair and walking sticks so we affectionately began calling them "Grandpa" and "Grandma".

⟷

As we continued to study their language and culture we noticed that another interesting thing about their culture was the way that they showed friendship. If there was someone visiting our hamlet from a different family clan that lived in a different area it was expected that he come with tobacco. As soon as he had greeted everyone he would sit down, pull a small bark like package from his string bag, open it up and pull out a couple strands of dried tobacco for each adult present. As he handed the strands to the other person he would say the word "*nemoomee*" which means "friend" in the Dao language. If his wife had come with him she would do the same with the other women. Then after the tobacco had been exchanged they would all smoke together and talk about any news that they had brought from other villages and areas.

We quickly came to the conclusion that tobacco and the regular exchange of it seemed like such a significant part of the Dao people's daily culture and interaction that it would be the equivalent to our shaking hands with someone as we greeted them back in our own country. Not only was tobacco used in greetings when visiting another area, every house in every village was lined on all four sides with tobacco plants. It was always the first thing they would plant at a new house site.

It was also exchanged in between two parties every time a significant trade of the Dao people's currency of shell money had gone on or any other tribal business transaction had taken place. Exchanging tobacco and smoking together afterwards was a sign that both parties were satisfied with a certain deal made between them. If two people had a disagreement or argument and it had to be worked out, after the disagreement had been talked through and settled the two parties would again exchange tobacco and smoke together to show that the disagreement had been settled.

On the other hand if you visited a village and wanted to state to the people there that a specific person was not a friend of yours or that you didn't like a certain person or had an unsettled disagreement with them you would purposely not give that individual tobacco or smoke with them to show your distaste for them.

I asked Jennie one day "If I walked up to an individual back in America and stuck out my hand for a handshake as I greeted him and he refused to shake my hand, wouldn't you think that was rude and that he was perhaps holding something against me?"

"Well yeah, I guess I would probably think that" she replied.

"So doesn't it seem that if there is a cultural way to show friendship in the Dao people group we should follow suit as much as possible, to show them that we are friends, not enemies and to show them that we respect them and their culture and have nothing against them?" I continued.

"Well yeah, as long as it doesn't conflict with the Word of God since that is the message we are trying to bring to them." she answered.

"So why don't we start growing tobacco around our house then just like all of them? And why don't we start exchanging it with them so that we can show them friendship in their own cultural way?" I asked.

The room grew uncomfortably silent as we both reflected on the question. We had been raised in a place that taught against things like the use of tobacco on the grounds that it was an un-Christian like activity. Besides that even the other expats and missionaries on this island were likely to have some very strong opinions on the subject. If they ever heard that we were doing anything to condone such an un-Christian activity we would likely be ostracized and reprimanded by them as well!

But who's teachings and opinions were we ultimately trying to teach these people? The belief system and teaching of our American Christian culture? Or the belief systems and teachings of Jesus? Neither of us were smokers, both of us in fact loathed even the smell of cigarettes. It seemed however that we had a decision before us. We had to decide if it was more important to us to show the Dao people friendship in their own cultural way during this very important time when we couldn't yet speak their language, or if it was more important to us to stick with the comfortable American

"Christian" culture and belief system that had been handed down to us where we were raised.

After a number of months the local people seemed a bit more used to our being there and we had grown used to many of the cultural differences of the Dao tribe. Despite the fact that we had settled into life in the jungle and learned to cope with things like limited water and electricity and an extremely limited and boring diet, the isolation from our families and the rest of the world was beginning to take its toll. The long hours of relentlessly studying the Dao language and culture turned into days. The long days of sunrise to sundown interaction with the Dao people and following the Dao diet of root types and leaves turned into weeks. Eventually we had been there in that little hole in the jungle hacking away at the Dao language for months.

The beautiful lines of tall jungle trees around our village started to seem less and less beautiful and began to feel a little more like prison bars. We had been here in this place so long and still felt like we could barely say anything at all in the Dao language. At first we didn't mind being laughed at when we said something wrong but now every time someone laughed at us when we talked wrong we cringed inside. "How long will it take us to learn this language? We have already been in this hole in the jungle for close to a year! Will it take years before we finally know enough to communicate what we are here to communicate?" we asked ourselves and wondered out loud.

From when we initially landed in Java, we had been in Indonesia nearly three years now and still hadn't been able to effectively communicate to a single tribal person the message that we were there to bring them. The stories we had read in the past about the great missionaries of old going overseas and telling thousands of people about their

Creator for the first time now made us feel like failures when we thought about them.

The Dao kids that always leaned up next to us and relentlessly petted our arms and tugged on our strange yellow hair didn't seem so cute anymore. In fact, we had both contracted scabies from the village kids and were itching relentlessly. These tribal people that didn't ever bathe didn't look quite so interesting or novel anymore either and we had been dealing with giardia and ameba from eating most our meals with them also. They didn't even wash the food they cooked or their hands either before they prepared meals. It was doubtless this was the reason we were always so sick.

After a while, when the people came up to our porch seeking medicine for the stinking, festering slashes on their backs and arms, yellow puss oozing out of them because they refused to bathe, it took everything in us to look on them with compassion anymore. "Why don't they just bathe or clean their cuts instead of spitting on them and sticking dirty jungle leaves on them? Why won't they just bathe their kids?" I would say to Jennie as I doctored a wound.

"They don't have to live this way! They choose to live this way and it's disgusting!" I thought to myself as I finished cleaning a machete wound of a Dao man and then moved on to the infected ears of one of the kids. Jennie and I worked together to flush the infected ears out with warm water to loosen up the crust and smelly puss. A teenager began to lean up against me as I cleaned his younger sibling's ears. His filthy hands caked with dirt and soot from the fires were on my shoulder and he was unknowingly wiping soot all over my shirt and neck.

At the same time another older woman was running up the trail to ask for some medicine water that we had given to her grand daughter a couple days before. It was just rehydration powder that we mixed into water and this older lady wasn't even sick! "She just wants it because it's a novelty here. There is nothing wrong with her!" Jennie said to me as the lady smiled up at me with a big toothless grin, her old flabby breasts hanging down as she rattled off another long line of Dao words that I didn't in the slightest way understand.

I was tired of being here. The job of learning this language was starting to seem impossible and my patience was wearing thin. We were here in the middle of nowhere for one reason: To tell them about Jesus. Sure, we were making a little progress and could understand some basic things in the Dao language but now so many people were coming for medical treatment that it seemed that half of every day was spent treating people's sicknesses and infections. We barely had time for anything else.

"What are we doing here?" I thought to myself as I lay in bed that night. "God, I don't love these people, and I don't think we can learn this language." I said as I listened to the cicada bugs and other creatures taking turns screaming out from the jungle. These jungle sounds used to lull me to sleep, now they would keep me awake at night. I didn't know how much longer we could last out there. Everything inside of me wanted to give up and it was obvious from our past few conversations that Jennie felt the same way.

⟷

The following morning as the sun came up I went out on the porch with a cup of warm coffee in hand and sat down. "Only a few more minutes to enjoy my morning and then it's the same old thing. Dirty people, festering, stinking cuts and unintelligible language!" I thought to myself as I heard the bushes moving about twenty feet down the trail. My attitude was terrible before the sun had even cleared the ridge in front of me.

I looked down the trail to see that unfortunately, our first patient for the day was already coming up to the house.

It was a man that called himself Apius. He was the only one that had pretty much kept his family in our village almost the entire time that we had been there. All the other families had regularly come and gone for about a week at a time as they were trying to keep up with their garden work in other villages and locations. Apius on the other hand had built gardens closer by when he saw us building our house here and he had also rebuilt a new house about a stone's throw down the hill from ours.

"Oh, great, what am I going to say to him when he gets to the porch" I muttered under my breath. I tried to quickly put together a few basic Dao sentences in my head as he walked up the trail so that I could try out some of the newest words I had learned. "*Epaoo nemoomee*" he said as he sat down on the porch beside me and stretched out his hand to snap knuckles with me three times. "*Aba, aba, aba*" I said as we snapped fingers in the typical Dao way of greeting.

There was silence for a few seconds and then I had worked out in my head a basic question I might know how to ask him. "I just have to get him talking. I can always understand more than I can say." I thought to myself. This seemed to be the case with the other languages I had studied in the past as well. It was just the way I learned. I looked at Apius and said to the best of my ability, speaking very slowly: "Friend, when we built a house here you also built a house here. Why did you build a house here, but most of the other Dao people did not build here but only visit instead?" I asked him. He seemed to understand my question and got a kind of half smile on his face, almost a grin as he thought for a moment about his reply.

After a few seconds he stretched out his arm next to him and held his hand about the height of his stomach if he would have been standing. "When I was about this high, just a young man, I woke up in the men's hut one morning and started cooking a sweet potato over the fire. My father was the last of the men in the house to wake up but when he woke he quickly sat up and said 'Wow! I had a really strange dream.'

'Well tell it to us' the other men said, because dreams are very important to us Dao people. My father continued on to say 'Oh, it was so strange. I saw pale skinned people hike up into our mountains. They hiked into our valley and somehow could speak our language. They said they had an important message for us and then they lived among us. Then after we had heard their message we became so close with these pale skinned people that they were like brothers and sisters to us, we became like family with them! And then I woke up! It was such a strange dream!' he said to the other men in the room." Apius explained.

Then looking up at my face and directly into my eyes, Apius continued. "Friend, when I saw you and your wife hike into our valley and I saw your pale skin, and then I saw you building a house here and trying to learn our language, and you told us you had an important message for us, I remembered my father's dream. Upon remembering the dream I decided I would do everything I could to help you learn our language as quickly as possible. I am here, living with you and helping you because I am waiting for the day I can hear your message. That is why I built my house here."

I could hardly believe what I was hearing. Apius was probably in his late thirties or early forties. His father had died years before we ever set foot into the Dao valley but from what Apius was saying, God had given his father a dream probably close to thirty years ago prophesying of our arrival in the Dao territory! Apius laughed as he saw the look on my face after I heard his story. He could probably tell that I didn't know what to think. I asked him to tell me the story again just in case I had been confused and was not understanding correctly because of my limited language ability but he said the same exact thing again the second time. This was incredible!

As Apius went back down to his house a little later and I went in and propped my door open once again for the day's traffic of giggly kids and festering wounds I realized something very important. I understood for the first time that morning that what was going on there in the Dao valley was so much bigger than me. It was about so much more than my wife and I and our measly efforts. This whole thing was not about us at all in fact!

God had a plan for these people since long before we ever arrived. Even though they had been forgotten by the rest of the world, God had not forgotten about them. Over the next few weeks we would hear this same story from other Dao people as well. Apius' father was not the only man in the Dao tribe to have this prophetic dream. In fact, this wasn't just a dream to these people at all. It was a prophecy that foretold future events! And because of our pale skin and claim from the beginning to carry a "great message" they saw us as the fulfillment to this prophecy!

Multiple men had experienced the same prophecy through dreams and passed it on to their children and clan also. God had been giving them these prophetic dreams to prepare them! He had been working out His plan here in the Dao valley. Before we had ever arrived here God's predetermined plan of having "people from every tongue, tribe, people and nation one day standing before his throne" as the Book of Revelation talks about, had been put into play! I realized that morning that God was even more committed to His Word than I was because if even one of the tribes was missing on that final day when everyone was standing before God's throne, that would make Him a liar. And God is not a liar, nor will He let Himself be made into one!

I had revived hope as did Jennie after we heard Apius' story because we realized that we would not fail if we would just let the Lord be the strength that we needed and keep on moving forward. Whether it was months from that point or even years, we would be able to learn this language one day and tell these Dao people about their Creator if we would just stick it out! Not because we were anything special or had what it takes to make someone place their faith in Jesus Christ but because God loved these people and was committed to His words. He would not let His purposes fail and He would not let Himself be made into a liar. We just had to be faithful and speak when God told us to speak. We had to let God be God and let Him do the rest.

Chapter 9

A New Friend and a New Name

Christianity has come to the point where we believe that there is no higher aspiration for the human soul than to be nice. We are producing a generation of men and women whose greatest virtue is that they don't offend anyone. Then we wonder why there is not more passion for Christ. How can we hunger and thirst after righteousness if we have ceased hungering and thirsting altogether?

John Eldredge,
Wild At Heart

Etokaatadi was as friendly as they come. A tall, slender, beautiful lady with petite features unusual to the average Dao women. She had small shoulders and a delicate frame. A slight reddish tint showed in her hair in the bright tropical sunlight and her young, two year old daughter Matauwoo was the spitting image of her.

Etokaatadi was usually very quiet and sat in a corner by herself while the other Dao women were chattering away. It seemed for some reason that most of the Dao women didn't like her very much. We didn't know why but Etokaatadi took a special interest in Jennie from the first couple weeks we were in Dao. She would come up and bring special foods from her garden just for Jennie and didn't hesitate to tell us her real name as most other Dao people did.

Etokaatadi would sit in our house with her young daughter Matauwoo for hours on end. She was patient and soft spoken as she taught Jennie new Dao language phrases and was always willing to repeat a word over and over again as Jennie tried to get the pronunciation of each word just right. Jennie was glad to have a friend like Etokaatadi that was so patient with her and so willing to spend large amounts of time teaching her the language. They were laughing together and spending most afternoons together in no time at all and it was easy to see that they genuinely enjoyed each other's company.

Her husband liked to be called Niko though we would find out later that his real name was Daokagi. He was an older, hard looking man with sandpaper skin and a rough demeanor about him. He looked to be about in his late forties or so. Daokagi had another wife also besides Etokaatadi that was much younger and more beautiful, his favorite of the two women. He had two kids from this other wife and seemed to spend all his time with those two kids and his younger wife while he wanted nothing to do with Etokaatadi and her daughter Matauwoo.

Polygamy is a very common practice in tribes all across this island so we were not surprised to also find it in Dao. It was very interesting to us however that when a man had two or more wives in this tribe, it seemed very rare that he treated them both equally and in love. Usually there was a favorite and in Daokagi's case it seemed that he not only loved his younger more beautiful wife as the favorite, but he absolutely despised his older wife Etokaatadi.

He constantly yelled at her and threatened her in front of the entire village and he was consistently harsh in his interaction with her. Sometimes he would throw things such as bamboo tongs or random coals at her while she cooked the evening meal and scream at her to leave. Perhaps this was the reason she spent so much time at our house with Jennie? Maybe she was just as happy as Jennie was to finally feel accepted. Perhaps our house had become a refuge to her in the midst of her bad relationship with her husband.

One day Daokagi walked up to our house in a somewhat somber mood. He was usually very loud and talkative but this specific day he seemed very quiet and contemplative. I had recently learned the different features that the Dao people would use in their language when they had a question so that specific day I was trying to use these features and practice simple questions about our surroundings. After a half hour or so of listening to me ask question after question about our surroundings in an attempt to practice the Dao language, Daokagi said "Friend, I have a question for you now." "Go ahead Daokagi, I will try to understand" I replied. "Do your people die?" he asked.

I thought that I had heard him wrong so I asked him to restate his question. "Do you pale skinned people die?" he again asked me with a very serious look on his face. "Well yes, of course we die. My grandfather is dead, as is my grandmother on my father's side. We will all eventually die just as your people die" I replied.

"Friend, I am afraid to die. What will happen to my spirit? Will it go to the place of demons to become an evil spirit as our ancestors tell us it will? What will happen to me? I do not know. I am very afraid of death," he continued and then looked at me with such a hopeless look on his face as if he didn't know what to do with himself.

"When you tell us the words from the Creator's leaf book, will you tell us of these things?" he asked. "Yes friend, we will tell you of these things" I nodded in agreement. "But we need to be able to speak well first. I want to tell you well so that you can completely understand the Creator's words. This is why we have moved here. This is why we are learning your language."

A grim smile stretched across his face. "I hope I live long enough to hear this message. I am so afraid of death," he said. Then he got up and slowly walked back down the jungle trail to his own house.

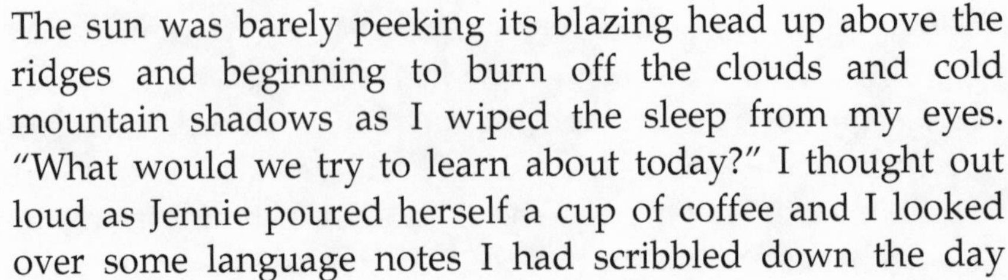

The sun was barely peeking its blazing head up above the ridges and beginning to burn off the clouds and cold mountain shadows as I wiped the sleep from my eyes. "What would we try to learn about today?" I thought out loud as Jennie poured herself a cup of coffee and I looked over some language notes I had scribbled down the day before.

"Well, we have learned most of the words concerning food and garden work and we seem to have exhausted the words and phrases used in house building" I continued. "Yeah, but we still can't even barely speak in basic sentences!" Jennie replied. "It doesn't matter if we can understand basic statements about their garden foods and houses if we can't speak in sentences! We probably sound like little children to them" she said in a frustrated voice.

"Well, all we can do is keep on studying and spending time with the people. It will come eventually, I know it!" I said as I tried to convince myself of the words coming out of my own mouth. We slurped up the rest of our coffee and got an early start on the day making our way down to a house that Totopwi's clan had built, about a hundred feet down the hill from ours.

"Epaoo nemomee! Epaoo" we heard ringing through the cool morning air as we got close enough for them to see us coming. "Greetings friend! Love to you all as well" we called back in their language as we approached the house. *"Aba, aba, aba"* I repeated in the Dao fashion as I stuck forward the knuckle of my index finger and we snapped each other's finger three times.

There were a couple newer Dao guys there that morning that we had seen hanging around during the time we were building our house but hadn't yet gotten to know that well. "These guys must have arrived yesterday evening just before we closed our door for the night" I said to Jennie as we found a place to sit down next to the fire.

We had learned by then that you never directly ask a Dao person their name. This might be the way we did it back in our country but to the Dao people names were something to be very careful with. Each Dao person had multiple names and they only offered their real name to those that they trusted. In their animistic belief system someone could take a name and use it to work sorcery. You only told someone your name if you truly trusted him or her as a close friend.

As we warmed ourselves by the fire under the little porch in front of the hut I leaned over towards my friend Apius and asked him what Jennie and I should call these newcomers that we were not yet too familiar with. This was the cultural way of asking for a name and Jennie and I already assumed we would be given false names for these two newcomers at first. "Well, the one with the head band on can be called Yakiyaa. The other younger one can be called by the name Arapius," he said as they both stretched forward their hands one at time and snapped knuckles with me and then with Jennie. "*Aba, aba, aba*" we repeated once again and then I reached into my bag and pulled out a strand of tobacco for each of them in order to show friendship in their own cultural way.

Big smiles stretched across their faces as they received the tobacco and replied "*Paamee nemoomee*" meaning "Thank you friend". Yakiyaa reached down and grabbed a warm sweet potato he had been cooking from under the ashes and handed it to me to show friendship back.

"Where are they from?" I asked Apius as I tried to use some of the newest language phrases I had recently learned. "They are from Totopwi's clan up in a village called Kodop," he replied as I broke the potato in half and gave a part of it to Jennie and then peeled some of the charred skin off the piece in my own hand and popped it into my mouth. We sat and listened to the two men and the other Dao people that were there rattle on in conversation as we munched away on sweet potato and enjoyed the warmth of the fire in the cold morning air.

From the first day we met him, Yakiyaa seemed softer spirited than the average Dao person. Though there was no way of telling for sure, it seemed he might have been about my age, possibly just a year or two older. The Dao people's counting system only went up to twenty seeing as how it was based on their fingers and toes, of which there are only twenty on the average person. Anything above twenty started over at one again. And even if they could count past twenty, they had no concept of years. They only knew and recognized days and months.

Yakiyaa seemed to try harder than the average Dao person to involve us in the conversations around the fire. When he could tell that the conversation was getting too fast for us to follow and our eyes were starting to glaze over in boredom he would often stop and ask a short simple question to either Jennie or myself so that we could be a part of what was going on again. He also had a wife named Moipi and he would encourage her to teach Jennie how to do the cultural things of the women like make grass skirts and string bags from the bark of a local tree.

Yakiyaa began spending a lot of time in our little village shortly after we had met him and would invite us along on garden trips frequently. He also invited us to garden a specific section of his own garden land and then told us part of the food in his garden was ours since we had helped in the clearing and planting.

He introduced us also to another close friend of his that liked to go by the name Yusupi and they even began to invite us on an occasional hunting trip. They would stealthily tiptoe down the jungle trails throwing out birdcalls and tree kangaroo calls. They were looking for cuscus and rat nests also to see if they couldn't find the owner of the nest and shoot it with their long bamboo arrows. They knew the local game so well that they could mimic any of hundreds of animal or bird types in that jungle. We were amazed at the sounds that they could make. More often than not we would clumsily fall on the slippery trail behind them or make too much noise and ruin the hunt but Yakiyaa and Yusupi were always patient with us. Yakiyaa especially never seemed to lose that soft spirited look on his face or that huge sweet smile.

One time as we were out hunting with them, all of the sudden our faithful dog Mili let out a sharp bark as she sniffed around the bottom of a large jungle tree. Yusupi looked up toward the top of the tree and motioned for us to quietly wait. He pulled back an arrow in his bow and then "Swoosh...tak!" he let it fly and it went right up into the branches and hit something in the tree. "Thud!" we heard something hit the ground about twenty feet from us. We looked up ahead to see that there was a multicolored, black, white and gold cuscus almost as big as our dog that had fallen out of the tree and hit the ground.

"Woo! Woo! Woo! Woo! Woo!" they hollered out in victory as we all jumped up and down and laughed with delight. "Your dog saw it! This is your kill too because it was Mili that found it!" they told us as they continued laughing in between sentences. "We will feast together on cuscus meat tonight and it will be good!" Yusupi said as he yanked his arrow from the warm cuscus body and then pulled a sharp piece of bamboo from his string bag to dismember it with. They proceeded to take the innards of the cuscus out and wrap them in some jungle leaves. They wrapped the cuscus carcass in a separate bundle and then Yusupi stuffed it into his string bag. Then we headed back towards the village with a spring in our step to feast on our kill!

From that point on, our language abilities rapidly improved. We had friends that we could spend time with who seemed to see us as more than just oddities. They saw and treated us just as much as real people and as valued parts of the community.

One evening as the smoke twirled up into the rafters from his tobacco cigarette, Yakiyaa and I sat across from each other in the men's house. He whittled away on a piece of bamboo that he was making into a new arrow tip. I sat across from him and studied his work very closely as I tried to mimic his movements. He skillfully carved the arrow tip just right and then inserted it into a bamboo shaft to make a perfect fit. Although I had tried time and time again I couldn't make arrows like they could. My work looked rough and almost comical compared to theirs.

Yakiyaa was unusually quiet that evening. He was usually smiling away and talking up a storm so I could tell that there was something on his mind. All of the sudden he stopped what he was doing and pulled the leaf cigarette from his mouth that he had rolled earlier with some of the strands of tobacco from his own string bag. He looked at me for a second across the fire and then held out the cigarette in front of him, pointing it towards me. "We heard recently that there is another man that is claiming to have the message of the Creator. He is teaching in the next tribe over but they say that he is from the Dani tribe many weeks walk from here.

We have heard that he teaches there is a place of fire that the enemies of the Creator One will go to. The man says that if we smoke tobacco and wear our decorative nosebones, if we carry our bows and arrows and wear our traditional dress, if we do not leave our ways behind and begin to wear the strange clothes of you pale skinned foreigners, we will go to this place of fire. Is this true? Does the Creator One that you have come to tell us about hate the way we look and the ways of our people? Will He send me to His place of fire because of this tobacco that I am smoking?" he somberly asked.

"Is this what it comes down to? Is this the message that these people think we are here to bring?" I thought to myself as I could feel my heart begin to race with disgust and even a bit of anger at what I was hearing. Jennie and I needed to show these people that we were not here to change their ways and culture! That we had not left our families and everything we loved on the other side of the world just to tell them that God hates their customs and clothing style and to teach them a false gospel! Everything within me wanted to fight against the false notion that God would love the Dao people more and would finally accept them if they only acted more American or looked more like us.

Many of the other missionaries and "evangelists" had taught these same lies in this country and even in other tribes on this island for years before we ever arrived and had led tens of thousands to spiritual destruction because of it. No doubt this Dani teacher had probably learned the lies he was teaching from people that had come from the same part of the world as Jennie and I had! We were here to teach them about Jesus and His words, the words of His book, not the random opinions of man or the American "Christian" church culture we had been raised in!

I thought for a second about how I had tried so hard to gain God's approval for so many years of my life through dressing up for church every Sunday and praying the special "Christian" prayers of penance which I thought would get me to heaven if I said them just right. I thought about how I had for so long completely missed the point that it was all about Jesus and His sacrifice, not about me and my pointless adherence to American church rituals and culture. These things couldn't save me and they sure couldn't save the Dao people either!

I reached across the room and grabbed the cigarette out of Yakiyaa's hand. I wanted so bad to show him that I didn't believe these lies they had been told by other tribes anymore than they should. I put the cigarette up to my lips and took a big puff. Nearly gagging on the smoke I began uncontrollably coughing, as I had never smoked a cigarette in my entire life. I exhaled and watched the smoke twirl up to the top of the room as Yakiyaa's eyes widened and he looked across the room with his jaw hanging wide open in shock.

"Well if this is what sends a person to the place of hellfire, I guess I am going there too since I also have now smoked some of your tobacco!" I said while looking him directly in the eyes. "But this is not the message that we bring Yakiyaa. The message that the Dani you have heard about is carrying around is a lie straight from the evil spirits themselves! It is not the message from the Creator's leaf book that saves someone from the place of fire! When we have learned your language well enough I will open up the leaf book of the Creator One. With your own eyes you will have the opportunity to see what the Creator One has to say about it. You and your people will finally hear about the one and only true trail to eternal life."

As Jennie and I lay in bed that evening I could hardly sleep for thinking about the conversation that had taken place in between Yakiyaa and I. I was reminded that there are many people and many religions in this world that believe and teach that it is what a person eats or drinks or wears that decides his or her eternal fate and right standing with God. Jennie and I were not some of those that believed such things and neither did we want to teach the Dao people to be.

I again reflected on my childhood and many of the lies I had heard growing up and been taught in "Christian" schools and churches. We made a decision that night that God's book would be our standard for what is right and what is wrong, not the church culture we had been raised in or the opinions of men that had been pushed on us and had distorted the truth in our own lives for so long. If it was to God's glory and the preservation of the true gospel on this island, we were even willing to smoke an occasional cigarette if need be. Through both our words and through our lives we wanted these people to know true good news and nothing else.

⟷

The next day we got some gourd seeds and planted them in our backyard and within a few months had a whole crop of gourds growing. This was so that we could provide the Dao men with new tribal style "clothes" should the gourd that they were presently wearing begin to break or wear out. We wanted them to know that we had nothing against their traditional dress. I even sported a gourd myself one day when there were only a few men around to see it. They laughed so hard at my pale, sun barren skin that I never tried wearing one again. Jennie learned from the women how to make a grass skirt like theirs and she began wearing it around the village for the time being to show the same thing to the women. I also carried a bow and arrows of my own from that day forward just as they did.

We took it upon ourselves to show them not just by our words but also by our actions and our daily lives that our message was different from the things that they had heard and would probably continue to hear coming from some of the other areas beyond their borders. We were there to teach them the Creator's ways, not our western or American culture or any culture for that matter.

They had made various comments since our arrival about how incredibly long our noses were compared to theirs. As we got better at their language they would occasionally joke about how our noses would look so much better and our faces would be so much more beautiful if we had our septums pierced as they did and wore the long decorative nosebones of their people.

We asked a lot of questions about if there were any animistic rituals surrounding the piercing of their noses or if they had any special beliefs surrounding that specific practice. When it was all said and done however, we came to the conclusion that the Dao people's nose piercings are for them a simple way to make themselves more beautiful. It was no different then the piercing of women's ears back in our homeland and most other parts of the developed world. One day a little while later when a couple of the tribal people came up to our porch one of them again made a comment in passing about our long noses.

"You would be so much more beautiful if you let us pierce your noses!" he casually mentioned and then continued on with his conversation as though he hadn't even said anything about it at all. "Well pierce it then!" I said. "What?" he replied as if he hadn't heard me right.

"Pierce our noses then! Do it! I am tired of being ugly!" I retorted with a laugh. "You want us to pierce your nose?" he replied. "Yeah! Why not? Go ahead and pierce my nose! I don't mind at all, then I will finally be beautiful like all you guys!" I said as I let out another nervous laugh. "Okay! We will do it but it will hurt! Your going to cry!" they said as they hooted and hollered with amusement.

One of the little naked tribal kids ran down to the middle of the village in his excitement to tell everyone else what was going on. Within minutes everyone in the village had run up and gathered on and around our porch to see what the commotion was all about and if we would really go through with it.

One of the men pulled a bone of a bat wing from a small bamboo container in his string bag. It had been sharpened on the end for use as a thick needle. It was about the thickness of a small ballpoint pen. He wiped the sharpened bone on his string bag to clean the dirt off. He then thrust the bone needle through the stem of a green plant a few feet away to coat it with a slimy goo-like substance for the piercing.

"Are you ready?" he asked as he grabbed on to my septum and pulled it down towards my upper lip as far as it would go. "Go ahead, I'm ready!" I hesitantly replied and then I saw stars and a quick flash of white for a second as he thrust the bat bone through my septum with a quick twisting motion. I could hear and feel the cartilage crack as he twisted the bone through.

When they saw the look on my face and the big long bone sticking through my nose they laughed so hard that they cried. "Your so beautiful! Your so beautiful!" they repeated over and over again as they laughed and the men took turns giving me good hearty pats on the back and shoulders. "We knew your long, pale skinned nose would look so good pierced!" they continued on.

"Your wife is next" they said as they looked up at Jennie. She hadn't necessarily planned on joining in on this event. "You want to be beautiful too don't you!" the women said as they got behind her and pushed her toward the tribal man doing the piercing.

"Okay, okay I will do it!" she said as she sat down and they once again repeated the procedure. Again the people hooted and howled with laughter as Jennie got her septum pierced as well. We couldn't smile for nearly a month it hurt so bad to move the muscles in our faces but from that day forward we wore the decorative nosebones of the Dao people and they absolutely loved it.

⟷

It was right around the time our noses were healing up that we were sitting in front of their houses one day and the Dao people present proclaimed that they had given us new names. They had always had problems pronouncing my name because "Scott" could not be said correctly in their language. The Dao language is one in which every word has vowels in between every consonant and every word also ends in a vowel. So the closest they could come to pronouncing my name was *Siko*. The closest they could come to saying Jennie's name was *Yeni* since there is also no *J* in the Dao language. Being that they couldn't even pronounce our names right, most of the time they just opted for calling us *nemoomee* which meant "friend".

They decided along that time however that we were like them now. We were part of the community and they wanted us to be called by their language and the ways of their people. They looked at me on that day and announced "From now on you will be called *Degapiyaa*." When I asked them what the Dao name meant, they pointed over to a tall white tree next to Totopwi's house that the entire village used for target practice. It must have had a hundred old arrows sticking out of it! I didn't know what to think about the arrows and when I nervously asked them about it they all laughed until they couldn't laugh anymore. They never gave me an answer as to why they had chosen that tree but nonetheless it was an honor to be called by my newly received Dao name, *Degapiyaa*.

They then gave Jennie a new name that day as well. "From now on we will call you *Ugiidataauwoo* they said. They went on to explain that they had named her after the small stream that ran down the side of the hill close by our house. Her name literally meant "water in a barren land". In their language, often women are named after streams of water and men are named after flower and tree types and so they had named us according to their Dao customs. From that day forward I was called "the tall white tree" *Degapiyaa,* and Jennie was called "the stream in a dry, barren land" or *Ugiidataauwoo.*

It finally seemed as if the people had begun to trust us more. They from that point on finally began giving us their real names as well! As we sat around the fires and spent time together day after day we started to hear the true names of the individual Dao people we were spending time with. Yakiyaa told me that from then on I could call him by his real name, *Wikipai.* Apius was *Apiyaawoogi,* Arapius was *Paatoma* and Yusupi was *Daapooi.* It was great to feel like we were finally being trusted. The people were finally beginning to see us as more than just an oddity. Many of them had begun seeing us as friends. Perhaps the day would come after all that the prophecies of their fathers and grandfathers would finally come true. Perhaps someday they would even call us family.

⟷

A few nights later when we got ready for bed it was a bit colder than average. Even though we were in the tropics of Indonesia it still would occasionally drop into the high fifties in those jungle highlands. Jennie put an extra blanket on the bed and we crawled in for the night and snuggled up together to get warm. We loved nights like this, it reminded us of winter back in the States. We had come to learn over time that another thing different about this part of the world was that there were not really seasons in those mountains. The leaves didn't change there and we hadn't seen the autumn colors for years. On cold evenings we would close our eyes and pretend that we were perhaps back in the hills of Tennessee where Jennie had grown up. We always slept deeper and sweeter on nights like these. It reminded us of home.

When we woke up bright and early the following morning, Jennie began to sleepily open her eyes from our bed in the loft and look up at the underside of the roof, which was only about two feet above our loft style bed. As she slowly wiped the sleep from her eyes and stretched she let out a good morning yawn and then all the sudden I heard her screech with terror.

"What's wrong? What is it!" I said as I frantically sat up and tried to figure out what was going on. "That is not funny Scott! Did you put that there? I can't believe you would try to scare me like that!" She said as she pointed to a white, fairly long cotton like strand of material hanging across two rafters a few feet above our heads.

"What are you talking about Jennie? I didn't put anything up there! Why would I get up in the middle of the night and hang something in the rafters? What are you pointing at?" I replied as I in my frustration got out of the bed and took a closer look.

There, within an arms reach above our heads, dangling in the rafters hung a nearly six-foot long, extremely large snakeskin. The snake wasn't there but he had left behind a souvenir for us to let us know he had joined us the night before. It seemed the fairly large snake had gotten cold during the night as well and decided to come into our warmer house and bed down for the night with us. Was it still in the house? We sure hoped not but how could we really know whether it was still there lurking behind a cabinet or under our bed or not? It could have been anywhere!

Chapter 10

The Theology of a Savage

The forces of hatred cannot be conquered by yet more hate. The rebellious principalities and powers of this world will not be undone by us trying to play their game. Victory comes only through love.

Lee C. Camp,
Mere Discipleship

Most nights in the Dao jungles the evening rains would come pitter-pattering on the roof of our little jungle house and lull us to sleep, and this night was no exception. We woke up the following morning to a beautiful double rainbow. I had never seen one so bright! Upon spotting it I immediately grabbed my camera and began to snap a few pictures. The deep green jungle mountains behind it seemed to contrast so beautifully with all of the rainbow's magnificent colors.

After snapping a few quick photos it occurred to me that I might get a better view of the rainbow from down in the center of the village. We grabbed our string bags along with our pens, notebooks and a few sweet potatoes and within a few minutes Jennie and I were headed down to the tribal houses to snap some more photos of the rainbow and have breakfast with our Dao friends. When we made it down to the houses though, for some unexplained reason no one was out on the porches cooking their breakfast foods like usual. It was strange to see the village so empty looking. Jennie went on in to the women's side of one of the tribal huts and I went into the men's side to see where everyone was. Wikipai was sitting next to the fire along with some other Dao men gazing into the fire. He and the others sat there silent with disturbed looks on their faces, none of them said a word.

"Did you see the sky this morning? Did you see it? It was beautiful wasn't it? Come outside and see!" I said to the others in my excitement as I turned to head back out the door. "Degapiyaa, no! Don't go back out there yet!" Wikipai yelled to me. "Why not? Don't you want to see the beautiful sky with me?" I asked. I had not yet learned the word for rainbow but I was sure they would be just as delighted as I was to see it.

"It is a bad sign in the skies today. Didn't you see the walking stick of the evil spirits?" they asked. "What are you talking about?" "Those colors, they are the walking stick of the evil spirits. We call them *paatamoo.*" he replied. "They are a bad omen, do not look at them! They could cause you sickness or even death! Stay in here until it is gone my friend. For your own good, do not look at it again Degapiyaa!" Wikipai replied.

It was obvious from the look on his face that he was very concerned for both his safety and mine. I sat there for a moment and thought about their word for rainbow. I had heard this variation of words before. The word for evil spirit was *paa*. I had learned that a few weeks before. *Tamoo* must have meant walking stick. It seemed they really did believe that this is what a rainbow was, the literal walking stick of an evil spirit!

We couldn't believe that they were so afraid of something so beautiful. Something that according to the message we wanted to bring them had been given as a sign of goodwill and of a promise from God to Noah and all of mankind. In the Dao culture, this sign of goodwill from God had been turned into a sign of the evil spirits, something that they believed could cause them harm and which was meant to bring sickness and even death.

⟷

A few days later as we sat in our houses studying language in between visitors, a little before noon we suddenly began to hear loud cries echoing up from down in the direction of the other houses. It sounded like someone was either in deep pain or extremely sad about something. Within moments other voices both male and female were chiming in crying and wailing.

Whatever was happening, we knew we needed to get down to our friends fast and see what was going on. Jennie and I ran down the trail towards where the cries were coming from and as we arrived I called out to Daokagi, the first man that I saw. "What is going on? Is everything okay?"

He was hunched over with his head on his knees crying along with Apiyaawoogi and some of the women in the village. He wouldn't answer me.

Just then I looked up and saw a group of men coming up the trail. It was Daapoi walking with a delegation of other men as he led little Matauwoo, the daughter of Etokaatadii by the hand. As usual, every man was carrying his bow and a fist full of arrows. Some also had their machetes but the looks on their faces were different this time. None of the men had their usual smiles as they entered the village and not a single one of them was greeting any of the others present or exchanging tobacco like they usually did.

"Where is Etokaatadii? I have never seen her apart from her daughter." I thought to myself. Jennie walked over to the women and asked them "What is going on? Why is everyone crying?" "Someone has died." one of the women replied. They began singing in a high disturbing wail as Matauwoo was led to her father Daokagi and put in his arms.

We had never heard them wailing and going on like this before. It was like a disturbing chant or drone of some sort. Drawn out and dark like a hollow, hopeless song mixed with deep painful cries. We have never forgotten it since. "I don't understand! Who died and what happened?" I asked one of the teenage guys close by named Kogipiyaa. "She wouldn't stop her witchcraft. She had been warned after she caused the death of that man up the valley a couple of moons ago but she didn't listen. She had to be killed." he said to me with a blank stare on his face and then continued wailing with a long drawn out moan.

"Was it Jennie's friend Etokaatadi they were talking about? Surely they hadn't killed her!" I wondered as my heartbeat quickened and I looked around for someone else to ask for an explanation. I looked over at my close friend Daapoi and the other men with him. They were all squatting in a clearing in between all of the houses clinging tightly to their bows and arrows and having what seemed to be an intense argument.

Then in a moment Daapoi quickly stood to his feet and angrily addressed all the others sitting around wailing in anguish. "We had to kill her don't you see! It had to be done!" Daokagi, the husband of Etokaatadii nodded in agreement. "Daapoi is right! It had to be done!" he added in with an almost sinister look on his face.

Then it hit me, Daokagi was in on it too! He had always treated Etokaatadi as if he would have been happier if she were dead. This murder had been planned from the very start and it was Etokaatadi's very husband that had probably instigated it! We found out the rest of the details as the day went on. The news they had received a few evenings before from a random traveler sparked the whole thing into play. The traveller had come from a different part of the Dao territory two days hike away. He had carried the news with him that two very prominent men had died of sickness within just a few days of each other back in his home village.

Daokagi in turn blamed the deaths on his older wife, Etokaatadi, who was already in disfavor with the tribe. After Daokagi blamed his wife Etokaatadi for the deaths, Daapoi knew what he had to do. He knew it was his responsibility being the younger brother of Daokagi to revenge these two deaths. There was no other way. He had to do it. He had to kill Etokaatadi for the witchcraft she had supposedly worked on these two men. This was what their animistic beliefs demanded of them.

After gathering a group of men to go down with him to her house, which was just down the mountain from ours, he confronted her there. "Why did you work your sorcery on those men!" he angrily yelled as one of the other men went and yanked her young daughter Matauwoo from her arms. "We will not let you do this any longer! We will stop you before you kill others!" he yelled as he placed one of the specially carved arrows designed for murdering enemies in his bowstring and drew it back.

The other men did the same following Daapoi's lead and the arrows flew at Etokaatadi striking her body one at a time. First in the shoulder and then two more through her chest which struck her with such force that they stuck out of her back after passing through her body. Another one hit her in the side and she slumped over dead as the blood flowed from her body. Her daughter, probably only two years old, had watched the whole thing along with all the other children in the village. Etokaatadi was dead.

Jennie broke down into uncontrollable tears as we heard the rest of the story. We couldn't believe what we were hearing. One of Jennie's best Dao friends had been killed in cold blood. Etokaatadi had never even had a chance to explain her side of the story or defend herself. Her daughter was taken from her and that was it. She was murdered. Now Matauwoo was left motherless and very obviously emotionally riveted. She would never be the same. She cried all day and all night for a long time. For days we listened to her from our house until late into the evening. Jennie did everything she could to comfort the young girl. Her cries echoed in our minds time and time again and we couldn't even sleep at night for hearing her pitiful wails over and over again.

They had only two ways of disposing of human bodies in the Dao culture. They would usually give someone an honorable funeral by placing them in the trees to decompose as the evil spirits came and ate their flesh. But in Etokaatadi's case they had given her the funeral of an enemy. They threw her body in the river to be carried down by the rapids into an evil place that they called *Sinipaa* and eaten by the fish, turtles and crocodiles of the swamplands.

That was a week we will never forget as long as we live. In those moments we were suddenly struck with the reality that these were the type of people we lived among. Daapoi, one of my best friends was a cold-blooded murderer along with most of the men that we spent most of our daily time with. How could I treat him or anyone else here the same from that point on? How could I still look at him as a friend? Jennie's closest friend was gone. What would keep them from doing the same to us or accusing us of witchcraft? What would keep them from blaming us for their sicknesses and then filling us full of arrows before we even got a chance to plead our case?

The questions raced through our minds for days until I feared for even the well being of Jennie and myself. I couldn't even look at a Dao man with his fist full of arrows without wondering who he might kill next. We couldn't look at a women or child without wondering if the same thing would happen to them eventually that happened to Matauwoo and her mother Etokaatadi. For a time, I couldn't even smile at a Dao person anymore. I constantly wondered if they had a plan to do the same thing to us. We didn't trust anyone anymore. If I were to make one of them angry or refuse one of their requests would they murder us too? We had to once again ask ourselves a question we had dealt with before: "Is our message really worth it?"

The bottom line was that if we were going to stay here and continue living among these people, we had to understand why they lived this way. We had to somehow find out why they thought the way they thought. Why they believed that the evil spirits controlled things like rainbows and natural phenomenon. Why they constantly sliced each other's backs and bodies and drained the blood until they were too weak to even stand. Why they murdered each other like this.

We had to get deeper into their mindset than just talking about going to the garden and making string bags. We needed to understand their belief system if we were ever going to tell them about ours. We had to understand where they were coming from at a deeper level, both emotionally and spiritually. We had to understand how they thought before we could translate into their language, with accuracy the message we had come there to bring them.

Things were different for us from that day forward in the way we approached our study of the Dao language. We purposely looked for opportunities to ask pointed questions about the evil spirits. We spent hours listening to them tell the stories of their ancestors. Stories that had been passed down from generation to generation by word of mouth for thousands of years in this unwritten language.

We asked them things like how they believed that man had even come to exist in the first place and who it was that their ancestors had told them created humankind. The old experienced men and most respected elders of the Dao tribe began to tell us more about their beliefs as we asked them question after question. They told us many of their folktales but the most intriguing story they told us was their account of the creation of mankind. Wikipai tried his best to explain it to me one afternoon.

"Our people believe that the very first humans on the earth were a mother and three sons. One day the middle son tried to commit incest with the mother and so the other brothers decided that they must kill him because of this evil act. They waited for just the right time when he least expected it. Then they shot him with their bows and arrows and killed him for his evil act.

It was then that the two remaining brothers decided that in order that there would be more people on earth they needed to split their murdered brothers body in half and separate it into different sections from which new groups of people could be born. So the older brother sent the younger into the jungle to gather the correct type of banana leaves in which to wrap the body parts. They would wrap the individual body parts of the murdered middle brother in these banana leaves after they had divided them into different groups according to types.

After hours and then days the younger brother still hadn't returned with the appropriate leaves and so the older brother grew angry and impatient. He decided he would not wait any longer and in his frustration he grabbed his half of the murdered middle brother's corpse and carried it over next to a large special type of tree by the river. He then grabbed the closest large leaves he could find and began separating that half of the middle brother's body into different groups. Just then the younger brother returned with the proper banana leaves but it was too late, the older brother had started without him! In his anger at the older brother the younger brother than grabbed his half of the corpse and carried it off into the highlands to divide the body by himself also.

Because the older brother had not been patient and had used the wrong type of leaves, some of the blood from the corpse dripped down into the ground next to that special tree which was next to that river. When it dripped down into the ground it seeped right into the mouth of a great evil spirit snake. For this very reason, even to this day we Dao people die. It is said that if there had not been that disagreement between the two brothers and that blood had not gone into the great serpent's mouth next to that special tree, we would live forever!" Wikipai explained.

This story sounded strangely familiar! A disagreement between two brothers? A special tree? A serpent that was responsible for the death of all mankind? It sounded like a very skewed version of the Bible's Genesis account and some of the events surrounding the Biblical account of the creation of mankind! This surely was strange!

This wasn't the only story they told us that had similarities to some of the stories told in the Old Testament. We would learn over the next few months that the belief system of the Dao people was not any less intricate than the most complicated theology of Christians in America or any other religion for that matter. In fact, to us, at times the belief system of the Dao people seemed even more intricate than any theology or belief system we had ever heard of before.

We also began making a detailed chart of the family tree and kin system of the Dao people. As Jennie sat next to her friend Wadamenaa, one day, an older man named Obapwi arrived from a long trip to another village. "Oh mother, I am so glad you have returned! Welcome mother!" Wadamenaa excitedley yelled as she ran and greeted him. "Mother? That's a man! How can that be your mother?" Jennie thought to herself as she sat there somewhat confused at what she was hearing. We made a chart over the next few weeks outlining how every individual person was related to the other living people in the tribe.

As it turned out, the brothers and sisters of Wadamenaa's mother were all referred to as her "mother" in the Dao kinship system. It was a distinct communal way of thinking unique to their people group and culture. The more we thought about it, the more it made sense as children in this semi-nomadic culture often moved from village to village as they got older in age and are raised by multiple people. Even though they knew their birth mother, they also saw all of the brothers and sisters of their birth mother as "mothers" and all the brothers of their father as "fathers".

Another very important thing we realized while studying the kinship system of the Dao people was that there was not a single person we had met in the entire Dao tribe approximately our age or above that still had both their father and mother living. Etokaatadi's murder had not been the first murder because of accused sorcery. Most of the men and women that looked to be in their mid-twenties and above had lost either one or both of their parents because of revenge killings, tribal warfare, or homicide of some sort. Even the majority of the teenagers and children in our village were being raised by only one of their real parents and his or her younger second or third spouse.

The reports from different areas of various murders continued to come in as people came through visiting from different villages. We started counting the murders and in only a couple of months we had counted over twenty more men and women that had been murdered, many of them people that we had known and spent time with. It seemed that the Dao people were killing each other off faster than we could even learn their language well enough to tell them about their Creator and the trail He had provided them to eternal life!

⟵⟶

This new wealth of information that we were gathering as we dove deeper and deeper into studying their belief system wasn't easy to deal with spiritually. We would often wake up in the middle of the night having had nightmares about evil spirits or about friends bodies being thrown into the river or decaying in the trees. If we heard the slightest sound outside our house or our dog Mili let out the tinniest bark in the middle of the night, we would wake up gasping for air, our hearts beating faster, wondering if someone else was being killed. We often wondered if someone would ever come after us or if we were seen as a separate entity from their usual system of revenge killings and tribal warfare.

One morning Jennie and I decided to take a walk at the top of a little hill a couple hundred feet from our house. We wanted to get some fresh air and exercise and we would occasionally walk circles along a trail at the top of the hill that was just long enough to stretch our legs a little. It was about seven in the morning as we walked along the little jungle path and discussed our plans for the day and what we would do in our language and culture studies.

Our faithful pup Mili was bounding around in the jungle as usual chasing grasshoppers and barking at bright red and green parrots and other jungle birds as they flew from tree to tree. All of the sudden she stopped about fifteen feet in front of us on the trail and started growling. We stopped dead in our tracks. "What do you think it is Jennie?" I whispered. "I don't know, maybe a wild pig or tree kangaroo?" she replied.

It was a bit foggy that morning as the clouds from the evening before had settled down in the jungle trees in front of us. We couldn't see more than twenty feet ahead but I knew that it couldn't be an animal Mili was growling at. She would always let out a distinct high pitched bark when there were animals around. The only time that she ever growled like she was in that moment was when there were people that she wasn't familiar with and didn't yet trust walking close by us or our house.

"We better head back to the house, I don't think it's an animal and I don't know who would be up here in the jungle at this time of the morning." I whispered to Jennie as we slowly turned around and started quietly and quickly making our way back down the jungle trail. We picked up our pace as we got closer and closer to the house and as Jennie went inside I ran down and told Wikipai about what we had heard. There had been rumors recently that a revenge killing was going to be carried out on a friend of ours. This friend and his son also were presently in our village. His name was Iyeepiyaa and his son was named Magabideedi.

Everyone waited inside their houses for a couple hours until the clouds had lifted and there was clear visibility. They then sent a couple of people up to look for tracks along the trails and in the jungle close by where Mili was growling earlier that morning. The Dao people were masters at reading tracks and signs in their jungles. Their daily food often depended on it. I was confident that they would be able to figure out what Mili had seen. Sure enough they found the tracks of at least five tribesmen from earlier that day. There had been a war party that had come to carry out a revenge killing. They probably had not been hiding in the jungle more than a few feet from Jennie and I. Most likely their bows were drawn and they were poised to release their arrows as they heard us coming.

It was not us that they were waiting for however. They were looking for Iyeepiyaa or perhaps his son or wife in hopes that they could murder one of his clan and gain the revenge that they had sought after. We thanked God for our trusty dog and made sure to keep her a little closer by from that point on.

⟵⟶

It was January again and it hadn't rained for over two weeks. This was the only month of the year that seemed different than all the rest in Dao. After a few years here we had noticed that January was a bit dryer and windier than all the other months. Our rain barrels were empty and we didn't always even have enough water to bathe or drink when we were thirsty. There was a small stream about twenty minutes hike down the mountain so for a couple of days now I had been carrying water back and forth up the mountain so that we could at least cook for ourselves and have enough drinking water to function. We would bathe in the stream and Jennie would wash our clothes there as well so that I didn't have to carry up as much water.

Just a few more months and we would be in Indonesia nearly three and a half years. The giardia and malaria was taking its toll. Jennie and I both were starting to look gaunt and the only clothes that I had were beginning to hang off me as if I were an old scarecrow. I had cut multiple new holes in my belt so that I could continue to even use it and my pants were pleated up in front of me because they were way to big for me anymore. When we had come to Indonesia I was over two hundred twenty pounds. Now I was nearing one-sixty and Jennie wasn't looking too healthy either.

This wasn't the first time that we experienced a water shortage. It seemed about every January or February this would happen multiple times. Though it was a hassle to deal with, it definitely taught us the value of even the simplest things. We would pray together at every meal asking God to provide the rain so that our barrels would fill once again and we would have enough clean drinking water. Then when He had finally answered our prayers and we had plenty of water we would find ourselves more often thanking God for the simple things such as rain and water because we had experienced many days where we had to go without it.

At other times we wouldn't see the sun come out for days because of all the tropical rain clouds. We would pray all day, every day for sun as we went about our work so that our solar panels could get a charge and we could have a little bit of electricity that evening. As a result even when we weren't experiencing power shortages and had plenty of sun we would often find ourselves thanking God for it because there had been plenty of times when we had been forced to go without lights for days in the evenings.

One of the games that we liked to play was what we called the American food game. Even though we did have the occasional supply and medicine drop from the helicopter pilots we had to use these supplies sparingly and we had often gone quite a while without eating much besides sweet potatoes and various root type vegetables and garden foods. We would be walking along the trail in between villages while going around to give someone medical treatment or just to visit some friends and one of us would ask the other, "Okay, it's your turn this time. If there were any one restaurant that could serve any food you wanted along this jungle trail what would you want the restaurant and the food to be?"

We spent a good while on the trail talking about the foods we couldn't wait to taste again when we got out into civilization. We played this food game so many times that I could pretty much predict what Jennie's reply was going to be and which mouthwatering food she was dreaming of before she even said it. She could do the same for me. I didn't even have to say what I was thinking.

The hardest times of the year where we missed our country and our own culture the most were no doubt the holidays. We could just picture the holiday spreads on the tables back in America and all of our brothers and sisters enjoying it without us. Mom's homemade stuffing or that big juicy turkey that our families were enjoying at Thanksgiving time, not to mention that pumpkin or pecan pie with whipped cream they were probably having for desert. Or those delicious frosted sugar cookies perfectly cut and decorated like little Christmas trees or snowmen that we used to eat every Christmas not long after my mom had pulled them from the oven.

At times we even wondered if we were healthy enough to stay in the jungle much longer. We would contact people from the city through a little shortwave radio that we had brought in and ask if anyone knew of a new medication we could try to get rid of the giardia. Sometimes we just wanted someone to speak English to and even some of the other foreigners and missionaries on the island thought we had been interior too long.

"Why don't you just go back to the States for now and recuperate. The Dao people aren't going anywhere! They will still be in the jungle when you get back! You should just take a furlough and take it easy for a while!" they would urge. "Perhaps a short furlough would help us get refreshed a bit…it would be so nice to see our families again." we would say to each other every once in a while as we dreamed of all the comforts of our homeland and all the good food we were missing out on. Perhaps the other missionaries were right, maybe we should go back to America…just for a little while?

We could never bring ourselves to take this advice though. It didn't sit right with our conscience. It seemed like we were getting more reports of new deaths every other week. How could we look the Dao people in the eyes and tell them "Once we learn your language well enough we will tell you the most important message that you will ever hear." but then take a vacation and take it easy for a while, in turn making it a longer period of time before they heard our "important message"?

It seemed like this was the new fad among missionaries in general. We would hear of people taking breaks every one and a half to two years on other islands and in other tribes in Indonesia before they had ever even learned the language of the people they were trying to teach. We knew of some tribes that had missionaries living among them for almost ten years already and they still hadn't heard the gospel for the first time because the missionaries hadn't yet learned the language! It actually made us sick to our stomachs when heard about things like this.

"What does this say about our message when we don't even care enough to endure through hardship so that people can hear it!" I would ask Jennie as we contemplated whether or not we should take it easy and go back to America for a while. "It says that Jesus isn't worth it to us, doesn't it? It says that our comforts and health and families and American foods are worth more than the our message doesn't it?" I would reason with Jennie and also with myself.

She agreed. We couldn't just speak about our message as if it were important to us, we had to live that it was important to us. We couldn't go back home no matter how tired and worn out we were, not now anyways. Perhaps the time would come when we felt the freedom to come and go from the Dao tribe freely but the time was not now! We couldn't go back to America and rest until our Dao friends had a chance to hear about Jesus and His trail to eternal life for the first time. They were hopeless without it. Even beyond that, our lives would not be consistent with our message were we to leave now and we knew it.

Chapter 11

Hungry for Human Flesh

My heaven is to please God and glorify Him and to give all to Him, and to be fully devoted to His glory: That is the heaven that I long for, that is my religion, that is my happiness, and always was ever since I suppose I had any true religion; and all those that are of that religion shall meet me in Heaven.

David Brainerd,
Life and Diary of David Brainerd

"Leave us! Go away from here! Stop causing us pain and sickness! Stop stabbing us with your spears and shooting us with your arrows! Leave us now and go to another place far away from here! Go! Go!" they yelled at the tops of their voices as Daokagi walked circles around Paatoma with a fist full of ashes from the fire. He made a circular motion over Paatoma's head with the ashes as strange growling and humming noises came up from the back of his throat.

Apiyaawogi's wife, Wadamenaa grabbed a sharp piece of bamboo with one hand while she pinched and puffed up a big tuft of skin on Paatoma's ankle with the other hand. In a quick sawing like motion she sliced him multiple times as another man, Uwokaatomaa grabbed a thick decorative arrow with a human killing tip and pulled it back on his bow string. Jennie turned her head as the blood spurted out of Paatoma's ankle, even I felt nauseous when I saw things like this.

Pointing his bow up toward the sky he released the arrow. Everyone grew silent as the arrow climbed up higher and higher into the sky slowly arching over the houses and began to descend back down into the jungle next to the stream at the bottom of the valley. As the arrow shot through the air he yelled a final "Go now you evil spirits! Bother Paatoma no longer!" The blood from Paatoma's ankle and foot dripped down into the ground for nearly an hour. When it had finally stopped dripping they dug up the dirt where his blood had spread down into the ground and threw it in the fire just in case it might attract evil spirits to the place where they had performed the spirit chasing ceremony.

This was the first time that we had seen this specific ceremony but it would by no means, be the last. As the people had begun to trust us and grown more comfortable with us being around and we had learned more about their language and culture, there was not much that they hid from us any longer. We had for the first time begun to understand why they have so many scars all over their bodies, why they constantly have wounds that are infected and we had to spend so much time cleaning out infected, oozing gashes day after day: this was their traditional medicine. This was their belief system.

This was the only way they knew and constantly turned to in order to get rid of sicknesses. It was the way their people had been treating the sick and wounded for centuries. Their animistic belief system combined with their lack of common knowledge concerning modern medicines demanded it of them. It was all their people had ever known. In their minds, it was the evil spirits that were to blame for all pain and sickness and these rituals were the only way to chase them away.

Paatoma wouldn't be walking anywhere for a while. He was involuntarily stuck in our village whether he wanted to be or not. He couldn't barely move his leg without wincing in pain they had sliced him so deeply. For him, a semi-nomadic Dao man whose whole way of life was wrapped up in wandering the jungle trails and hunting as he traveled to his multiple gardens, this was nearly torture.

We felt bad for him. At the same time though, this might get Jennie and I an opportunity to dig even deeper into the belief system of the Dao people. Perhaps Paatoma would give us new insight into the ceremonies we had seen taking place that day. Why had he been sliced specifically by a woman, Wadamenaa? Where did Uwokaatomaa and Daokagi first learn the incantations and rituals they had performed on him and were they the only ones that knew these specific incantations? Was this really the only way that they could scare the spirits away or were there other ways also?

The next morning we headed down bright and early to the hut where we knew Paatoma was staying. There he was, sitting by the fire by himself. The others had already left for their gardens and wouldn't be returning until later in the afternoon. "How are you today, friend? How does your foot feel?" I asked as I squatted down beside him and pulled some medicated ointment from my string bag to help keep the infection down.

"Oh look at it friend, it is swollen out in pain. Curse you evil spirits!" he replied as he hopelessly looked at us and then at the deep, fresh gashes again. That was the opportunity we were waiting for. "Which evil spirit was it Paatoma? And why do they do this to you?" I curiously asked.

"Who can know which one it was? I surely do not know. It could have been any of them. They never leave us alone! They always seek whatever opportunity they can to do us harm. Not a single one of those spirits is good! Curse them! They are all evil! Look at what they did to my foot! This is why people here are always sick. It's their fault! Surely I have been stabbed with their walking sticks or shot with their arrows. Otherwise my foot would not be like this." he said while looking down at the ground disheartened and depressed.

"Do you know how many there are? Is there a certain number of spirits and are they really all bad? Every single one of them?" I asked probing for more information.

"There are too many to count! They live in the trees and in the roots of the trees as well. They are under the rocks and in the caves, they are in the rivers and under the ground. They are all around. They are everywhere," he continued as the smoke from his cigarette twirled up into the rafters. "Are they male or female? What do they look like?" I asked.

"There are both male and female evil spirits of course! They look like us, they carry bows and arrows just like us, they walk the trails and jungles just as we do. But they are hungry for our flesh. We are their food and this is why they hunt us as they do, this is why they shoot us with their arrows and stab us and cause us sickness.

They want us to die so that they can feast on our bodies. We will become their food. Our loved ones will wrap us in our bark rain capes and place us in the trees when we die and the evil spirits will feast on our bodies until we are no more." He continued with a look of horror on his face. "They are all evil. There is not a single spirit that is good. Curse them all!"

For days Jennie and I talked through and hashed over what we heard that day from Paatoma. "Cannibal spirits! Can you believe it Jennie? How are we supposed to convey to them that God the Creator is spirit and that He is good when the only spirits they have ever known are evil and want to do them harm?" We had come to the realization that the message we travelled all the way from the other side of the world to tell them about was in many ways the exact opposite of everything they had ever known and believed.

After diving deeper into their animistic beliefs and seeing firsthand the way that the Dao people daily lived in fear trying to manipulate the evil spirits, there was no doubt in our minds that they needed the message we had come here to bring them. It was the only thing that would set them free from the daily fears and manipulation they had always been enslaved to. We even knew that we were fulfilling a prophecy given to the Dao people in the form of a dream by being there. A prophecy that had been given to the Dao people a generation before our arrival! But still we doubted whether or not they would really be able to accept the teachings we had come to bring them of a loving Creator and a way of salvation.

Their people group had believed so differently for so incredibly long. Unless God opened up their eyes and did what we as mere message bearers could never ourselves do, our being there and our leaving behind everything that we had ever known was in vain. God would have to do a miracle in the Dao people's hearts and minds if anything at all would ever change in this dark place.

A few days later my good friend Wikipai was back from a trip to another village, his wife Moipi and their new baby boy, which they had given the name Simbo was also with them. Simbo was their first child and he had only been born a few months before but his personality was beginning to show already. He was sweet and joyful just like his father and as we spent time with him we came to love him as if he were one of our own.

"There is hardly a thing I say anymore that you don't understand Degapiyaa!" Wikipai said to me after we had talked a little about the recent news he had heard from other surrounding areas on his journey. "Has the time come yet?" he then casually asked.

"What do you mean has the time come yet? Time for what?" I asked somewhat confused. "You have always told us that when you knew our language well you would tell us of the message from the Creator's leaf book. The words that will show us the trail to eternal life! You speak well enough now, don't you? When will you finally tell us the words of Creator's leaf book? Will it be soon?" he asked with an inquisitive look in his eyes.

He was right. We had been in Indonesia for over three and a half years now. We had been studying the Dao language day in and day out for months upon months. We still didn't speak as fast and well as they did, nor did we feel adequate to begin translating or teaching in their language, but they needed to know. We were continuing to get reports almost weekly of more Dao men and women dying through revenge killings, tribal warfare, homicide and sickness.

"How many more of the Dao people will die before they have even had their first chance to hear about their Creator and what He has done to provide them with eternal life?" I thought as I looked Wikipai in the eyes.

"Friend, in order to be able to tell you the words of the Creator One's book we must first write down these words in your language so that they can be told to your people. We do not know your language well enough to write them in the way that you would say them. We are foreigners, we still often make mistakes and speak as little children sometimes." I replied.

"Don't worry about that Degapiyaa, I will help you. We need those words. This is a big talk isn't it? I will stay here if you want me to. I will not walk the trails or travel to other villages until every last word is in our language. I want to hear the whole story from start to finish. My ancestors and my grandmother and my father all died without ever having even heard the true name of the Creator One. My people die in hate and in fear because we have not yet heard this talk. I do not want to die in hate and fear, without knowing the trail to eternal life as my ancestors did! Don't you see, Degapiyaa? I want to die well! It is for this reason that I will stay and help you put these words into our language. I will do whatever it takes." he concluded.

That was the day that we finally knew it was time. God wasn't working in only us now. Despite our doubts and despite how incredibly daunting the task seemed of explaining such deep Biblical concepts to such an animistic, remote group of people, it was obvious that God was also already working in the Dao people and beginning to draw them to Himself. He was preparing them for His message and many of them were waiting for His words! It seemed His message was irresistible to Wikipai. As if it called to him like a long lost treasure that he had been waiting for and dreaming of.

Besides that, Wikipai wasn't the only one! There were others that had not forgotten our promises to teach the words of the Creator's leaf book that we had made on our first foot surveys. Daapoi, the one that had murdered Etokaatadi was also asking us when we would begin teaching, as well as Daokagi and Totopwi. Over the next few days, Wadamenaa along with Moipi and some other women also agreed to help Jennie translate should she need their help.

Jennie and I talked one evening shortly afterwards and made a plan to start in the following week working with the Dao people to begin translating God's story into their language. We began strategizing about what we would translate first and which of us would be the main translator. It had become completely obvious to us both over the last few years of studying both the Indonesian language and also the Dao language that Jennie had way more of an aptitude than I did for paying attention to important details and grammar structures in languages.

I had always been the type to just learn languages in what I like to call "crash and burn" style. I would just say things wrong a hundred times and let people laugh at me until they told me the way to say it right. I would learn fast because of this and was always a step ahead of Jennie in my speaking ability. Jennie on the other hand would listen and study how to say a single phrase perfectly for days before she would ever attempt to say it out loud for even the first time. For this reason, even though she couldn't rattle off language like I could, whenever she did speak she would say things very correct and precise and would understand every tiny little prefix, suffix and grammar feature for every paragraph she said. It seemed that though God had gifted her to be the main translator, He had just as much gifted me to teach. We found out before long that we both thoroughly enjoyed these roles and they seemed to compliment our personalities as well.

We also sorted through the sounds that were used in the Dao language and with the people's help wrote out an alphabet to match their language. This was so that from that point forward we would have the ability to write things down precisely and accurately with an alphabetical system that could also be used by the Dao people themselves. This new alphabet for the Dao language could also serve the purpose of helping them to preserve their language through writing in future generations. We had heard of many other languages on the island that were literally going extinct because of the national Indonesian language moving in and replacing the tribal languages all together!

As we talked through the beliefs and culture of the Dao people in preparation to begin translating, we also came to the conclusion that we could not just start translating and teaching in the New Testament with the life of Christ. These were animistic people and they believed that there were literally hundreds of spirits that infiltrated everything and every aspect of life. Every one of these spirits had to be manipulated specific ways and according to the Dao belief system, every single one of the spirits was evil and ultimately sought to do them harm.

They had no concept of one great Creator spirit that was good in nature, more powerful than all others and ultimately sovereign over all things, both good and evil. If we began right off the bat teaching about Jesus, the Son of God but neglected to first teach them about the good and holy character of the Creator God, they would simply throw Jesus in with the rest of their spirits and then perhaps have a thousand and one spirits to manipulate instead of just a thousand.

Unlike many of the other missionaries that had worked in other tribes on this island and in Indonesia in the past, we had to lay a correct foundation and begin teaching from the Creation account in the book of Genesis. We had to lay a solid foundation for the understanding of God's character through the Old Testament stories or the Dao people might end up even worse off than before. If we did not start from Genesis and the concept of one good Creator God over all things, then the Dao tribe would likely just turn into a group of people that sought to appease the American "Jesus Spirit" along with all the other spirits.

Just as some of the other tribes on the island that had already had missionaries were already trying to do, they would simply end up trying to appease this new "Jesus Spirit" by not smoking tobacco or by not drinking taboo drinks. They would try to appease Him by dressing up for church every Sunday in the clothes of the foreigners and by meeting in the special foreigner's building where they would pray special prayers to gain this new spirit's approval. This was not what we wanted. We hadn't traveled across land and sea to make them worse off than they were before. The last thing we wanted was to make a bunch of false converts that did nothing more than dress up and play church every Sunday in hopes of manipulating God.

Jennie and I sat down and talked through a specific outline that we would follow for translating key portions of the Old and New Testament for the Dao people and then teaching them. We would first translate the majority of the book of Genesis and then other key Old Testament stories all throughout the Old Testament that pointed forward to Jesus, "The promised Redeemer". Before we ever said a word about Jesus coming down to earth we would make sure they had met the good Creator God and understood His promise to one day redeem mankind.

We also began asking ourselves and key close friends like Wikipai questions like "When a Dao person has something important to say how does he say it and in which setting does he say it? Does he tell everyone at once or does he tell only the biggest and most respected men first? Does he tell the important news casually while smoking some tobacco and while everyone is sitting around the fire? Or does he stand up in the middle of the village and shout at his audience while occasionally tapping one of his hunting arrows on the ground in front of him every time he hits a main point? Does he do anything out of the ordinary in order to keep everybody's attention or does he just talk like he always normally talks? What is it that shows a message is important in the culture and speech of a Dao person?" We listened carefully to Wikipai's answers and studied all these things in preparation for telling the story of the Creator's leaf book for the first time.

After Jennie began translating portions of scriptures I would take what she had translated and make a sort of lesson based on that portion of scripture. A few of the Dao women would help Jennie as she translated but her main two helpers that seemed to have a good knack for helping her explain things in the Dao language were Daokagi's young wife Topeawa and Daapoi's wife Otopina. They would sit for hours in our house or somewhere else in the village talking through verse after verse and chapter after chapter trying to find the perfect way to say things in the Dao language. Then one phrase at a time Jennie would write everything down clearly and accurately and then pass it on to me.

Wikipai and Daapoi were the two men that agreed to help me make the lessons and we would, just like Jennie and the women helping her, sit around and talk through the stories of the Old Testament one by one chronologically for hours. I tried to pay special attention to the way a Dao listener would perceive the stories being told according to his tribal animistic background and would ask a lot of questions to Wikipai and Daapoi after they had heard a section of my lessons. If they didn't seem to be understanding a point that I was trying to get across about an individual story or truth about the character of God we would stop and discuss it sometimes for hours until we had figured out a clear and accurate way to explain it to the Dao people as a whole.

Wikipai and Daapoi would be the first two people in the history of the Dao people to hear the story from start to finish. From the scriptures Jennie translated, I would work together with those two men to write down from start to finish the story of the Creator and the promised Redeemer, His Son Jesus. Our plan was that when we had translated and written the entire story down in a clear and accurate way in their language, we would call all the Dao people together that were within hiking distance to come gather in our village and would teach the entire group as a whole through the lessons Wikipai, Daapoi and I had together made.

I will never forget the very first day Wikipai, Daapoi and I met together to begin writing lessons based on the Creation account of Genesis. They sat down completely silent as if they were afraid to speak and they were going to meet their Creator for the first time face to face right then and there. They had a silent reverence and knew that something great was about to happen as I read the first verse that Jennie had translated into the Dao language.

"Long long ago, in the very beginning, the Creator One created the heavens and the earth..." I read and then continued on reading in the Dao language up through the end of the section. Daapoi and Wikipai looked at each other, their eyes wide as saucers. They looked back at me, their mouths slightly open as if they had just seen a ghost. They seemed almost afraid to speak.

"All things? He created all the heavens and the earth? One Creator being with enough power to speak into being everything that we see? One being responsible for the sun and the moon and the stars and all that is in heavens and on the earth?" They gawked in amazement. The simplest of truths that I had heard my entire life hit them like a ton of bricks. Over and over this would be their reaction as I would look up from my notes at their faces after I read.

We worked our way through the creation account and also talked of how God had along that time created the angels. I told them how the Creator's book says that the angels He created rejoiced and praised Him as they watched Him create all other things. We worked through the story chronologically and touched on the story of the fall of Lucifer and his followers that had come into disfavor with God and then been kicked out of heaven and become the enemies of God.

We then came to the story of Adam and Eve and they heard of the perfect garden that God had made and then freely given without charge to them. This also blew them away. "Imagine doing all the work to make a garden and finally have food in it and then just giving it away free of charge like that! We Dao people would never do such a thing would we!" Daapoi said as he laughed out loud. "Yes, the Creator One surely is not like us is He? He is so powerful that He can merely speak and things come into existence. He surely is more powerful than any other isn't He!" Wikipai chimed in. They were understanding! Already they were seeing that this great Creator God is not like any of the spirits they had ever heard of before. He is in a class of His own!

As we worked our way through the story of the fall of Lucifer and how Satan had taken the form of a serpent for the purpose of deceiving Adam and Eve, Wikipai and Daapoi sat on the very edge of their seats in anticipation of what would happen next. They had heard the warnings of God about touching the fruit of that forbidden tree. They knew the consequences that awaited Eve should she give in to the tricks of the snake and eat the fruit. I needed to make sure they were understanding what was going on and that I was communicating clearly so I stopped and asked them a simple question. "Who is this serpent and why is he trying to convince Eve to eat the fruit that God told them not to eat?" I asked.

"I know exactly who he is and why he was doing it!" Daapoi replied without the slightest bit of hesitation. "He is an evil spirit! He knew that if Eve ate the fruit that the good

Creator told her not to, she would die and he was hungry to feast on the flesh of Eve. That is why he was trying to get her to eat the fruit!" he confidently replied.

I thought back through what I had just said and looked at my notes again. "Surely I didn't say anything about the serpent being hungry for human flesh did I?" I thought to myself. Then I remembered that according to the beliefs of the Dao people this is the ultimate goal of every evil spirit. This was what they believed happened to their bodies as they decayed in the trees.

At first I didn't know what to say. This false assumption that Satan survives off of the flesh of deceased human bodies had to be addressed, but how? I thought about it for a second and then another question came to mind. "According to the Creator's book, who were the only other beings besides God Himself that were present during the Creation of the world and who sang His praises as He created all things including things edible and inedible?" I asked.

"The angels of course!" Daapoi replied. "And what was Lucifer, the evil spirit that took on the form of the serpent before he fell into disfavor with God?" "He was also an angel." Wikipai added in. So if the angels are spirit beings as God is spirit, and they existed before things both edible and inedible were created then do they need a source of food to survive as we do?" I asked.

"Well, no, I guess they don't." Daapoi responded with a thoughtful look on his face. "Then why would he seek to deceive Eve and do her harm if he didn't need to eat her flesh in order to survive?" I asked.

"I guess simply because he is the enemy of the Creator God as are the other evil spirits! That must be why they tried to deceive Adam and Eve. Because they belonged to the Creator one, the Creator loved them, and they are the enemies of the great Creator!" Daapoi responded.

The following day Wikipai and Daapoi were once again there on my porch bright and early ready to start helping me put the next part of the story into their language. They were excited to hear about the things we were talking through and were eager to get started. That morning we started by talking through how everything in the Garden of Eden was perfect and there was not a single bad thing, not even a thorn or sickness there that did Adam and Eve harm. We then talked through the fall and how Eve and then also Adam had fallen for Satan's tricks and sinned against God. Their faces completely lost any expression of hope as they heard about the demise of mankind. They just couldn't believe it. They cursed at the snake right then and there.

Jennie and I took a trip to help Wikipai and his wife Moipi do their garden work later on that day and to work our section of their garden. "If it wasn't for that stupid evil serpent! Oh how different things would be now!" Wikipai said out loud as we walked along the jungle trail and across the ridge towards his garden. He just couldn't stop thinking about it.

As we were in his garden pulling up weeds a thorn dug into his hand. "Would you look at this Degapiyaa! Look at this thorn in my hand! We have been deceived! We would not have things like this in our gardens were it not for the bad choice of Adam and Eve to not listen to the Creator one. My people die in sickness because we were deceived by that evil spirit! If only Adam and Eve had listened to God, it would be so different for us all!"

It seemed from that day on that these types of things were all Wikipai and Daapoi could ever talk about. They had never heard anything like it but their hearts gave testimony that the stories they were hearing were true. The next day we worked our way through the story of Cain and Abel where they heard of the first acceptable sacrifice of a lamb. Then we went on to the story of Noah and the ark where they saw God's character once again through his judgment of sin, as they had previously seen when Adam and Eve were kicked out of the garden.

They heard the story of the great flood and of God's judgment on mankind, but they also saw how He delivered Noah and his family, as Noah trusted Him and His words. They once again saw Noah's acceptable sacrifice of a lamb in Praise to God and learned about the true significance of the rainbow and how it represented a promise from God to mankind that He would never flood the earth again. They laughed with joy as they were freed from their fear of one of the most beautiful natural phenomena that regularly occurs in the rainforests of Indonesia.

The evening of the very day they had heard the story of Noah and the ark for the first time a beautiful rainbow stretched across the sky behind the village and we all rejoiced together with Wikipai and Daapoi as they yelled out loud in the middle of the village: "Thanks to the Creator One for the rainbow!" instead of running into their houses in fear of it. The rest of the village however stayed in their huts and looked out at us as if we were crazy because they hadn't yet heard the story of Noah as Wikipai and Daapoi had.

As the weeks went by it wasn't long before we were working our way through the key stories of Exodus. Wikipai and Daapoi continued to learn more and more about the character of the all-powerful Creator as we continued forming chronological Bible lessons together in the Dao language. When they heard the story of Moses it really struck home with them but especially with Daapoi.

"Moses was a murderer and God still used him as a tool to speak His message?" he asked me with shame in his voice. He had heard about God's judgment on Cain for the murder of his brother and knew that he had likewise offended God when he had led the war party to kill Jennie's friend Etokaatadi not too long ago. "If there is hope for Moses, then there surely is still hope for me also, isn't there Degapiyaa?" he asked with deep conviction on his face. For him, the story of Moses had given him hope that perhaps he was not too far gone for God to love him after all.

They heard about the plagues that God sent to Egypt because the pharaoh would not obey Him but they also heard about how God watched over and saved the Israelites because they had trusted Him and obeyed His request to provide the Passover lamb and put the blood on their doorposts. Then they heard about how God delivered the Israelites time and time again in the wilderness despite the fact that they turned against Him over and over again.

They understood that not only the Israelites, but they too had fallen short of God's standard of perfection given in the Ten Commandments. They knew that they as well as the whole Dao people group were in disfavor with God and that they had offended their Creator by breaking His law. They also saw in God's character that He never makes a promise that He does not keep and He never gives a prophecy that doesn't come true. Through those Old Testament stories that we worked through, they saw God's character reflected in His promises. He had promised the Israelites freedom from their oppressors in Egypt and a good land to live in also and then over time He had delivered on His promise!

God had also promised them a Deliverer and Redeemer that would usher in a new age and take the place of the sacrificial lamb. Wikipai and Daapoi were convinced that this promise of a coming Redeemer was also one that was bound to be fulfilled. They knew that God does not lie. They knew that He was righteous and hated sin and most important of all they had seen that those who trust in Him are never disappointed. God had delivered on His promises time and time again and He would deliver on His promise of a Redeemer and Sin Bearer as well!

After they had seen His character shine through time and time again for literally weeks of Old Testament stories we continued reading together through the key writings of the other Old Testament prophets as well as Jennie continued to translate new scripture portions for us. Daapoi and Wikipai heard about how King David, Isaiah, Daniel, Jeremiah, Zechariah and Micah all individually prophesied about the Redeemer that was supposed to come and take away the sins of the world.

The Creator had given a promise in His leaf book that this coming Redeemer would show mankind a way we could be made right with God despite our wrong doings. Because we went through the Old Testament prophecies of the coming redeemer chronologically before getting to the New Testament, before I ever said the name of the promised Messiah even once they knew where He would be born, what family He would be the descendant of, which Israelite tribe He would be a part of, that He would be born from a virgin, that He would go to Egypt, that He would be without sin, that He would be betrayed by a friend for thirty pieces of silver and hated by the Jews, that He would be mocked, executed and beaten, that He would be pierced on His hands and feet and then killed, that not a single bone of His body would be broken during the crucifixion, that He would be buried in a rich man's tomb and finally, that He would be raised from the dead and ascend into heaven.

It wasn't until after they had heard through every one of these Old Testament prophecies that we finally began to teach them the first stories from the New Testament. Then we started at the beginning of the New Testament with the story about Mary and Joseph and the star over Bethlehem. As soon as they heard the very mention of the name of the place where He would be born Wikipai and Daapoi realized what was beginning to happen. They listened to every detail with excited anticipation. Could this possibly be the birth of the Redeemer they had been waiting for?

Jennie faced her fair share of challenges in the whole process of translation. Sometimes I came back to our little jungle house to find her absolutely baffled at the concepts she had to figure out a way to explain. "How will I explain that they sacrificed a lamb when the Dao people have never even heard of or seen a lamb in the entire history of their people group?" or "How will I write this section that says 'they crossed the sea in a boat' when my Dao helpers have never even seen the sea and most of them live too far up in the mountains to have ever seen a boat? They don't even have a verb in their language for 'row' or 'swim'!" she said as she shook her head in frustration.

Another time when she couldn't figure out how to translate the word donkey because there was no such thing as a donkey in that part of the world, I held a picture of a donkey up in front of Wikipai and asked him to explain what he saw and what he would call this creature in his language. "It's fur looks like a dog but it's body looks like a pig and it has got the ears of a tree kangaroo. Yet it's tail looks like that of a cuscus. I am scared of that thing! Does it eat people?" he asked. I nearly fell over laughing but the fact of the matter was that he had never seen a donkey or anything similar to it. When I explained to him that these creatures would actually let you climb up on their backs and give you a ride around if they had been trained right, he really didn't know what to think!

Another day when we sat down and began to read through the stories for that day, I had just finished reading a new section that Jennie translated for us and then "Crack! Crack!" the whole house we were sitting in began to violently jolt back and forth. I could hear some of the rafters pop and snap like they were going to split. It was another earthquake! I quickly jumped up as the floor continued to move underneath us nearly making me lose my balance. "Should we go outside? The house could fall on us!" I began to yell to Daapoi and Wikipai.

They both just sat there and looked at me like I was crazy. The earthquake only lasted for about ten seconds and then subsided but I knew that there were almost always aftershocks as well. "Don't you want to go outside for a while in case there are more of them?" I asked. Daapoi looked at me with a grin on his face and started to laugh. "Oh Degapiyaa, after hearing about how powerful the Creator One is all this time I am not scared of a little earthquake! I believe that God wants us to hear His message and He will not let this house fall on us because we haven't yet heard the end of His story! Sit back down and let's keep reading!" he replied with a grin. I stood there speechless for a second and then sat back down and continued reading.

Later on that day as things were drawing to a close and the people were going into their houses for the night I could hear Wikipai and Daapoi laughing around the fire and see the smoke from their fires seeping up through the cracks of the leaves and bark on their roofs. I continued to think about their reaction to the earthquake earlier that day. I had flashbacks to those first foot surveys a few years back when we had seen those same men running around in circles in fear, trying to stomp on the ground to get the great "spirit snake" to leave them. What a stark contrast I had seen that morning between the way they viewed these things now and the way they had viewed them in the past.

It was simple faith in the Creator. They were already beginning to taste their first bits of spiritual freedom. They were already a tiny bit at a time being set free from fears that had held their tribe captive for centuries. It was faith that I had seen shaken into action. "Will they really understand the work of Jesus the Messiah when I tell them about His life, death, burial and resurrection and what it has accomplished? Will they really be able to fathom what Jesus has done for them?" I thought to myself as the sun slowly went down behind the dark green jungle mountains. "I suppose we will soon find out." I said to Jennie as we also went into our little jungle house and closed the door for the evening.

Chapter 12

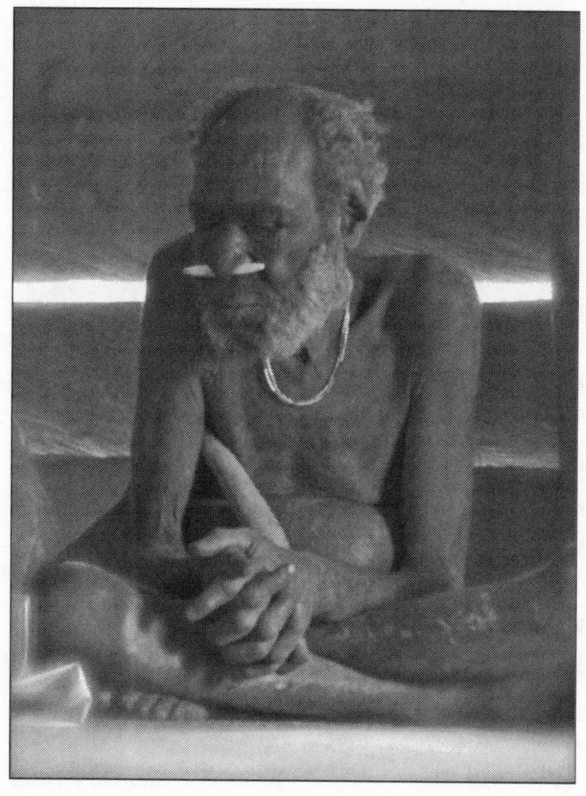

Dark Eyes and Dried Up Muscles

No man on earth, unless endued with the Holy Ghost, ever in his heart knows of or believes in or longs for eternal salvation even if he harps on it by tongue and pen.

Martin Luther,
The Bondage Of The Will

Obapwi sat staring at the fire, his back hunched over from old age, his thinning grey hair framed his old weathered face. In any modern country he would probably have already been retired to an old folk's home or be pushing around a walker. In Dao however, things like retirement homes and social security didn't exist. It was plain and simple: if a man doesn't work, he doesn't eat.

Obapwi was pretty impressive for his old age even despite the hunched back and balding head. He could still hike with the best of them, even if it was with the loudly popping and cracking knees of an old man. He still proudly carried his bow and arrows as if he were a great warrior from the past. Not too long ago he had made one of the hardest hikes in Dao territory to an area called Kupee Kuyee and had lived to tell about it. That specific stretch of mountains and much of the trails to get there were said to be lined with jagged limestone cliffs. One miss-step on that thin winding trail could cost you your life. There were only two men that I knew of in our area that had grey hair and were still alive and well. Obapwi was one of the two and the other was his good friend Totopwi, the one that had originally given us his permission to move into their lands and live among them and his word that they would help us learn their language.

"Degapiyaa, I am old. My eyes are dark with age and my muscles have dried up. I am no longer like the other younger men. It is for this reason that I fear that when the time comes for all of us to begin hearing the Creator's message and the big talk that you have promised to tell us, I will not be able to understand these words like the others. Is it possible that this talk is one that is meant for everyone? A talk that can even be understood by the old ones? Would even an old man like me be able to hear and understand?" he asked as he fidgeted with his string bag while looking back and forth between it and then at me again.

He was not the only one that had voiced these concerns to us over the past few months. Some of the women voiced their concern that this would be a talk only for the men. Some of the men even mentioned that they were concerned it would be a message too complex for the children. It seemed that the closer the time drew for everyone to gather and be taught and the nearer Wikipai, Daapoi and myself came to the completion of the lessons that would teach all the way from the Creation of all things up through the life of Jesus Christ, the more nervous the people got.

So many of them were so fearful that they were perhaps too backwoods or even too stupid to understand. When it was all said and done, they knew that they were the dregs of the island and possibly even of the world. They had begun hearing stories from other tribes about the fascinating things that existed in the outside world and beyond their borders. They had begun to understand that the rest of the world had left them far, far behind.

"Obapwi, the words of the Creator are not for any one type of person or gender of person. The words of the Creator's leaf book are not only for some tribes and not others or for only some clans and not other clans. This message is for men, women and children from the youngest to the oldest. It is not for only the strong men or those that still have strong muscles and clear eyes. Do not think that this message is not for you old friend, the Creator God loves you just as much as He loves me or anyone else. You are His creation just as much as I am. If you come and listen when the teaching begins you will not be disappointed. Trust me!" I replied.

⟷

"Today, you will finally hear his name" I announced as Wikipai and Daapoi sat across from me getting ready to hear the first newly translated section of scripture for the day.

Their silence was nearly unbearable and the suspense had been building for weeks. They had asked me time and time again in the past if I knew the name of the Redeemer Messiah that they had been waiting for.

They had heard through the Old Testament prophecies and they knew that Jennie and I had already read the end of the story. After Wikipai heard the first prophecy of the coming Messiah weeks before he had reasoned with me saying, "If you didn't already know the conclusion to the story, you wouldn't have known it was so important that it was worth bringing to us from such a far away land right?"

They had been waiting for this day for a long time and today was the day that they would hear about the New Testament account of His birth. They knew from the lesson the day before that Mary was a virgin and a miracle had occurred in order that she became pregnant. They knew that she had gone to Bethlehem to give birth just as the prophecies had foretold. They knew that today was the day. You could have heard a pin drop as I read the words to them that Jennie had finished translating just a few days before from the book of Matthew: "She gave birth to a son, and they called his name...*Yesusi*". I stopped and let them soak it in for a minute.

"Yesusi...Yesusi...Yesusi.." they repeated over and over again to each other with a reverent whisper as if the very speaking of His name was a demonstration of such a long awaited for hope, a demonstration of the Creator's power. When using the Dao alphabet and the sounds of the Dao language this is the way that His name was pronounced. In their language He could be called by no other name. He had entered the Dao language for the first time and his name was *Yesusi*.

We started into the life of Jesus from that day forward and in no time at all *Yesusi* was all that Daapoi and Wikipai could talk about. Even when we weren't working through these lessons together and preparing them for the others it seemed all they wanted to do was sit on our porch or around the fire for hours talking about this one Man.

When they heard how John the Baptist had called Him "The lamb of God that takes away the sin of the world" they rejoiced that even John the Baptist had confirmed this was the One they had been waiting for. When they would hear about how He could merely speak a word and the evil spirits would flee they would talk about how useless the rituals and incantations handed down from their ancestors were to chase away the evil spirits in comparison to the power of Jesus.

When they heard story after story about Jesus curing people's sicknesses by merely saying a word or laying his hands on them they would talk about how ineffective their traditional practices of slicing each other with bamboo knives were in comparison to the healing power of Jesus. When they heard about how He commanded the winds and the storms to be silent and even these things obeyed His command they thought back to the stories they had heard in Genesis and Exodus about the Creator Himself. They commented that the Creator was the only other One they had heard of having power over even natural phenomena and seas.

In no time at all they were saying again and again that surely Yesusi must be the Son of God because if He weren't He couldn't have done these things that only the Creator God had done in the past. When they heard His teachings and how Jesus said that he was "the trail (the way), the truth and the life" and that no one could come to the Father except by Him they were overjoyed at the thought that even Jesus Himself proclaimed that he was "the trail" to eternal life that they had been waiting for!

As Wikipai and Daapoi heard the teachings of Jesus day in and day out they themselves even began to change and others in the village began to notice it. It was a common practice to be very careful with things like the leaf cigarette butts of the end of used cigarettes in the Dao culture. They would store the cigarette butts in their net bags or burn them or even eat them so as to make sure they hadn't left anything behind on the trail that the evil spirits could get a hold of. They feared that the evil spirits would find and then use a dropped cigarette to cause them harm or work sorcery on them.

I was walking behind Daapoi on the trail in between my house and his one afternoon. As he finished up the rolled tobacco he had been smoking while we walked he accidentally dropped his cigarette butt in the bushes. He stopped for a second and began to frantically search for it and then all the sudden he stopped and started laughing.

"What is going on Daapoi? Are you all right? What are you laughing at?" I asked. "Oh nothing, I dropped my cigarette butt and was concerned for a second that the evil spirits might find it, but then I thought to myself 'Why am I afraid? Yesusi is more powerful than the evil spirits and I know about Him now! I don't need to fear those evil spirits!'" he said and then began casually walking on up the trail again.

When we had worked most of the way through writing down lessons based on all the key stories of the life of Jesus in the New Testament they couldn't stand it any longer! They wanted at least their wives to hear what they were hearing. "Degapiyaa, our wives and the others have got to hear these stories! They have got to hear about Yesusi like we are! Can we please bring them with us tomorrow? We go back to our villages every night and try to tell them what we have heard but we can't read directly from the Creator's leaf book like you can and we want them to understand well like we are! You have to let us bring them along! They have to hear about Yesusi!" they pleaded with me.

"Guys, we are almost to the end of the story! Only a couple more days and you will hear the end. Then we can work together to tell them the story well. They will be able to hear it all just like you have from start to finish. All the way from the Creation of all things to Adam and Eve and then through Noah, Abraham, Isaac, Moses, David, the Old Testament prophecies about Jesus and everything else that you have heard and then they will understand well just as you have! Just be patient, I want them to understand well also just like you okay? They need to hear the whole story, not just a small part of it!"

They nodded in agreement, excited that they would soon hear the end of the story and at the same time eager that soon their wives and friends would also have a chance to hear.

⟷

Finally the day had arrived when the first two people in the Dao people group would hear the conclusion to the story of what happened to Jesus at the end of His time on earth. We worked our way from His last supper with the disciples and His betrayal by Judas up through His arrest and trial.

Daapoi as well as Wikipai were absolutely appalled at what they heard. They couldn't believe that a man that had done nothing but good would be treated like this. They sat there with their jaws hanging open as they heard about His incredible torture by the soldiers and then His crucifixion. They were absolutely astounded at what Jesus went through. It was nearly unbearable for them to even listen to.

"Degapiyaa, the words that you are telling me make my heart hurt, this is a talk that would make us cry. Jesus could have easily fled from those men or even killed them all by merely speaking a word couldn't He have? But He didn't!" Daapoi responded with anger in his voice as he heard that the nails were driven into Jesus hands and feet and then he was lifted up on the "crossed wood". As they heard up through the death of Jesus they just couldn't understand why He wouldn't fight back but instead let those people kill Him. They had seen His power demonstrated time and time again. Why wasn't He demonstrating His power just one last time and defending Himself?

Then there was a key realization point in the story. They heard how the Bible says that the ground shook with earthquakes and the sky was covered over with darkness at the moment that Jesus died. This was a very significant thing in Dao culture. Even when the Dao people themselves would tell a story in their language they would often talk of a natural phenomena that had happened just before the climax of the story when the most important part was taking place.

For instance, if one of them was telling a hunting story or a tribal warfare story where something or someone was to be killed, just before the wild pig was shot or the enemy was killed there would be a marker in the story such as a strong wind blowing or dark rain clouds moving in overhead or an earthquake taking place. This was the Dao people's cultural way of telling the listeners that the story had hit its climax. They were cultural cues for the listeners. Likewise, when Wikipai and Daapoi heard that Jesus yelled up into the sky "Oh God, my God why have you forsaken me?" and then breathed His last breath, then the earth quaked and the vail in the temple ripped, and the skies covered over with darkness they realized what was happening. To them, this was the Creator's cue to them that His story had hit its climax, its main point!

They suddenly began to remember the prophecies they had heard for weeks before hand, how the Messiah would become as a sacrificial lamb for the sins of the world. They remembered that it had been prophesied that He would be betrayed and sold for thirty pieces of silver, that He would die between two sinners and that He would serve the same purpose as the lambs that had been sacrificed by Abel, and then again by Abraham and Isaac and once again in Egypt at

Passover by the Jews, then all throughout the Old Testament under the sacrificial system of the Jews at the temple.

These things were all pointing towards Yesusi, the Lamb of God! There was no mistaking it! They sat there completely amazed as we continued on talking that day through the burial of Jesus in the rich man's tomb as this too had been prophesied. Then they heard that He rose again from the dead three days later! "Only the Son of God could do something like that! Only Yesusi could come back from death! Is there anything at all that He is unable to do? I don't think so!" Wikipai nearly yelled as he laughed out loud and excitedly flailed his arms with expression.

We continued on reading that morning through how Jesus appeared again to His disciples and walked the earth another forty days to prove He had conquered sin and death itself. These two Dao men were soaking it all in with smiles on their faces as they heard that Yesusi had come out victorious and conquered even death itself! I began to question them to make sure that they understood what they were hearing. I had to make sure they understood why all of this had taken place. I asked them what they thought about what they had heard.

Daapoi was the first to respond. "I realize now why He didn't fight back! He took that pain for us, to become our sacrifice. If it were not for Yesusi, our wrongdoings would have never been cleared away. If Yesusi had not become the Lamb of God, sacrificed for us, we would have faced eternal punishment! I believe that this message is true, I believe that He died for me!" he replied. I could see the joy on his face as he was realizing for the first time that his past had been forgiven and that because of what Jesus Christ had done, he was now part of God's family and would spend eternity with Him some day.

At this point Wikipai chimed in "If the sacrifice of Yesusi would not have been enough, God would have never raised him from the dead. If Yesusi and His sacrifice had not been enough then the curtain in the temple would have never been ripped in half to signify that we can now come into God's presence even without the sacrificial lamb. I also believe that Yesusi and His death on the crossed wood was for my wrong-doings and that His sacrifice was sufficient!" He excitedly concluded.

I did not ask them to stop and "repeat a special 'sinners prayer' after me" or to make a commitment to from that point on give up smoking and alcohol, or to quit wearing the traditional dress of their people and start dressing a little more like me. There was no American "Christian" church ritual needed and there never would be. Simple faith had been expressed in the sacrifice of Jesus Christ on their behalf. It was completely obvious not only from the words that came out of their mouths but also because of the joy in their hearts and the hope that I could see in their eyes that they had experienced the saving grace of the Great Creator and His Son Yesusi. Nothing they could do would add to it or take away from it.

As we closed the conversation that day we ended by reading through the verses in Acts where Yesusi gave one last command to "Go into all the world and share the Creators message with all the others that have not yet heard". The section explained that after Jesus had said these words, He then ascended up into heaven.

Wikipai and Daaopi got even more excited when they heard this and kept on getting up and jumping up and down as if they were also ascending. They were trying to act out what they were hearing about Jesus ascending back into the heavens. The last verse that we covered was from Acts where the angels asked the disciples "Men of Galilee, why are you standing here looking into the sky? Yesusi, who you saw taken up into heaven will come back in the same way you saw Him go!"

At that moment Wikipai and Daapoi immediately began asking "When will He come back? Will He come back today? Tomorrow? Will he come back quickly?" to which I responded "Well according to the writings of Yesusi's disciples Peter and also John, He is patiently waiting for others to hear His message before He comes back again. He will come back when there has been people that have believed from every language and group of people and everybody that He has called to believe has heard His message and believed."

They immediately replied "Well then we have to tell the others! We have to tell our families! We have to tell the Kupee Kuyee clans and the Mokotaka clans! We have to tell the Taomi clans too so that Yesusi will come back! Anybody that hasn't heard, we have to tell them His message!" They were right.

⟷

There was only one type of great feast gathering that the Dao people regularly had in their culture. It was called a "*yoo*" and they usually held one about every one to two years. People from miles around would come together and there was always feasting, singing, dancing and any significant business that needed to be talked about as a tribe was discussed and settled. This was the Dao way of talking about big news and making communal decisions as a tribe. The people would talk about a *yoo* and spread the word about it anywhere from a couple months to a year in advance so that everyone was aware and had time to prepare for the event. They would count down the months together by watching the moon move back and forth across the ridge.

"Only two more moons till the *yoo* takes place…Only one more moon until the *yoo* begins!" we would hear from the men and women and children as they sat around the fire and excitedly talked about it day after day. Then when there was only a couple more weeks until the event, it was cultural for a representative to be sent out from the village hosting the *yoo,* to spread the word that the event was about to begin and that it was time to start gathering.

We had been telling the Dao people ever since our arrival a few years before that when we learned their language well enough, we would tell them the message of the Creator One's leaf book. We had been working together with Wikipai and Daapoi to put the message into their language for about five months. The word had already gotten out that the time was drawing close as everyone heard that Daapoi and Wikipai had already been working with us daily to put the words of the Creator's leaf book into their language.

We set the date for beginning to teach the Dao tribe as a whole at approximately one month from the day that Wikipai and Daapoi had heard the conclusion to the story of Jesus. Then we followed the Dao cultural model for announcing a *yoo* as we announced to the Dao tribe when the teaching would begin. If there was any one cultural way that would state to everyone in the tribe that the teaching of the Creators leaf book was a very important event, this would.

Daapoi and Wikipai took pieces of jungle vine and tied knots in them and made a plan to hike around the Dao territory handing one jungle vine out to each village. They would tell the individual villages to cut one knot off of the vine each day until they were all gone and then show up in our village on the day the last knot was cut. Then everyone would be gathered at the same time and on the following day the great story from the words of the Creator's leaf book would begin!

Wikipai and Daapoi would be the forerunners of Jesus' message for their people as John the Baptist had been the first forerunner of Jesus and His message for the Jews. Daapoi agreed to head one direction down valley the following morning and Wikipai would head the other direction up valley. They planned on spreading the word and gathering their people! It had all come down to this.

The Dao tribe, for the first time in its history had its first two believers. Wikipai and Daapoi had trusted in the finished work of Yesusi on the crossed wood and they would do everything in their power to try and bring their families, friends and relatives all throughout the Dao territory to trust in this same great Man. The man that they had fallen in love with from the first mention of His name. This Man that had finally, through His teachings and life, given them the message that their people had so long been waiting for, the message about the one and only true "trail to eternal life".

⟷

The wound was so deep that I could actually see his skull as I was cleaning away the blood, dirt and grime. Had it been any deeper Sigapiya very possibly could have died. The attack on his clan left him without a wife but at least he still had his own life.

The war party that had gathered together for the attack on Sigapiya's clan had come from a different valley multiple days hike away. They had come with the intent to kill Sigapiya and to steal a wife for a man from their own clan named Sedaomenaa. The attack was because of a past disagreement in between their two clans over some shell money. They beat Sigapiya so badly with their machetes and wooden clubs that he could not even open his eyes for a full three days because his head was so swollen. The war party's plan to steal Sigapiya's wife had succeeded but their plan to kill Sigapiya had failed.

Five days after the attack took place Sigapiya along with a few of his friends showed up on our porch seeking medical attention. The wound was festering and smelt so badly that I could barely clean it without thinking I was going to lose my breakfast. As Jennie and I cleaned the wound and scraped away the dirt and blood from his skull I asked God for His grace and wisdom as I knew that Sigapiya and his clan were not only seeking our medical attention but would also be seeking our blessing on their possible future counter attack on Sedaomenaa and his clan.

"We love all of the Dao people. We don't want to see any of you die! We are here in order to tell you what will happen after death and to help bring an end to your killing each other, not to support it!" I told Sigapiya. "Had you died from that machete wound it would have been very bad for you after you died. You have still not heard the Creator's talk and so you are not ready for death!" I continued.

"If Sedaomena and his clan come back to finish you off what will happen to you after they kill you? You have not yet heard the Creator's message and maybe this is the very reason why you didn't die during their first attack. It may very well have been that the Creator wants you to hear His message and so He watched over you so that you did not die! You are not yet prepared for death!" I said in conclusion.

We realized that day that even though Wikipai and Daapoi were doing everything they could at that very moment to gather their tribe to hear the message that would be able to change them forever, there was also another force at work here. Satan would not give up these precious people without a fight. He would do whatever he could to stop the Dao people from hearing this message. He would even try to kill them if he had to. He would also do everything he could to keep us from teaching it even if it meant stirring up old grudges in between clans. The Dao people were on the verge of once again breaking out into the tribal warfare and killings that we had so often seen in the past.

"Would the semi-nomadic Dao people really gather in one place to listen to literally months of stories? Would they come together despite old grudges in between clans? They had to continue to work their gardens and it was their very nature to constantly be on the move and walking the jungle trails. Besides that, their usual *yoo* only lasted a week or so and we would be asking them to stay and listen for months! Would they really see this as something important enough that some of them would hike from areas three to four days away to hear it?" Jennie and I wondered.

As the time for the teaching to begin drew closer and closer, and our village cut the knots from their jungle vine one at a time, even Jennie and I had our doubts that it was even possible for such a semi-nomadic group of hunters and gardeners in such a remote place to gather for such a long period of time.

Chapter 13

A Miracle in the Making

The gospel starts by teaching us that we, as creatures, are absolutely dependent on God, and that He, as Creator has an absolute claim on us. Only when we have learned this can we see what sin is, and only when we see what sin is can we understand the good news of salvation from sin. We must know what it means to call God Creator before we can grasp what it means to speak of Him as Redeemer.

J.I. Packer,
Evangelism and the Sovereignty of God

The air was thick with excitement. Word had spread for miles around that there was a *"yoo"* about to begin. This is the only cultural event of the Dao people in which all of the people that are within a reasonable distance gather together in one place at the same time. Clan after clan had piled into our village, each group announcing their arrival through chants and yells as they entered the clearing in between the small thatched and bark roof houses.

There would be singing and laughing and especially feasting, boy would there be feasting! Everything from grub worms, frogs and lizards to sweet potatoes, bird, tree kangaroo, cuscus and wild pig meat had been gathered. The odor was so strong that even in our own house, Jennie and I could smell the hair being burnt off the animal carcasses as they were roasted. We sat in the midst of all the people gathered around both young and old. Men in traditional gourds, women half clothed with grass skirts as usual, young mothers cradling infants and young men proudly grasping their bows and arrows. Old warriors were exchanging stories and news from their different areas and old friends were seeing each other for the first time in months.

Today would be the kick off to this much-anticipated event. Wikipai and Daapoi had done their job well! Word had spread all throughout the Dao valley and by the end of the evening it looked like everyone within a day's hike plus others from even as far as three day's hike away had gathered for the event. There were barely enough houses for everyone to have a place to sleep!

After that initial night of feasting the people gathered at sunrise the following morning and were all ready and waiting for the story to begin. Daapoi and Wikipai had excitedly gathered everyone in the village and couldn't wait to start. They could hardly contain themselves. After the last and oldest member of the village had finally hobbled in the door, they gave me the cue that I should begin.

I slowly stood, extremely nervous and praying hard under my breath that God would give me the right words so that they would understand. To signify that this was a great event I did something that I had seen other Dao men do before as they gathered for important talks. Just as the rest of the Dao men, I had brought along my bow and arrows and my string bag also to the gathering place. Jennie and I also wore our nicest traditional nose bones for the big day, as did many of the people that had gathered to listen.

Reaching over to my left I grabbed hold of my bow and arrows. I held the bow out in front of me and before saying a word, firmly held it in place with one hand while releasing the bowstring from the top of the bow with my other hand. This was a statement to the Dao people. This signified in the Dao culture that a talk was going to take place in the village that was so important that I would not even think of hunting or warfare or walking the trails on such a day. It was a talk so big that it was to take priority over all other events!

"The words from the Creator One's leaf book which you will begin hearing today are more important than any other words you will ever hear in your lifetime! This is a message so big that it is to be contemplated and discussed as it is spoken. It is a talk so important that even the bowstring from my bow has been removed to show this event's importance! There is no other thing you or I can do that is more important than listening to and carefully contemplating the words of these leaf pages and so do not be sidetracked by other things! Think hard about the words that you will hear, they are the most important words that will ever enter your ears!"

I continued "This will not be a talk that is quick and is soon over in just a day or two! It is one that starts with the very beginning of man himself and goes all the way up to our present time. It is a talk that requires patience. But if you stay and listen through the entire story of the Creator's leaf book, you will understand well! Why are there evil spirits?

Why do they seek to cause us harm? What is the true reason that we people of the earth die? What will happen to a Dao person's spirit after death? The answers to all these questions are in the leaf book of the Creator that sits before you. If you stay and continue to listen to the words of these leaf pages, you will hear and understand a talk bigger and more important than anything you have ever heard before!" I said to the crowd after I removed the string from my bow and then placed it along with my arrows to the side.

Daapoi stood and spoke out in agreement: "It is true! Wikipai and I have heard this talk from start to finish and this is a message that all Dao people need to hear. These are the words that we have been waiting for!" he spoke out while slightly raising his voice so that everyone could hear him. I had not anticipated that things would happen this way but from the very first day that I began reading through the stories of Genesis, Wikipai and Daapoi also took it upon themselves to help me explain the Creator's story to their people. In the grand scope of things, I was not the main teacher by any means. Since these two Dao men had heard the story from start to finish they knew every detail and it seemed that they couldn't have shut up about it even if they wanted to. When an exciting verse was read about God creating the trees of the Garden of Eden or the animals they would excitedly make comments about the verse before I could even get a chance to catch my breath after reading and comment on it myself.

"Can you believe it? If the Great Creator had not created light how would we see anything? We would walk in the cold darkness! If He had not created the ground where would we plant our gardens and what would we eat? If He hadn't created the trees how would we build houses or make arrows or make fire to warm ourselves? How would we survive? Only the Great Creator could merely speak a few words and cause these things to be!" they would chime in.

Every day after the teaching time they sat around the fires and went from house to house for hours, answering people's questions and trying to help the listeners understand. Jennie and her two translation helpers that had heard a good amount of the scriptures in the months before also did the same. They would remember key sections they had heard and talk with the other Dao men, women and children about how they related to the lesson Wikipai, Daapoi and I had taught earlier that day. Whether we wanted them to or not, these few key Dao people were helping us teach. In fact, most the time it seemed the other way around, like we were merely helping them as they told their own people about this message that they had been absolutely riveted by just a few months before.

⟵⟶

"Don't stop teaching! We want to hear more!" Every single day that we taught that first week this is what we heard. The Dao people themselves had decided that we needed to teach them at least five days a week for at least two to three hours a day. We would teach for one hour and they would want us to keep teaching for another hour.

"We want you to keep teaching us until our knees are sore because we have been sitting too long!" Obapwi, one of the oldest men in the room called out from the back of the crowd after my voice had grown hoarse from talking for hours. The Dao people couldn't get enough of the Creator's message. They were excited about the things that they had heard up to that point and even though we had only been teaching for one full week it seemed that their very hearts were screaming to them that the things they were hearing were true.

The majority of them expressed the same reaction that Daapoi and Wikipai had when they heard about the deception of Satan in the Garden of Eden. It was all making sense. They could look around and see evidence in their own surroundings, culture and experiences that this story was true. They could see that they also had been severely affected by the curse placed on their ancestors: the first humans, Adam and Eve. We could already see cracks forming and changes occurring in the animistic worldview of the Dao people even though theirs was a system of belief nearly thousands of years old! The Words of those pages were alive! The translated portions of scripture were communicating clearly and were speaking with power!

"I have never seen the 'child-like faith' that Jesus talks about displayed more vibrantly than I have in this very first week of teaching the Dao people." I told Jennie as we lay in bed one evening at the end of that first week. Little by little they were beginning to understand not only which part of their belief systems were inconsistent with the teachings of the Creator's book, but they were also learning that there is a good Creator God that is even greater than the evil spirits themselves. That this very Creator was unlike any spirit being they had ever heard of before. He was the most powerful of all, He loved them deeply, and that He was their only hope.

After three weeks of teaching, the listeners had been brought up through the story of creation and the fall of mankind. They had also heard Wikipai, Daapoi and myself teach through the story of Cain and Abel. After the story of Cain and Abel, we then taught on through the story of God's judgment on the world in the great flood and the life of Noah. For the first time, they were set free from their traditional fear of the rainbow and rejoiced at the thought that this beautiful, common occurrence in the Indonesian rainforest was a sign of goodwill and promise from their Creator, not a tool of the evil spirits to be feared.

We continued on teaching through some of the other key stories of the Old Testament as well and they began hearing the very first promises of a coming Redeemer that would come for the purpose of making us right before God despite the curse that had been placed upon mankind during the fall of Adam and Eve. They were little by little beginning to understand that this message would change everything!

As the old chief, Totopwi heard the first mention of the coming Redeemer and what purpose and promise He would fulfill he spoke out in agreement in the middle of one of the teaching sessions: "Only God could create the world and the things in it. We Dao people could never do such a thing! Only God could breathe the breath of life into man and then create woman as well for him. We people could never do such a thing could we! In the same way, only God can fix our bad hearts and erase the bad things we have done! We could never make our hearts right again! Only God could do something like this!" He had realized before even the first mention of Jesus what the Messiah and coming Redeemer would come to accomplish!

God was doing a great work in the hearts of the Dao people and Jennie and I couldn't believe that we were the ones that had the privilege of being there and seeing it first hand. He was working to gather His elect and a people for His name from this people group just as He promised in the book of Revelation and He was doing it right in front of our eyes. God was doing the work that we knew we ourselves could never do: He was drawing the Dao people to Himself! The dreams and prophecies that God had given the Dao people a generation before our arrival were beginning to come true!

The listeners continued to ask Wikipai, Daapoi and myself to teach five days a week and as they ran out of food they would spend the weekends returning to their closest gardens to gather more. Some of these gardens were as far as a full day's hike away and so some mothers and fathers were carrying their children barefoot up and down four thousand foot mountains to gather food for the following week so that they could continue to listen to us teach.

Many of them voiced that even though they must take these weekly trips to their gardens, they felt that this was a message that was well worth it and that they would continue to make sacrifices such as these so that they could hear what the Creator had to say to them. They were making personal sacrifices and literally hiking mountains barefoot with fifty pound bags of sweet potatoes, garden foods and whatever else they could kill to eat just so that they could keep hearing the words of the Creator's leaf book.

After over a month teaching it was daily becoming more and more evident that Satan was trying to do whatever he could to hold on to the Dao territory. If it were possible, Satan would keep these precious people in his grasp for all eternity! There were families from thirteen different hamlets, villages and clans that had been faithfully gathering every week for the teaching. The majority of the people were still very excited about what they were hearing and had voiced to us that they were willing do whatever it took to be able to hear the rest of the "Creator's Talk". Then on a Wednesday morning, as the people were all gathering to hear the days lesson, for the very first time since the teaching had begun there were a small group of three women that decided they no longer wanted to attend the teaching or hear the lessons anymore.

They got together early in the morning just as the sun was coming up and after gathering together their net bags and belongings they left. When the woman's husbands found out about it they were pretty upset. Some of the other listeners came to us at various times throughout the day voicing their concerns over the matter and asking for advice on how they should handle the situation.

We reminded them of some of the different Old Testament stories they had heard about how there were people groups where some had taken God's message seriously and others had left God's Word behind. We talked with them about how every person must decide for themselves what they want to do with the Creator's talk but we will all individually have to stand before the Creator Himself someday and give account for our actions.

One of the three husbands spoke out to us and the other Dao people about what he thought of the situation. "We have heard about Adam and Eve in the garden. We have heard about how the serpent first came to the woman and told her that the Creator's words were not true and that eating the fruit was more important than listening to what the Creator had said. She was deceived and as a result so was her husband! Her children also had to pay the consequences for her bad decisions, as do we as their descendants. Now just as Satan deceived Eve, he is trying to deceive us Dao people and our women. He is trying these same old tricks on us! We must not make the same bad decisions. The Dao women as well as us men must put the Creator's words first and listen to His message." he concluded.

As the day went on and those three women returned to their houses from their gardens many individual Dao people took it upon themselves to go to the women and share their thoughts on the matter. Many people individually went to these women and sincerely encouraged them to return to the teaching sessions for their own good. As a result, the three women once again decided to rejoin the teaching the next day and the other Dao people that had come to the teaching during the day that those three women missed caught them up on everything they had missed out on hearing. The Dao people were taking it upon themselves to look out for one another as a community and encourage each other to keep on faithfully coming to the teaching until all of them had heard all that their Creator had to say.

A few days later I once again contracted malaria. Those same old pounding headaches, cold sweats and constant vomiting fits were taking their toll on my body once again. The pain was incredible. "Oh God, how will I teach the people in this state?" I thought as I lay in bed in between vomiting. Since Jennie and I had both experienced malaria so many times we both recognized the symptoms much earlier on and were prepared with the best medicine available for the sickness. I started to take the medication early on in the day, only a couple hours after the symptoms began and we both prayed all day as I lay in bed that God would take it away quickly so that I could continue to teach the following day.

Many of the Dao people sat on our porch all day long checking on us and trying to offer their pity. "Oh Degapiyaa, if you do not recover, who will read from the Creator's book for us? None of our people can yet read as you can read?" they would call to me as I lay in my house. This wasn't really helping me to get any rest but I was thankful for their concern nonetheless.

The next morning I woke up without any headaches and the nausea was gone! My fever broke in the middle of the teaching time and the listeners watched the sweat pour down my face and onto my beard and notes as I read the Old Testament portions for them that day. I had never felt this well this fast during a bout of malaria. God was watching over me and demonstrating His power to the Dao people even through our sicknesses and suffering. The Dao people were seeing the worth of our message firsthand in the fact that we continued teaching them even in the midst of physical pain and sickness.

A couple days after that some people came up to our house and asked us if we had seen the war party coming through earlier that day. It was the end of the week and most of the listeners were off gathering food so they could come back for the following week of teaching. We had not seen the war party but apparently there was a group of men from a different valley and language dialect that had hiked through the jungle and along a stream about a hundred meters from our house once again looking for Sigapiya, the man that had been attacked and nearly killed when he took a machete blow to the head a couple months before.

They had previously stolen his wife and nearly taken his life as well but Sigapiya had been faithfully coming to the teaching sessions since we began teaching anyways. He was taking my words to heart that "God had spared him for a reason" and that he should come and listen to the Creator's message when we taught it. Apparently the original war party that attacked him the first time had gathered again and come back with even a few more men for a final attack and to finish the job. Luckily they didn't find him as he had traveled to a different hamlet for the weekend to gather food so that he could come back and continue to hear the lessons the following week.

When Sigapiya returned for the teaching the following day he heard the news that this group of men were looking for him with the intent of murdering him so he quickly gathered together his things and left immediately with two other men from his clan. He wanted to continue to hear the teaching but he knew that most likely doing so would cost him his life. He was forced to go hide out in the jungle until he knew the war party had departed again for the valley from which they had come. Only then would it again be safe for him to walk the trails and return to our village. He told the other Dao people he would return when it was safe for him to do so. It seemed that this was one more way that Satan was trying to put a stop to the teaching and it seemed that for now, in some small sense he had prevailed as far as Sigapiya's clan was concerned.

Just when we thought perhaps things couldn't get any worse and there couldn't be any more distractions then there already were, Satan seemed to begin attacking the families that were helping us teach. Wikipai's young son Simbo became very sick with a mystery illness that we couldn't figure out. He didn't eat for five days and his little body was hot to the touch. He grew weaker and weaker until he was drifting in and out of consciousness. He kept throwing up any medicine we would attempt to give him and so it wasn't doing him any good.

After one of the morning teaching times all the women and many of the men were gathered around the little boy crying. They told us that over the past few years there had been three other women that had all three lost children of the same size to what seemed like the same sickness. "He will for sure be dead within one to two days" they told Jennie and I.

"Perhaps the helicopter that is out in Wamena would be willing to come and get him so he can get medical attention in the city? But his parents don't know Indonesian so one of us would have to go with them to translate in between the parents and the Indonesian doctor." I said to Jennie. Jennie and I were the only two people in the world that were fluent in this little monolingual dialect as well as the Indonesian language so it was up to one of us to be a go in between if we were going to send him to a hospital.

"I will go with them and you and Daapoi keep on teaching. I don't want to be separate from you but it seems to be our only choice if Wikipai's son is going to live." Jennie replied after a few moments of deliberation. Luckily, we were able to get ahold of the pilots on the radio that morning and tell them of our dire situation. Jennie quickly gathered together a backpack with some clothes and basic essentials in it. A couple hours later we heard the old familiar "Thud! Thud! Thud!" of the helicopter as it noisily rumbled down through the Dao Valley from the southeast.

Jennie, with Simbo cradled in her arms and his mother Moipi and father Wikipai trailing closely behind jumped in the helicopter after it had touched down in the middle of the village. Moments later it smoothly lifted off again, then steeply turned back into the wind and headed up valley for the closest hospital. We didn't know how long it would take the child to recover or when Jennie along with the family would be able to return from the city.

It could have been days, weeks or even months. Perhaps little Simbo would not survive or return at all. But one thing this did specifically mean for the Dao people was that if I or Daapoi got sick or got another bout of malaria or whatever else then the teaching would not be able to continue. I was emotionally worn thin with Jennie gone. As far as continuing on with the teaching, it felt as if we were barely hanging on by a thread.

⟷

A few days later we finally received word via radio about what was going on with Simbo. After they made it to the hospital and the Indonesian doctors had run a number of tests on him they came to the conclusion that both Simbo and also his mother Moipi had very bad lung infections possibly mixed with some other tropical sicknesses. "Given the remoteness of your location and inability to give medicine intravenously the child almost indefinitely would have died because of the sickness. It is a good thing you came out!" the doctors told Jennie.

The child and mother were both started on medicine and within a week little Simbo was back to laughing again and babbling on and on in a dialect of the Dao language that only his mother could understand! He gained almost four pounds in one week after they started him on medicine and before long he was almost up to running around again like he used to. Then the helicopter flew Jennie and Simbo along with his mother and father back in to be happily reunited with the rest of the tribe after another week.

Wikipai, Moipi and Simbo had been the first of their tribe to go out to the city of Wamena where the hospital was located so needless to say they came back with loads and loads of stories to tell the others about all the crazy things they had seen. Everything they saw from pedal bikes, motorcycles, cars and dump trucks to the fried foods, huge stores, televisions, and mass amounts of people all in one place in that city had absolutely blown them away.

On the day of their return to our village, Wikipai told me that he and his wife had barely been able to even sleep at night the entire time they were in the city for all the strange noises, city lights and commotion that surrounded them. As they tried to explain to the other Dao people what they had seen and experienced, their language was barely even sufficient to describe all of the strange foods they had tasted and the interesting sights, everyday city events and vast amounts of people that they had seen.

By the time a couple weeks in the outside world had passed, they were nearly begging Jennie to convince the helicopter pilot to take them back home. They couldn't barely stand another day in that unfamiliar, weird concrete village eating those uncanny foods and sleeping in the cold, bright lighted, concrete houses of those peculiar city people instead of by the crackling fire in the dark, cozy little thatch roofed huts they were used to!

Daapoi and I had been able to continue teaching daily and had taught through the Old Testament sacrificial system of the Israelites and also all the Old Testament prophecies of the coming Redeemer while they were gone. Just as Wikipai and Daapoi had months earlier, the Dao listeners were hearing how King David, Isaiah, Daniel, Jeremiah, Zechariah and Micah all individually prophesied about the Redeemer that was supposed to come and take away the sins of the world. They heard about how their Creator had given a promise in His book that this coming Redeemer and Sin bearer would show us a way we could be made right with God despite our wrong doings.

Once again, before Daapoi or I had ever said the name of the promised Messiah even once, the listeners knew where He would be born, what family He would be the descendant of, which Israelite tribe He would be a part of, that He would be born from a virgin, that He would go to Egypt, that He would be without sin, that He would be betrayed by a friend for thirty pieces of silver and hated by the Jews, that He would be mocked, executed and beaten, that He would be pierced on His hands and feet and then killed, that not a single bone of His body would be broken during the crucifixion, that He would be buried in a rich mans tomb, and finally that He would be raised from the dead to prove he was who he said he was! Every single one of these things had been clearly prophesied before the promised Redeemer ever even set a foot on the earth!

Once again, it wasn't until after they had heard through every one of these Old Testament prophecies that we finally began to teach them the first stories from the New Testament. It seemed as if things were beginning to look up again! God had given Daapoi and I the ability to continue teaching, and now Wikipai and his family along with Jennie were back! We had now been teaching through the Old Testament for close to two months straight and the semi-nomadic Dao people were still continuing to excitedly attend the daily teachings and were longing to hear more. It truly was a miracle that the Dao people were still attending after all this time!

Within another week of teaching we were well into the life of Yesusi! Just as Wikipai and Daapoi had, the rest of the listeners were hearing for the very first time about this incredible man. They were daily getting more and more excited about what they were hearing as Yesusi proved He was the Son of the Creator One over and over again through both the fulfilling of the prophecies and also through the power He displayed over sicknesses, evil spirits and even death itself!

They heard through the stories of the gospels about how He even raised a man from the dead and they hooted and hollered with joy and laughter as they heard that Lazarus walked out of the tomb after Yesusi commanded: "Lazarus come forth!" It was no exaggeration at all to say that Yesusi was quickly becoming the hero of the Dao tribe. Every day all we would hear down at the houses were people talking about Yesusi and another one of the amazing things He had done in the lesson that day.

The lights were coming on for a lot of them. Just as Wikipai and Daapoi had in the past, they were beginning to ask a lot of questions and make a lot of interesting comments as they had already been taught thoroughly through the Old Testament about the function of a sacrificial lamb. Many of the listeners had now begun to put together that Yesusi, the promised Redeemer was meant to fulfill that same exact function since John the Baptist had called him "The lamb of God that takes away the sins of the world." They were once again holding on to every word and daily asking to hear more.

Also, little animistic beliefs that the Dao people had lived in fear of for thousands of years were continuing to be challenged. As Jennie was sitting in one of the huts around the cooking fire with the other women one afternoon, she noticed that in the course of their conversation, the Dao women were openly and freely using the names of people that had died in the past few years. Up until this point we had never heard this before as the Dao people traditionally believe that if you say the name of a deceased person it could stir up evil spirit activity. They would often blame bad weather or heavy rains or even sicknesses and death on this belief and accuse each other of saying the names of deceased people and in turn causing these bad events.

"Why are you now saying the names of deceased people freely and openly when you were scared to say them in the past?" Jennie asked the women. "Well, Degapiyaa has been teaching us for months now from the Creators leaf book and has been saying the names of deceased people such as Adam and Eve and Noah and Moses and the others over and over and over again. And look! Nothing has happened to him! So why should we be afraid?" one of the Dao women sitting by the fire replied. All the other women hooted and laughed in agreement.

A few more weeks of teaching through the events of the life of Christ and we had finally entered into what looked like it would be the very last few days of the life of Yesusi and the climax of the story of what the Creator had done for them. Nearly everybody within a day's hike that had been coming to the daily lessons for two and a half months was still attending! They were finally about to hear the conclusion to the story of the Creator's leaf book.

They would finally, for the very first time as an entire community hear about what Yesusi had accomplished on behalf of those that trust in Him. The battle wasn't over however. We hadn't seen it coming, but there was one final trial that had to be faced before the end of the story was taught. One last attempt by the enemy to thwart our plan to tell about the trail to eternal life that Yesusi had provided for them.

⟵⟶

It was Thursday morning. I got up early and began looking over my notes for the day's lesson as I sipped on a cup of coffee and tried to prepare myself mentally to teach. To Wikipai, Daapoi, Jennie and myself, these were some of the most important days in the history of the Dao people group. These next few days of teaching would sum up our entire reason for coming here. They were the days Jennie and I had waited for all this time and crossed land and sea and left behind friends and family in order to finally see take place. The days that the Dao people as a whole would have the very first opportunity to reject or accept as truth the finished work of Jesus Christ!

I flipped on the radio that was in our house to check in with some friends in the city and give them a report of what was going on in Dao. There was a core group of pilots and some other expat friends and their families that had been praying for the Dao listeners and us as well this entire time of teaching. They knew that the next few days were very important ones and they would also want to know whether or not Wikipai's son Simbo was continuing to recover well from the life threatening illness he had faced a few weeks before.

It was then that we received some news that we hadn't anticipated. My mom was facing the first signs of congestive heart failure and she would have to have an operation that very evening. They told me my Dad had contacted them with the news and that if there were complications, the operation had the possibility of being life threatening. I couldn't believe what I was hearing. My mom could die that very evening!

All kinds of questions began to race through our minds. I hadn't seen my family in years now. "Oh God why now? How are we supposed to handle this? Are we really going to have to choose in between attending a funeral or finishing the last week of the lessons so that the Dao people can finally hear the end of the story?" We had no idea what to do.

We went to the gathering place after we received the news and I shared with Wikipai and Daapoi what we had just heard about my mom. We prayed about it together and asked the Lord to give us wisdom in what we should do and then went ahead and taught the lesson for the day about the last few miracles that Jesus did before he went to Jerusalem for the Passover feast, the place where he would ultimately be betrayed and arrested. Once again the Dao people hung on to every word.

As we finished up the days teaching time and the day went on, I continued to think about my mom and the surgery she would face that evening. Then, out of nowhere a verse from the New Testament came to mind that I had often thought about throughout my life and wondered exactly what it meant. It was a verse from the book of Luke in chapter nine. Then once I thought about it, the verse would not leave me alone. It kept gnawing at me relentlessly. Those words were nearly all I could think about. "Let the dead bury the dead, but you go and preach the kingdom of God." was all that the verse said. That phrase just wouldn't leave the forefront of my mind. Was this what God was trying to tell me?

Jennie and I talked about it as we lay in our jungle house that evening while listening to the soft, tropical evening rains begin to fall on our roof. We knew deep down inside what we had to do. We couldn't have lived without regret with any other decision. Once again we knew we had to stay. We made the decision together that night that no matter what lie in our path, we would not give up. Even if it meant never seeing my mom or our parents or loved ones again on the face of this earth, this message was worth staying for.

No matter how the operation turned out for my mom, no matter whether there were complications or not, whether there was soon to be a funeral or not, we would not leave the Dao people until they had heard the end of the story. Nothing else would show the worth of our message more in our lives than this. We believed that this was the decision that God would have us make. He wouldn't let our consciences rest with anything less.

The next morning when it came time to teach, before we jumped into the daily lesson we shared with the Dao people about the situation my mom was in and our decision to stay and finish telling them the end of the Creator's story no matter what lay before us. We openly told them that we had made this decision simply because this message was the most important message that they would ever hear and that we believed it is a message that is well worth any hardship we may face in order to bring it to them. Then with tears in my eyes at the though of never seeing my mom again on this earth, I opened up my notes and continued to teach.

It wasn't two days after we shared about my mom with the Dao people that they themselves began facing what seemed to be the very first death in their community since the teaching had begun more than two and a half months earlier. Messengers had come to our hamlet from just over a day's hike away bearing the news that an important Dao woman with many family ties to the people attending the teaching seemed to be on her death bed.

The people that had gathered in our village to attend the teaching couldn't believe what they were hearing. They immediately responded by sending runners down to the dying woman to see what was going on, one of the two runners being the nephew of the dying woman. Late in the evening as we began to hear the wailing and death chants coming up from the various houses in our local village we knew that those distinctive chants could only mean one thing. They meant that the runners had returned and that the women had passed away.

As we heard the story from the local people the following morning, the two men appointed as runners had left our area around eight o'clock in the morning the day before and literally ran all the way to the dying woman's hamlet. All together they would end up covering what would take the usual Dao traveler at least two days of travel, in only approximately thirteen and a half hours. After they arrived at the woman's hamlet the two men stayed at the home of the woman just long enough to see that she had already died just a few hours before their arrival. After mourning her loss for a short while with the others that were gathered around her body they turned right back around to run another thirteen and a half hours to get back up to our hamlet before the next morning of teaching.

As it came time to teach the following morning, despite the fact that in Dao culture when someone dies there is usually a good two to three days of mourning where no one does anything except sit in their houses and mourn their loss, to our surprise every single person had gathered to hear that days lesson and there wasn't a single person missing. Some even came to the teaching session with tears in their eyes and trickling down their faces because of their loss but they still insisted that we continue with the teaching.

After teaching the lesson that day we along with all the local Dao people gathered around a clearing amongst the houses to hear what the people had decided concerning attending or not attending the funeral of the dead woman. Perhaps even after everything else we had been through to see the teaching finished and tell the end of the story of their Creator, this would be the straw that would break the camel's back. This could be the end of it all.

Totopwi was the first to speak after everyone had gathered around: "Was it not three days ago that Degapiyaa told us of his mother's sickness and possible death? Did they not tell us that this message was important enough that even if his own mother died they would not leave us? Are he and his wife not still here at this very moment sitting amongst us and keeping their word to finish telling us the Creator's talk even though his mother could have died as well? We need to stay! We need to put The Creator's talk first. If it is a big enough message for Degapiyaa to stay it will also become an important enough message for us to stay! Those people that have not come to hear the Creator's talk and live in the place where this woman died can be the ones to perform the funeral for that woman but as for us this should be a message worth staying for!"

The next day, again many of the men and women came to the teaching with tears running down their faces because of their loss. Nonetheless it seemed that the same thing that God had been teaching me, was what he was teaching them. "Let the dead bury the dead." I thought to myself as we started the lesson that day. Needless to say, I was still very concerned for my mother, but a few days later we received word she had made it through the surgery just fine.

God had used even her surgery back in America and the hardship and trials of being separated from our families to be a direct source of encouragement to a stone-age tribe in the darkest of jungles on the other side of the world. It had become a challenge and inspiration to the Dao listeners to continue to place His Word first. They were all gathered for the final day of teaching. They would finally hear the conclusion of the story. As a community, they would hear for the first time in the history of their tribe about the sacrifice of Yesusi on the crossed wood.

⟷

The air was thick with emotion as we explained to the listeners the betrayal of Jesus by one of his twelve closest friends. The silence in the room was nearly deafening as I told about the torture that Yesusi was put through at the hands of the Roman soldiers, the insults hurled at Him, the beatings and whipping of His body as He stood there and took it without saying a word, the crown of thorns that was pounded down onto His skull, the blood pouring down from His wounds, the public humiliation and mockery that He took from the crowd, then finally about the nails driven through His hands and feet and into the crossed wood.

They couldn't believe that this had all been done to such a good Man. The fact that He allowed it all to happen when He could have stopped it with a single word was even worse. This man that had given only healing and life to others, this man that had become a hero to them and a symbol of hope was being murdered before their very eyes. Then came the words that the listeners seemed to fear.

"It is finished!" they heard Yesusi yell out as He breathed His last breath and then hung there on that crossed wood limp and lifeless. The earth shook with earthquakes and the darkness moved in. The sky rumbled and the veil in the temple ripped. Then finally, all in a moment the lights began to come on for many of the listeners. Just as Wikipai and Daapoi had in the months before, so many of the other Dao listeners recognized the earthquakes, darkness and other unusual natural phenomena during the death of Christ as signs from their Creator that the climax of the story had been reached!

We continued on explaining through the burial of Yesusi in a rich man's tomb and how not a single one of His bones had been broken during His gruesome crucifixion. They recognized one Old Testament prophecy after another that He had fulfilled and started smiling and talking among themselves as they listened. As I continued to teach and read from the final lesson I began hearing the hum of excited chatter in the room as the Dao people began making comments to one another about what they were hearing.

When I told them of how the followers of Yesusi discovered the stone from the tomb rolled to the side and also discovered Him risen from the dead some of the Dao listeners seemed as if they could hardly contain themselves any longer! So I stopped and asked them to say what they were thinking. "What do you have to say about what you are hearing? Go ahead, speak it out!" I encouraged them.

"It's true! This is a true talk! Yesusi has cleared away our wrong doings!" shouted Totopwi. Then Wusimpaa,

Apiyaawogi, and Obapwi started to chime in: "I believe this is true as well! I also believe! Yesusi is the Son of God!" Another man spoke out: "Yesusi has done a very big thing for us! If His sacrifice on the crossed wood hadn't been sufficient then the veil in the temple wouldn't have torn in two and the Creator wouldn't have raised Him from the dead!"

A few seconds later Wadamenaa, one of the women added in: "This really is a big and true talk! Only Yesusi could do this!" People continued to excitedly add in from all over the crowd. They broke out into a spontaneous time of testimony, some of them standing up to share their personal belief in what Christ had done with the rest of the group, while others just listened and grinned from ear to ear while nodding in agreement. Almost the entire group of Dao people that had been coming to the teaching faithfully for these past few months was right in front of our eyes expressing faith in the sacrifice of Yesusi on the crossed wood. They were speaking out about what Jesus has done on their behalf.

Jennie and I spent the rest of the day among the people, sitting in their houses and around the fires questioning many of the men and women on what they had heard. We continued to rejoice together with them over their new found faith and just laughed with joy as we listened to them speak out to both us and each other of their love for Yesusi and what He had accomplished on their behalf. We couldn't help but smile as we watched God doing what Jesus said in Mark chapter ten was "humanly impossible" for we ourselves to do. He was creating saving faith in and transforming the hearts of this first group of Dao people.

Once again, we didn't stop at the end of the final lesson and asked anybody to "Pray a special sinners prayer" or "Repeat these special words after me". We didn't tell them that there were any special weekly rituals they needed to perform for God's approval or that from now on they would have to dress like foreigners and stop smoking their tobacco or drinking certain drinks.

There was no talk of leaving behind their traditional dress and nose bones or their bows and arrows. They knew as well as we did that the sacrifice of Jesus was completely sufficient. Jesus alone was enough. It was all about what He had accomplished for them on that crossed wood and no one could take this away from them! It was a miracle that God had done in the hearts of the Dao people right before our very eyes. It was a miracle that only the great Creator Himself could have done!

Chapter 14

Totopwi's Ladder

When God is the blazing sun at the center of your solar system, All the planets of your life come into proper orbit.

John Piper,
The Blazing Center

"I thought I would never live long enough to hear this talk. I thought that I was too old already and that I would die before you had ever learned our language well enough to speak to us this great message that I have heard over these past couple moons. I used to think 'Well, I will not get to hear the big talk, but at least my children and grandchildren will get to hear it and will know the trail to God's good place above the sky.' But now I have heard the Creator's message to us. I have heard of His Son Yesusi and what He has done for me and it is good! Jesus paid for our wrong doings on that crossed wood and I believe He did that for me." Totopwi said as he looked over at me with that classic toothless grin.

He was right, I wasn't sure he would live long enough to hear the message either but I was glad that he had. He had always been one of the sweetest and most cheerful old men I had ever known. He had done a lot to help us over the last few years and now, the prophetic dreams given to his people long before we ever arrived had come true, we were brothers! He had become part of God's family.

After that initial, nearly three month stretch of daily teaching took place all the Dao people dispersed back into their own areas carrying the message to whoever they came across. They were still hungry to hear more of the Creator's leaf book however and so they decided that we would continue coming together and meeting once a week to hear from His book. This was quite the challenge for a semi-nomadic people group that had no concept of a week though. Sometimes people would show up two days late for the weekly gathering thinking they had shown up on the right day. Other times they would show up a day or two early thinking they had come at exactly the right time.

In the Dao culture and language, there are no calendars or individual specific names for the days of the week so this became an ongoing problem for quite a while. Eventually, we once again began tying knots in small pieces of jungle vine for the people that just couldn't seem to show up on the right day. Cutting one knot off of a seven-knot vine each day and showing up when the knots were gone, they eventually began to catch on to the concept of a week and finally began showing up on the right day.

Jennie continued working together with the women translating in the book of Acts because we figured this would show the new group of believers how to function according to the model of the first church body in the New Testament. They heard how the early believers had praised God with songs together when they met and the Dao believers likewise wanted to do the same.

There were a few older men in the tribe however that felt the Dao language was not good enough to praise the great Creator. They felt as though we should teach them songs from our language and country or from the Indonesian language because perhaps these other languages were more important than theirs and would be more fitting to praise the Creator God with.

We openly disagreed with them on this point. We refused to teach them songs from our language and culture because we knew that if we did, they would never see their own language as good enough. We encouraged them to write and sing songs in their own language and in their own cultural way but for a good couple months they refused. For some reason they just couldn't bring themselves to see their language as good enough.

Finally, one week when we gathered to hear another section from the book of Acts we had a breakthrough. Once again I asked them if anyone had made a song with which to praise the Creator and to our surprise a young boy, probably not more than ten years old at the time named Yoni spoke out. "I have one Degapiyaa, the other boys and I made it together this last week." The other boys were too embarrassed to join him at first so Yoni started singing by himself in a very apprehensive, quiet voice:

"Yesusi, Yesusi, Ebeatamee Yoopaa Yesusi.
Yesusi, Yesusi, Ebeatamee Yoopaa Yesusi.
Magaa to kaa eseta Mée, Ebeatamee Yoopaa Yesusi.
Magaa to kaa eseta Mée, Ebeatamee Yoopaa Yesusi!"

He sang it out over and over again until the other boys and children had joined in and then eventually the whole gathering was singing it together with him. The words were simple: *"Jesus, Jesus, He is the One that is the Creators Son. Jesus, Jesus, He is the One that is the Creators Son. He is the One that came down to earth from up above, He is the Creators Son, He is Jesus. He is the One that came down to earth from up above, He is the Creators Son, He is Jesus."* It was the first song that was sung in the Dao language to the praise of their Creator and His Son Jesus and from that day forward there seemed to be new songs every week.

At the gathering after that two young men named Debaatomaa and Kogipiyaa sang a song they had written about the seven days of Creation. The song went through each individual day of Genesis 1 in detail and described what God created and then thanked Him for it. The week after that Daapoi and Wikipai made another new song about how the Creator's leaf book is only truth and that it is the biggest of talks in many different lands. The Dao people eventually began to understand that God is worthy of being praised in every language and that He loves their language and culture just as much as He does any other. He had created it after all, so it was His language just as much as it was theirs, wasn't it?

⟷

As we continued on through the book of Acts the new believers also saw that the early church had baptized people as a sign to the community that they were following Jesus now. The Dao people likewise wanted to follow this example. They had come to the conclusion that whatever the early church in the Creator's leaf book had done was what they also wanted to do.

Wikipai, Daapoi and myself together studied the symbolism of baptism and then the following week decided we would teach the lesson at the closest stream so that anybody that wanted to could have the opportunity to be baptized. There was a problem though. The mountain stream close by our village was extremely shallow. We would have to somehow figure out how to baptize people in only two feet of water.

Another concern Jennie and I had was concerning all the traditional beliefs that the Dao people had surrounding evil spirits and water. They had made clear to us in the past that they believed there was a specific powerful female evil spirit that lived in the rivers and would do them harm should they bathe or spend time near certain streams. This was one of the main reasons why they seldom bathed or washed their cuts and were usually caked with dirt and ash from the fires. This was an age-old belief and fear that had a grip on the Dao people for literally thousands of years before we ever arrived.

The following week as we all gathered Wikipai and Daapoi led the way and the entire group of believers walked down to the stream together hooting and whooping in a rhythmic song-like fashion to show that a big event was about to take place. Then when we all got down to the streamside all the men and women began working together lifting good size boulders and placing them in a line across the stream to make a dam. They finished the dam in about twenty minutes and while we were waiting for the little handmade pool to fill up with water we taught a lesson on baptism from the book of Acts.

As we finished the lesson that day, to our surprise and despite the age old fears they had of a female evil spirit living in the waters, the Dao believers stepped forward one at a time to be baptized in testimony of their faith in the sacrifice of Yesusi. Then another thing that we weren't expecting took place also on that memorable day. Three new people also stepped forward to be baptized who had just in the past couple months arrived in our village. We knew that they had not heard the original teaching time because they were from areas too far away to attend. They had recently moved to our area.

We questioned them in detail about what they understood concerning the Creator's message and the sacrifice of His Son Yesusi. "Perhaps they are just copying everybody else and don't really understand the significance of this event." Jennie and I though to ourselves. To our surprise however, upon questioning the three individuals we realized that they understood completely what Jesus had done, why He had done it and that He had done it for them! After asking more questions to the others gathered it came out that the Dao believers had been on their own, and in their own houses, every day teaching these three people through the message chronologically from start to finish since these three newcomers had arrived in our village a few months before. These three new believers were the first fruits of the Dao people beginning to teach their own people group! It was awesome to us how quickly the Dao people were beginning to reach out and take responsibility for sharing about Jesus with others in their tribe that hadn't yet heard!

The Dao people also saw in the book of Acts that the first group of believers had also regularly taken communion together in remembrance and honor of Jesus and what He had accomplished. So along that time we also had the first communion service in the Dao tribe. They wanted to share the "wine" and "bread" together in remembrance of what Jesus has done for them just like the early church. In these jungles however, it was nearly impossible to come up with things such as wine and bread. After thinking and talking about it, some of the men got together and decided that sweet potatoes and water would have to suffice seeing as how it is the remembrance of what Yesusi has done that is the key issue, not the actual wine and bread.

When it came time to all gather together that week and we celebrated communion for the first time, the people had brought sweet potatoes that they cooked over the fire in their huts earlier that morning. They also brought a small container of water, which was to be passed around as the "wine". Everything was prepared and the small group of Dao believers were understanding the purpose of communion well as a few other Dao men and myself began sharing the message that we had prepared a few days before.

Everything was going smoothly until it came time to pass out the sweet potato in remembrance of Jesus body. When we were preparing to pass out the potato it was brought to our attention that there were four visitors in the gathering that had not yet completely understood the point of Jesus sacrifice on the crossed wood nor had they placed their trust in what He had accomplished for them. This posed a serious problem for the Dao body of believers. They realized from the message that communion was a time set aside for only believers to take part in and they had heard the verses that said "If anyone partakes unworthily, they are drinking judgment upon themselves." The Dao people are so communal in their way of life and culture though that they share everything, especially food and tobacco.

In their culture, to purposely single out specific individuals and not share with them even though you are sharing with everyone else and there is plenty to go around is to purposely state to all those present: "This person is my enemy." It is an act that in their culture is regularly and purposely used to make a serious and offensive statement. Because of the underlying statement that it would make, it was something that the Dao believers felt very uncomfortable with and that went against their very cultural grid and everything inside of them.

When it came time to hand out the sweet potato there was an awkward silence for a short while. Then Wikipai, Daapooi and some of the other believers in the room began taking turns sharing with these four visitors that it was not because they were our enemies or because we didn't love them that we would not share the sweet potato and water with them as we passed it around. It was actually out of love and concern for them that we did not want them to partake.

We shared with them how they needed to trust in Yesusi and His sacrifice for them on the crossed wood so that they also would become right with their Creator and become part of His family. We told them that it is because we love them that we were telling them these things. Then after sharing this with them everyone in the service except for these four people went ahead and took communion together and then we sang some songs of praise together thanking our Creator for what He had done for us in providing a trail to eternal life through His son Yesusi.

One of those four guys in the weekly gathering that day was deeply affected by what he had seen and heard. Exactly one week after that first communion time he came up to our house to get some medicine for a sore tooth. Then as we were sitting there talking he began to share with us that after the communion time that previous week he had begun thinking about how he was not yet part of God's family and that this was not good. He told us that he had gone to talk to Wikipai and Daapoi about his concerns and they used the opportunity to go back through and once again re-explain to him his need for placing his trust in the sacrifice of Yesusi on the cross to clear away all of his wrongdoings. It was through that conversation with Wikipai and Daapoi that day that he for the first time personally realized his need of Jesus sacrifice.

"Now I am part of God's family! I have completely believed what Yesusi has done for me. Yesusi has thrown away my wrongdoings through his death!" he told Jennie and I as we sat on the porch together. We praised God together for what He had done because what started out as a very uncomfortable and culturally controversial situation for the Dao believers ended up as a tool to bring another person to understand and place their trust in the finished work of Jesus.

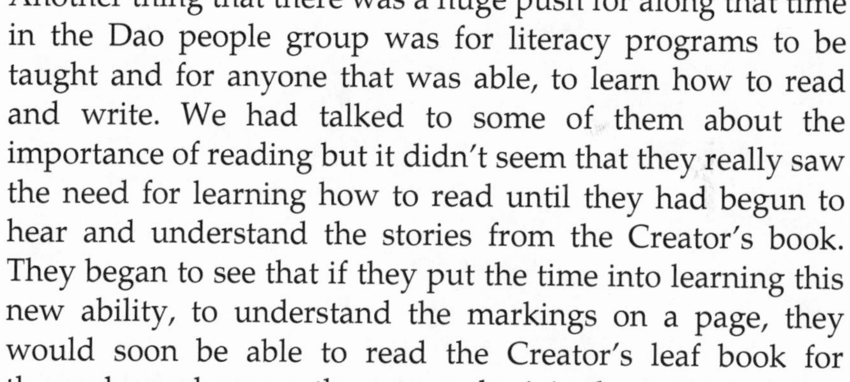

Another thing that there was a huge push for along that time in the Dao people group was for literacy programs to be taught and for anyone that was able, to learn how to read and write. We had talked to some of them about the importance of reading but it didn't seem that they really saw the need for learning how to read until they had begun to hear and understand the stories from the Creator's book. They began to see that if they put the time into learning this new ability, to understand the markings on a page, they would soon be able to read the Creator's leaf book for themselves whenever they wanted to! At the point that they understood that one simple truth, the literacy program began to absolutely take off!

We worked together with Wikipai to make simple schoolbooks to teach people how to read and write in the Dao language. Jennie and I made a series of small booklets that covered the entire Dao alphabet, which we had formed a couple years before that point. We then followed a system of teaching the people through the symbols that represented the sounds of the Dao language one at a time. This was our literacy program and only a few months later the first group of Dao people had completed the first class and we had our first group of good solid readers. The Dao people and especially the children and teenagers had turned out to be incredibly fast learners.

Although it was a significant challenge for the kids to gather everyday for classes, and we had to patiently teach even grown men and women how to perform simple tasks such as holding a pencil correctly, in a matter of only a few months many of the Dao people were reading their own language. They would take the little scripture portion booklets back to their houses and even up to different villages and read them by the fire in their huts for hours.

Now everybody in the village, both old and young, literate and illiterate had a way to hear stories from the Creator's leaf book in their own gardens and houses! These little books and scripture portions that Jennie had worked so hard to translate and I had labored to teach were now being regularly carried in the string bags of the Dao people for miles upon miles and read all over the Dao territory. The people loved reading the stories for themselves and for others that didn't yet have the ability to read for themselves or were too young or too old to read.

As more and more of them were learning to read God's Word for themselves and we had then gone through a second and then a third literacy class teaching new groups of Dao people to read something else very important also took place in the minds of the Dao people. They began to for the first time see a need to raise up their own indigenous teachers and send them out so that these literacy classes could be taught in new areas and villages as well. They started doing just that and before we knew it the literacy program had quadrupled and there were multiple teachers and literacy programs going on in two different dialects and three other different villages. Many of the people were prioritizing the literacy program simply because they wanted to read and understand the Creators leaf book for themselves.

Daapoi summed it up well when at one of the weekly gatherings he stated to all those gathered: "Just as our garden food provides nourishment for the stomach and makes us strong, the Creator's leaf book and His words within it are like the sweet potato for our souls by which our souls can become strong and we can live well."

⟷

Things were dramatically changing in the Dao valley. The people were struggling to sift through their old ways and expose those practices that went against the Creator's book and at the same time continue on with those cultural practices that didn't. Old beliefs were being weekly challenged as they learned more and more and heard the stories of the early church in the New Testament. Some of the believers were stepping forward and boldly calling out those old rituals that didn't line up with the things they were hearing in the Creators book.

One specific week there had been a lot of talk going on about evil spirits and how perhaps because of the recent death of a young man named Bonanimenaa, the evil spirits could be stirred up and seeking to cause harm to some of the people that had come into contact with him before his death. Their traditional Dao beliefs told them that there is no such thing as a "natural" death but rather every death is caused by the evil spirits, by witchcraft or by murder. In their minds, every evil spirits' ultimate goal was to cause them death whether it be through sickness or any other means possible.

Jennie and I knew it was not our place and neither was it true to tell the Dao people that these evil spirits don't exist. The Bible is clear that even Jesus and many of His followers had regular encounters with evil spirits of various types. The people had been weekly hearing of the many accounts in both the Gospels and the book of Acts where "by the power of Yesusi" evil spirits were cast out of people that had been tormented for years. They couldn't help but see Jesus as a man with ultimate authority and power unlike anything they had heard of in the past!

It was on a Monday that a man named Paina came up to our porch early in the morning. He wanted to tell us that he and his family were headed to one of his garden houses about half a day's hike away. The name of the small village was Emopo. "We're all afraid that there are spirits in the Emopo house because it was one of the last places that Bonanimenaa went before he died!" he told us. We reminded Paina of some of the many stories he had been hearing in the journeys of Paul and Barnabas over the past few weeks in the book of Acts. I shared with him that now that he had believed the Creator's message and was part of God's family, that he no longer needed to live in fear of such spirits but should rather place his trust in the power of Yesusi to protect him from the evil spirits that he feared.

"You can call out to Yesusi at the times you come into contact with these evil spirits just as Paul did during his journeys! He will hear you just as He heard Paul. You are part of His family now and He is greater than all and so you no longer need to live in fear!" I encouraged him.

"I believe what your telling me Degapiya but I am still fearful. Would you come with me to my garden house and together with me and my family pray against the evil spirits that I believe are waiting to torment us in that place?" he asked. After talking it over Jennie and I decided that this would be a great opportunity to perhaps model to the Dao people how to trust in Jesus and His authority as they faced such situations.

A few minutes later I had grabbed my backpack and headed down the trail along with Wikipai to go with Paina's family to their garden house. We headed over the first of a series of steep mountain ridges, slippery logs and small rivers that needed to be crossed in order to make it to the garden house where these spirits were said to be residing. I myself was even a bit nervous and uncomfortable with the situation as I also had never been involved in anything like this before. I was simply following the example of the New Testament believers we had been reading about in the weekly gatherings just as they were.

When we arrived at the garden house that afternoon there was already a good sized group of people from other hamlets gathered there, many of which had not yet had teaching in their villages or heard about their Creator for the first time. Many of them had travelled to Emopo specifically for the reason of performing what the Dao call *"paa mpaa see"* which could be translated as, "spirit chasing" or "an exorcism". Traditionally the most powerful men and women would come and perform various rituals in a situation like this and that is what these people from farther away areas had come to do.

They would speak special incantations handed down from their ancestors and place fetishes such as a certain type of ants nests or the strong smelling leaves of a certain tree in different places around the house in order to chase away the evil spirits. Before these rituals were to begin however Wikipai stood up and announced to all of those present that we had come with the intention of sharing with them what the Creator One's leaf book had to say about such situations.

It was about four o'clock in the evening when everyone sat down in front of the main thatched roof hut and next to the fires to hear what we had to say. Wikipai and I shared from the book of Mark, which Jennie had recently completed and we had printed in the Dao language for the new readers. We read from the Dao scriptures through three different stories from Mark chapters one, five and nine for all of those present.

We told about how Yesusi had commanded evil spirits to leave and the spirits had fled in fear because they recognized His authority as the Son of the Great Creator. We ended the talk by telling the believers present that now that they were part of the Creator's family, they were to trust in His power and authority, which is greater than all other earthly authorities to protect them against such things. Then Wikipai closed the talk by calling out to His Creator in prayer in the midst of everyone gathered.

"Creator One, You are greater than the greatest, You are bigger than the biggest! You are more powerful than the most powerful! And we know that there is nothing that You cannot do! Today we that have gathered here are afraid of the evil spirits and because we know that Yesusi has the power to cause these evil spirits to flee from this place, we are asking You to protect us and cause them to leave! Thank you Yesusi for watching over us. Please continue to watch over us because only You are the One that can do anything." Wikipai prayed out in the middle of all those gathered.

When he finished his prayer you could hear various people speaking out in agreement and gratitude to what had been shared. Then as the night went on we didn't see any more of those traditional spirit chasing rituals take place that we had seen take place in other situations in the past. The next morning there was still talk going on about how all those present had slept well and how they had not been bothered by any evil spirits although they had slept in the very house that was said to be full of evil spirits just the day before. It was an incredible time of testimony to the power of the Creators message and a time that God used to prove Himself to the Dao people.

A few months later, after we had finished teaching through the book of Acts, a good friend of ours named Wusimpaa seriously injured his leg one afternoon when he was out in his garden. As the result of an accidental blow to the knee with his machete, the main tendons and ligaments in his right leg had been severely severed. He could no longer walk.

For months Wusimpaa hobbled around our village, hopeless and pitiful looking, using a wooden staff to help him get around. He couldn't even go back and forth to his garden to get food and was desperate for help from anybody that could offer it. In his desperation Wusimpaa tried old rituals, calling out to spirits and many other traditional remedies to get his leg healed up but it just wasn't recovering. It wasn't long before atrophy kicked in. Nothing seemed to be enough.

Then one day another believer went down to Wusimpaa's house and sat with him for a little while. He placed his hands on the injury, the leg itself deformed from the atrophy. He prayed for God's healing and then he stood up and looked at Wusimpaa's leg saying: "I believe that the Creator will heal this leg and I look forward to seeing the leg again after He has!"

It was just a few days after that there was one afternoon I noticed Wusimpaa wasn't limping anymore. Neither was he using the wooden stick to help him get around that he had been using for many months. In fact, both of his legs looked nearly the same strength and size and no longer was there any sign of atrophy at all! "Friend, where is your walking stick? Do you no longer have any pain? What has happened to your leg to where you can walk well again?" I asked.

"Things haven't been the same since I was prayed for and we called on Yesusi to heal me a few days ago! From that moment on my leg began getting stronger and the swollen damaged parts started shrinking a little at a time. Now I can walk again and I believe that it is the Creator that has heard our prayers and caused this to happen!" He replied.

Not long after that incident with Wusimpaa, there was one afternoon our old, grey haired friend Obapwi went out to set traps in his garden with the hopes of catching a cuscus or wild pig. But then one of the traps in his garden went off while he was setting it. The very sharp edge of a stick came flying right up into his left eye! Within minutes the entire eye was nearly swelling out of his head and had turned blood red.

"Oh man, Obapwi already constantly talks about how he can't see well because of his old age. This is going to be bad for him!" I thought as I heard about it. A few days later he came to our house for medical attention. As Jennie and I looked at the swollen, blood red eye He told us that he hadn't even seen out of it for a couple days. He had pretty much gone blind in his left eye. All we had for eye injuries was a little bit of antibiotic ointment so we rubbed it in the damaged eye and prayed over him asking Jesus to heal him. Then over the next few days other believers including Daapoi, Wikipai and Kogipiyaa all took turns praying for him on a regular basis.

One day about a week later Obapwi excitedly came running up the jungle trail to our house as fast as an old man can run. "The Creator healed me! I can see again!" he told Jennie and I. We took another close look at his eye and almost couldn't believe what we were seeing. His eye had been completely restored! At the believers gathering the following week nobody could stop talking about it. Some even jokingly started calling Obapwi "Old Bartimeus" instead of Obapwi as they equated him with the story of Yesusi healing the blind man named Bartimeus in the New Testament. God was doing great things in the Dao valley and proving His power over and over again to the Dao people.

Jennie and I had never seen anything like it before even back in America. Even our faith was being strengthened because of what we saw God doing for the Dao people!

⟷

Another way that the Dao believers and what God was doing in their lives profoundly affected Jennie and I was through their reaction to Jesus' teachings on "loving your enemies". They saw the example of Jesus love for His enemies even to the point where he was hanging from a cross, scarcely recognizable as a human being because of the torture that he had faced, yet still saying out loud *"Father forgive these men that have done these things to me because they do not realize what they are doing!"* Many of the Dao believers could not help but to be deeply affected by what they saw and heard in these stories.

They were more convicted than ever before when they went on to hear of great men like Stephen in the book of Acts who followed the example of Yesusi and as he was being stoned to death, fell to his knees and said the same words as Jesus, pleading with God to forgive the very men that were killing him because they *"know not what they are doing"*. This message of extreme love only got all that more intense as we moved into the life of Paul in both the second half of Acts and Romans and they saw Paul being beaten and whipped by his enemies over and over again. Then Paul would turn around and tell the very people that had only minutes earlier had a part in beating him, of the love Yesusi had for them.

In the Apostle Paul they saw the attitude of a man that teaches not only with his words but also with his life things like *"Do not ever repay anyone evil for evil."* and *"Never avenge yourselves but let God do the avenging!"* They began to understand what it looked like to live out the verses that said *"If your enemies are hungry feed them."* and *"Do not be overcome by evil, but overcome evil with good!"* They admired such extreme love, which seemed to go against every system they had ever known or lived in their people group.

Then one weekend these teachings became that much more real and personal to the believers. A very important man from a far away branch of the Dao territory that had yet to be taught God's message for the first time got sick and died. The people from that clan blamed his death on one of the clans in our area that had been taught and become believers. Then they sent a war party to our area to avenge the death.

"It was in the middle of the night that they came. I knew that they were there because I could hear voices outside of my hut and I could hear them walking around on the other side of the piece of tree bark that I place in front of my door each night. Then they came right up to the bark door and began tapping and scratching on the bark trying to get me to come out. I knew that if I went out that they most likely would start shooting arrows at me and I would want to shoot back." A young believer named Uwokaatoma told Jennie and I.

Uwokaatoma continue on, "I knew from what we have learned from the Creator's leaf book that our Creator alone is the most powerful and that He could protect me if He wanted to and so I prayed out to Him 'Oh great Creator, please show me what to do! I do not want to fight with these enemies! Please protect my family and cause these enemies to go away so that we will not have to fight each other' and then I just waited.

They came a second time and began tapping and scratching on the door once again and trying to get me to come out and fight them but I just waited and kept praying. They came a third time and tried again to get me to come out and war with them. Then finally, they left. The next morning I made sure that they were not around before my family and I went outside and then when we finally did go out we found that they had dug up and stolen some of the food from our garden. But I just stood there and thanked the Creator because He had protected both me and my family and made a way so that I did not have to war with these enemies that had come down to our village in order to kill us."

Later on that Saturday afternoon another Dao believer named Debatomaa came and told us his thoughts on the situation: "It is because we now follow the teachings of Yesusi as Stephen and Paul and Peter did that we are not doing what we would have done in the past in this situation: We are not likewise hunting this war party down and trying to kill them first! In fact, even if they come and shoot me tonight, as I am laying on the ground and while the blood is pouring from my body I will look up and thank the Creator One because He has made a way for me to be with Him when I die. Then when my spirit leaves my body it will go up to His good place above the sky to be with Him. Because of what Yesusi has done for me, I have no fear of death."

That evening everyone in our area was still worried that another attack might occur so Jennie and I went down to the middle of the village and prayed together with the people gathered that God would watch over them. We prayed that God would calm any fears they may have and that if it were His will, that He would protect them and spare their lives in the midst of this hard situation. No attack happened that evening although everyone expected one. Then the next morning all of the believers gathered together like usual for our weekly teaching time. Uwokaatoma, in representation of all of the believers that had gathered to hear God's word again prayed for their enemies and pleaded with His Creator.

"Oh Creator One, please see our situation, change our enemies hearts, please take away their hatred and their desire to kill us. Please take away their wanting to shoot us with their arrows. We know now that they only do these things because they have not yet heard Your message and that in the past we were no different than them. *Forgive them because they don't know what they are doing.* Take the hate from their hearts as You have taken the hate from our hearts. Change them as You have changed us."

His prayer was so different from anything Jennie or I had ever seen or heard growing up in the church back in America. Even at the very moment Uwokaatoma was crying these words out our "Christian" country was sending more troops to Iraq and Afghanistan and to other Middle Eastern countries in retaliation for their attacks on us. Reports were coming in regularly on the news in our homeland of unreached women and children being killed in the crossfire. Where we were from, returning evil for evil had become the norm. It was called "heroic" to return evil for evil, not sin.

After the meeting was over that day, with tears in my eyes I approached Uwokaatoma. "Thank you friend because this morning you have shown me how to do the same as Yesusi. You showed me how to do the same as Stephen and Paul and Peter. You showed my wife and I how to pray for our enemies in the same way that Yesusi prayed for His!" I told him.

As Jennie and I walked away from the believers gathering that day, we thought about our own hearts and attitudes and the way we had talked of and treated the enemies of our people in the past. Whether those enemies were in America, across the village, in the Middle East, or anywhere else in the world for that matter, Jennie and I walked back to our little jungle house that day realizing that our attitude and the attitude of most of those from our own country had not been the attitude of Jesus. As we walked down the jungle trail, we asked God to change us and thanked Him that even though some might call us "missionaries" to the Dao people, God was actually now using the Dao people to reach and change us.

⟷

One of the first big events that the Dao people wanted to celebrate after they heard the Creator's talk that first time was Christmas. Up until that time, they had heard how other tribes had great celebrations once a year, but they didn't know what those celebrations were about or why the people were celebrating. But after they had heard what their Creator had done for them through sending His Son Yesusi they began to understand what it was all about. They decided that they also wanted to celebrate with a great feast for this event.

They called it in their language the *"Yesusi onee daata naagoo"* which translated means "The day that Jesus' cord was cut." They started out planning for the event months in advance. They began passing the news all throughout the valley and to different villages as to where and when they would have this great celebration. They also began hunting for cuscus, tree kangaroo, wild pig, cassowary and birds. They gathered foods and started to store the various foods and supplies in our village for the big event.

When the day had finally come to celebrate, they came hooting and hollering in their cultural way. Then when a good amount of them had gathered, the men began working together to create a special structure for the feast in which they would cook all the food and celebrate. The women worked gathering wood to cook with. The children ran around picking flowers and decorating the place where we gathered weekly to hear from the Creator's leaf book and where they had initially heard about Yesusi for the first time.

Finally, when all had been completed, they gathered on Christmas Eve to once again hear the story of the birth, death, burial, and resurrection of Yesusi so that they could be reminded of the special reason for this celebration day. After we had once again read through the story the Dao people present began to create and sing songs about Yesusi one after the other for hours. All night long, all the way up until the next morning when the sun came up they praised their Creator and His son Yesusi in song. This was their cultural way of showing appreciation to Yesusi for what He had done for them.

The following morning they began cooking as soon as the sun was up. Then when everything had been cooked and a number of very expensive pigs had all been shot and cooked as well, Wikipai stood and prayed. He once again thanked the Creator for sending His Son Yesusi and thanked Yesusi for dying on the crossed wood in their place. Though there were no presents, lights, Christmas trees or little figurines of Santa Clause around, it was a very special day because it was the very first time in the history of the Dao people group that they had ever celebrated the birth of Jesus on Christmas. Jennie and I sat by the fires and listened to the people talking after the Christmas celebration was over and all the feasting was winding down to a close.

"If the day the cord of Yesusi was cut had never taken place, how different things would be for us Dao people today! We would even now be living as if we didn't have any eyes. In fact we would be as a person without any head at all because we would be as those who couldn't see, couldn't hear about, believe, or even follow the good trail that Yesusi brought us, the trail that leads to eternal life!" we heard one young believer speak out to all the others.

Since the time that we first moved into the Dao Territory we had seen many different sides of death, the causes being everything from homicide and malaria to malnutrition and old age. In fact, not long after that first Christmas we had seen Omaniwo, an older woman and another close friend of Jennie die from what we could only guess was throat cancer. We did everything we could to help her but in the end we watched her slowly waste away as she literally starved to death because she could no longer swallow food.

A few weeks after that we once again found ourselves along with the rest of the Dao people grieving the potential loss of another close friend. Our local chief, Totopwi was said to be dying. When we had first stepped foot in the Dao valley a few years back after riding the muddy lowland rivers and hiking into the foothills of their territory, Totopwi had been one of the first to actually welcome us with his huge toothless smile and invite us to stay in their lands.

From day one he had been supportive of our coming and the telling of the Creator's talk. He had sent his sons and daughters to help us learn their language and then when the day finally came that we were to begin teaching them in their own language he had made sure that his entire clan was there and listening. He made sure that they stayed until the very last day of the nearly three month long daily teaching time all the way from Creation to the completion of the story.

It was on a Sunday afternoon that two of Totopwi's daughters came to our house at first light, bearing the news that Totopwi was very weak and that he believed that he was going to die. "He wants you to come and read the Creator's leaf book with him one last time before his spirit departs from his body and he goes up to the good place above the sky to be with the Creator One!" they told us.

We immediately grabbed our backpacks and a few supplies as quickly as we could and began heading down the jungle trail and along the mountainside to Totopwi's hamlet. He was a very special friend to us and it was hard to think of the Dao valley without him. Half a day's hike later as we were just arriving at his village we could hear the traditional death chants and cries coming up from the houses. We went directly into the small smoke-filled, men's hut where Totopwi was laying on his leaf mat.

All his friends and family were gathered around. When he saw that we had arrived, in a soft voice he looked over at some of his sons and asked them to help him sit up. He was too weak to sit up by himself. As his sons held him up, Totopwi then looked over at us and began telling us that he had sent for us because he had seen a dream the night before. It was a dream which he believed was an omen from the Creator One. An omen that in Totopwi's words, he "would soon be departing for the place above the sky and that Yesusi was the only way to get there."

We asked him to describe what he had seen in the dream. In a very soft and fragile voice he began, "I saw in my dream the same ladder that Jacob saw in the story that we heard during the Creator's talk. This time however, it was not Jacob at the bottom of the ladder, It was me. I began climbing up the ladder in between the angels. I climbed from Dao land up into the good place above the sky. Yesusi was waiting for me at the top of the ladder, I was going up the ladder to meet Yesusi and go into the Creator's good place."

As Totopwi finished describing his dream he then looked around at his sons and family and at the others sitting around the room. In a weak voice he began: "The Creator's talk is big and there is nothing bigger. I will soon die and my spirit will not carry with it any of my belongings. I will leave all of my shell money behind. I will leave my pigs and my gardens and my houses and my wives also behind. Nothing will go with me, not even my body. My spirit will go up alone. All of those things I once thought so important will no longer even belong to me and so I say to you hold onto the words of the Creator's leaf book and never let them go! Do not run after those other things that you also will leave behind when you die someday. Instead run after and hold onto the Creator's talk because your spirit is the only thing that will go up to heaven in the end."

After he said these things, I opened up my little tattered Bible that had been with me all over these trails and also a copy of the Gospel of Mark in the Dao language. I shared with all those in the room from chapter sixteen about the promise of eternal life that Yesusi has given to all of us that trust in what He has done on our behalf to clear away our wrong doings. Then we prayed together for Totopwi that God's will would be done and we thanked our Creator for the hope that He has given all those who believe, through the work of His son Yesusi. Then we cried together there as we sat around Totopwi and said our goodbyes.

I reached out and snapped knuckles with Totopwi one last time and as he smiled up at me from his leaf mat with that kind, toothless smile. With the tears streaming down my face I said to him: "Friend, I do not know whether I will see you again on this earth or not but if I do not see you again on the earth, I will see you when we are both together with the Creator One in His good place above the sky."

During the following night Totopwi's spirit left his body and went up to be with his Creator just as he had foretold. His dream had been prophetic just as he told us and the others the day before his death. Both believers and unbelievers all over the Dao territory heard the story of Totopwi's dream and his last words. People from miles around hiked to his village and gathered to mourn his death and it was an incredible time of testimony for the entire tribe. The dream that Totopwi had so boldly talked about was a clear message to him, his family and the entire tribe that there is only one ladder, one trail, and one way to eternal life: the Great Creator's only Son Yesusi.

Chapter 15

Death Threats and True Life

The occasion that best stimulates us to call on God is when distressed by our own need, we are troubled by the greatest unrest and are almost driven out of our senses until faith opportunely comes to our relief. For among such tribulations God's goodness so shines upon us that even when we groan with weariness under the weight of our present ills, and are also troubled and tormented by the fear of greater ones, yet relying upon His goodness, we are relieved of the difficulty of bearing them.

John Calvin,
Institutes of The Christian Religion

I believe in Christianity as I believe the sun has risen, not only because I see it, but because by it I see everything else.

C.S. Lewis,
The Weight of Glory

It was still the same beautiful, intriguing, yet hard to get along with remote jungle. The same incredibly steep mountains and muddy trails. The same leeches, mosquitos, malaria and jungle sicknesses, but everything had changed. The people used to sit on our porches for hours talking about only string bags, pigs and shell money. Now there was a core group of people for whom a new thing seemed to dominate the majority of their conversation.

Sure, they still talked about all the same things of the Dao culture that others were talking about, but all these other everyday things were merely second priority to the greatest thing. They knew the reason all these other things existed. They knew that all these things were because of their Creator and they knew that none of these things held a candle in comparison to their greatest treasure, Yesusi!

There was a group of strong believers now in the Dao territory that had been dramatically and forever changed and this made us all the happier to be there. We finally had true, deep fellowship with many of the Dao people that we had never had before. The prophecies of their ancestors had really come true: "Though our skin was pale and we came from a far away land, after they heard our message, we had become like brothers and sisters with one another. We were like family."

Not to mention the fact that we had in many ways adapted to life in the jungle. Now, when we found a snake in the house as we still regularly would, we knew how to handle it. I would grab my bow and arrows and pin the snake to the wall or the rafter and then Jennie would grab her machete and chop its head off! We were a good team and things like snakes and leeches didn't seem as big a deal anymore. God had helped us overcome even our fear of the simple things like snakes, spiders, centipedes and tarantulas over the years. We finally felt like we had a family here in Indonesia. When we were in these jungles together with the Dao people, we felt like we were "home".

We moved on from translating and studying together the book of Acts and the Gospels at our weekly gatherings to studying in the book of Romans. Romans had a lot of deep truths in it that once again the Dao people would discuss for hours as they walked the jungle trails to and from their gardens or as they sat around the fires in their houses.

As Wikipai, Daapoi and myself continued to together teach the others on a weekly basis we also invited a few other men that had learned how to read and write to begin working with us developing new lessons and helping us teach. We regularly sat around together discussing the following weeks section of scripture that was going to be shared at the weekly gathering. We spent a lot of time searching for cultural illustrations of the passage to be taught as it seemed cultural illustrations always helped the Dao listeners better understand the deep truths of books like Romans, which were at times harder to understand.

One of the illustrations we together came up with was that of comparing dirty, crooked twigs to our sinful condition as humans. In the middle of one of the lessons Wikipai pulled a large piece of straight, hollow, clean bamboo from his string bag and then held it up in front of the listeners while saying "Look at this piece of bamboo. It is perfectly straight. It is not even a little bit crooked. It is new and clean. It can be used to represent Yesusi because He is completely sinless. He is the Son of the Creator and He is the only One that is perfect, clean and has a straight heart in His Father's sight."

Wikipai then gathered a handful of dirty, crooked twigs from the ground and placed them inside the clean straight hollow piece of bamboo. "This is what Yesusi accomplished for us when we trusted in what He has done for us on the crossed wood. Though we were dirty, crooked and sinful in the Creator's sight, because we are in Yesusi we now are seen by Him as straight and new. We are clean in the

Creator's sight because of what Yesusi has done for us." Wikipai concluded.

The listeners always laughed with joy when we shared illustrations like this. God was speaking through the things of their surroundings and culture and they loved it! Many of them were growing in their understanding of Jesus. There were a few however that weren't continuing to grow in their faith. The same as anywhere else the message of Jesus is shared in the world, there were those that grew cynical over time and began to lose interest in coming to the weekly gatherings as other things competed for their attention.

It was exactly like the parable of the sower that Jesus had shared in the Gospels and specifically in Mark chapter four. There were different hearts that were like different types of soil. Many of the people had hearts like the good soil that after it had received the good news grew well and *"produced much fruit"*. But some of them had hearts like the rocky soil and the thorny soil Jesus had described. The soil that even though it had at first received the message with joy, the seed had seemed to be *"choked out by the cares of this world."*

One week after the Dao teachers and myself taught the weekly lesson together Daapoi came to me and mentioned, "There are a few women down in my home village of Kegatabo that have been either too sick or too old to make the half a day's hike up the mountain. For this reason they have not been able to join in and hear the words of the Creator together with us at the weekly gatherings. Would it be okay if I taught a second time every week down in Kegatabo from our notes?" he asked.

"That's a great idea! We need to take care of them and make sure that they also have spiritual food! I will start making extra copies of our notes so you can take them with you" I told him and the next week he began taking the notes and also teaching weekly at his village down in Kegatabo. Those women really appreciated it and seemed to be just soaking it up but not everyone down in that village was happy about what Daapoi was doing.

"How can you sit there and tell me that you know for sure these things will happen in the future! How can you sit here in Kegatabo and speak so confidently about what will happen to our spirits! I am sick of hearing about it! All you do is talk about the things you have been reading about in your books and I don't want to hear these things anymore!" shouted Magabeotoma with his fists clenched.

"These are not my words older brother, they are the Creator's words. That is how I know these things will happen! And I will never stop talking about the Creator and His message here in Kegatabo or anywhere else!" replied Daapoi.

Magabeotoma had hit his bursting point, he couldn't believe what he was hearing! He grabbed the closest good-sized piece of wood that he could find and started towards his younger brother Daapoi with his arm raised, ready to strike a blow that he expected would settle the issue for good.

"Go ahead and hit me! It would be no worse than what happened to Stephen in the book of Acts when he was stoned for preaching the Creator's words! It would be no worse than what happened to Paul and Peter and the other ones that spoke the Creator's words and were beaten for it!" Daapoi yelled out as Magabeotoma angrily walked towards him, club in his hand and threats coming from his mouth.

It was when Magabeotoma heard those words that he decided there could only be one solution to this problem. He dropped the club and went for his bow and arrows. Within seconds he had an arrow pulled back in his bow, pointed directly at Daapoi and angrily yelled "I will not just strike you younger brother! I will kill you! Do not ever speak of these things here in Kegatabo again!"

With his older brother Magabeotoma's bow drawn and the sharp bamboo tipped arrow pointed directly at his chest from only a few feet away Daapoi gave one final reply: "I cannot and will not stop preaching the Creator's words. I do not fear death and what you are doing right now to me is no different from what happened in between Abel and his older brother Cain. You are my older brother and you like Cain have chosen not to follow the Creator. I am like Abel and I have chosen to follow and believe the Creator's words and so you want to kill me. So go ahead and shoot! In the future, when you and I are both dead and gone and are standing before the Creator One, you will see then that His words are true!"

"I thought those moments were my last" Daapoi said to Jennie and I the following day as he and his wife Otopina sat on our porch visibly shaken from what had occurred. "I would have been shot in the chest right then and there if it wasn't for a man from another village called Taomi that ran in from the side and grabbed the arms of my older brother so that he couldn't release the arrow."

Jennie and I just sat there astounded at what we were hearing as we listened to them tell us those things had taken place. We knew that many people had been murdered here in the past. It was no exaggeration to say that Daapoi was moments away from being the first Dao martyr. I don't know that we really expected to hear however that something like this had taken place in the Dao Valley on account of someone sharing about Jesus.

It did remind us however that the enemy was not happy with what was going on in the Dao people group and he had not yet given up. He would do anything that he could to stop the gospel from moving forward to new villages in this dark, unreached corner of the world. What had long seemingly been the evil spirit's territory was now being taken back for the true King and Satan didn't like it one bit.

⟷

A couple weeks later Wikipai and Daapoi were talking about how they needed to do a first major outreach to carry the Creator's message to a group of neighboring clans that lived nearly two days hike away. The area was called Taomi and at that time, it was the only lowlands village in Dao territory. The village of Taomi had a significantly larger amount of exposure to malaria and the other harsh tropical diseases that are more prominent in the hotter lowlands. Wikipai and Daapoi knew this. They wouldn't let it deter them however from making plans to carry the "big talk" about the Creator and His Son Yesusi down to this village. They knew that the people there needed the message of Jesus just as much as they had needed it. They needed to know of what their Creator had done for them.

Daapoi's wife had to be close to nine months pregnant. She looked like she was about to pop as her pregnant belly swelled out in front of her. This being the case Wikipai said that he would go down first with his wife Moipi and their two young children and begin teaching the people there the first lessons. Daapoi agreed with the plan that after his wife had given birth they also would travel down and join Wikipai and his family in the outreach.

The following week Wikipai along with his family were excitedly preparing for their journey down to the lowlands to teach the people in Taomi about their Creator for the first time. During the last weekly gathering before he left for Taomi we all gathered around him with the other believers and prayed together for him and his family and those that they would be teaching. Then we sent Wikipai along with his wife and children out as the first Dao missionaries to the Taomi people.

"I know that my kids could get sick and die or my family might not have enough food and I am not looking forward to living in a village that is so far from my own home but God's message is a big message. I know that the Taomi people need to hear as well and so I will go. God's message is worth it!" Moipi told Jennie and I after we had prayed for them that afternoon. We couldn't believe how far the Dao people had come. Just a few years before they had never even heard the name of their Creator or His son Yesusi for the first time. Now they had heard and taken to heart the things they learned from the Creators leaf book, had learned how to read and write, and were going out as message carriers to reach a new branch of their own people!

A few weeks later a group of believers led by Daapoi went down to Taomi to check on the outreach and encourage Wikipai, and his family. They took with them some supplies as well so that they could support Wikipai and his family as they had learned that the New Testament church supported Paul in his evangelistic journey's as well. When Daapoi and the others returned we were finally able to hear the first news on how things were going!

Wikipai wrote in a letter to us that he sent up with Daapoi: "There are so many students attending the literacy classes and meetings that there are two people to every one literacy book. The students are hungry for what we are teaching and are learning quickly and so we are having classes in both the morning and afternoon as well, and there are both young and older ones coming to the classes wanting to learn how to read and write!" This was the first step in seeing the Taomi people able to someday read the words of the Creators book for themselves. It was exactly the type of news we were hoping and praying for! Along with this good news however we also received some fairly concerning news from the ones that carried the letter up to us.

According to Daapoi, after they spent a few days down at the outreach area with Wikipai and his family, on the night before they left to come back up to our village both Wikipai and one of their two young children, Simbo had gotten very sick. This was one of the things that Wikipai and

Moipi had talked openly about their fears of before they left to do the outreach. They knew before they ever left that Taomi would be more of a lowlands area. They knew that village would have much higher daily temperatures and a lot more malaria and tropical diseases than where they usually live up in the mountains. They chose to go anyways. Wikipai had told us with his own mouth: "The message we carry will be worth the hardships."

Kogipiyaa told us that if we wanted him to, he was up for making the hike back down to Taomi and so we sent down medicines, supplies and also some letters of encouragement to Wikipai and his family telling them we were praying for them. As we continued praying about the situation though over the next few days, and we thought about the fact that Wikipai's family had been going strong on their own in Taomi for close to a month now, we felt that we needed to do more to encourage them in their outreach than just send letters and supplies.

Wikipai and Moipi were very close friends of ours. Their children had become like our own. I thought about the many times that Jennie or I had held little Simbo in our arms and played games with him as he babbled on and on in that sweet little Dao voice. We couldn't stop talking about them and neither of us slept well at night because we kept on waking up thinking about them. We decided that we would go ahead and hike down to Taomi ourselves and try to be a support to them there at the outreach area for a time. Perhaps this would also encourage the listeners that he was teaching to continue to be faithful in their attendance of the daily teaching times.

This would be a challenging trip, two days to get there, two to three days at the outreach area, and two days to hike back, approximately one week total. We knew from previous trips that this trail was very steep and even involved some hand-over-hand climbing, holding onto roots and trees along the mountainside. The leeches, mosquitos and biting flies would take their toll in blood as we passed through their jungles.

We also knew about the very sketchy and challenging rattan vine bridge at the half way point which we would again have to cross in order to make it over the river and to our destination. We knew we would be spending a lot of time in smoked filled huts, eating mostly sweet potatoes, other root like garden foods and various greens and leaves. Not to mention we would be trying to get much needed sleep on some pretty hard and uncomfortable ground. It was nothing God hadn't given us the strength to handle in the past though. We knew He would be with us every step of the way as He had always been. We were confident He would provide us with the strength that we needed to complete such a journey.

One of Wikipai's younger brothers named Paatoma also agreed to join us for the journey. And though we had nothing to go by on this long jungle trail, though we had no maps, no compass and no GPS, we had been here in these stone age jungles long enough to know beyond a shadow of a doubt that Paatoma was all we needed. We set out on the jungle trail early in the morning, before the sun was even up, amidst the jungle sounds of screeching cockatoos and the squawks of brightly colored red and green jungle parrots.

I will never forget seeing Wikipai smiling up at me from the little lean to beside that jungle stream. The image is burned in my mind like a still photograph. We hadn't realized how serious things were until we finally made it down to Taomi and caught our first glimpse of his sickness worn, emaciated body. To this day there isn't nearly a week that goes by that I still don't think about those words that he said to us the day that we finally made it down to Him.

With the little bit of strength he had remaining in his body he had said those words to us in almost a whisper. *"Oh friend, do not cry for me. Do not cry for me. Yes, it is true that my body is wasting away. I am like a jungle stream that has not been fed by the rain for many days, but although my body is very weak, my spirit is strong. I know what the Creator One's Son has done for me. And if I die here in this place then the Creator One has chosen that for me. I am ready to go... do not cry for me."* He had said every word with such a sweet smile on his face.

We cooked for him and his wife and children for days and gave him medicine until he felt well enough to try to make the hike back to the highlands. I had never prayed so hard in my life. Wikipai had become my best friend in Dao. I couldn't even begin to imagine life there without him. He had been such a help all these years in so many different ways. He had been one of the first two Dao people of his tribe to trust in the finished work of Jesus and had worked hard alongside Jennie and I to put the Creator's story into the Dao language for the first time.

When he finally seemed strong enough to try to make the return hike to his village up in the cooler elevations of the mountains, we carried his belongings for him the entire way, back up two mountains and into the highlands. He seemed to stop every few feet to catch his breath. He used a walking stick to help hold himself up. A strong wind probably could have blown him off of the trail he was so thin. We went slowly so that he could keep up with the pace and stopped at quite a few different places on the trail so that Wikipai could rest and catch his breath. He was having a very hard time and it was obvious to both us and his family that he wasn't doing well.

"God You have to heal him!" I pleaded over and over again under my breath for hours as we made our way farther and farther up into the mountains one tiny stretch at a time. Finally we made it back up to Wikipai's village. Jennie and I thought for sure that God was going to spare him and restore his strength. "Surely God wouldn't take Wikipai of all people!" I reasoned with myself but even after we made it back up to the highlands and were able to get him back to his village, he wasn't recovering. Day after day I spent nearly all day sitting with him, cooking for him and trying to administer medicine.

"No man knows the day that I will die, but the Creator knows. Will I die soon while I still am young? Will I die while my wife and I have only cut the cords of two children? Will I die when I am old and have lived a good long life? No man can know such things, but the Creator knows. And if I die while I am still young, then the Creator has chosen that for me. I am ready to go up to that good place above the sky and live with Yesusi." he said to me a few days later as I sat with him next to the fire in his little thatch roofed house. Then a little while later he lay down on his weaved leaf mat and breathed his last breath.

"Why God! I don't understand! Of all the people that work against you that you could have taken why did you have to take him?" I screamed in my mind. I felt as if God Himself had slapped me in the face. After all the trials and hardships Jennie and I had been through to bring God's Word to the Dao people, this was the trial that nearly destroyed me.

I took long walks alone in the jungle trying to work through my frustration and anger at the situation. Jennie could even see that I was at my breaking point. Moipi and their two kids would be left without their father at such a young age. The Dao believers would be missing one of their best teachers at a time when they were just getting on their feet and I felt as if I was the one that should bear the blame. I was the one after all that had encouraged him to go to Taomi in the first place and had led the believers in sending him out.

"And what about the Taomi people? What will happen with them now God?! Do you actually want to be mocked and doubted in this place? Do you actually want people to think that what happened to Wikipai will happen to them also if they listen to your message? What are you doing God!" I asked over and over again. I felt like even though I had given my best and prayed like I had never prayed before for God's intervention and for the sparing of my best Dao friend, I had been betrayed by God Himself.

Even in the midst of this struggle I knew deep down inside that somehow God would work even this out for His own glory and for the Dao people's good. I knew that God had sovereignly chosen this for Wikipai. After all, if God could for our good and His own glory, watch from heaven and simply stand by and do nothing as His own son Jesus was crucified, even after having known that it would happen for eternity past, why wouldn't He choose the same for Wikipai? But it was just so hard to let go and trust that He was doing what was best. For a time I could hardly even pray any more for the whirlwind of emotions that would well up inside me when I tried to talk to God.

⟷

Nearly four months later I heard a voice calling me from outside the house one afternoon. *"Degapiyaa! Degapiyaa Wae!"* I heard in the typical Dao fashion. It was Paatoma the younger brother of Wikipai that was standing there when I went to the door. He had a somber look on his face and told me that we needed to talk. He had been hanging around our village a lot lately and was building a new house for his family not far down the hill from us. Paatoma was a very soft spoken man for the most part just like his older brother Wikipai was. They looked similar as well and it was hard for me to spend time with Paatoma without constantly thinking of the recent loss of my best friend Wikipai.

"What is it you want to talk about Paatoma? Do you need to borrow a tool for your house building? What is it?" I asked him. "I want to join the literacy classes and learn how to read and write, and my wife does too." he replied.

"Well that's great Paatoma. If you do that you will soon be reading the Creator's book for yourself and won't have to depend on others to read for you. But I don't understand, why do you all the sudden now want to learn to read and write when we have been teaching these classes for a long time now and you never cared about them in the past?" I asked him.

He paused for a moment and looked down at the ground. He then looked back at me and very intently asked: "Do you remember the words that my older brother Wikipai said to us when we hiked down to give medicine in Taomi a while back?"

"Yes Paatoma, I remember. I think about those words nearly every day. Wikipai said *'Do not cry for me. Yes, it is true that my body is wasting away. I am like a jungle stream that has not been fed by the rain for many days, but although my body is very weak, my spirit is strong. I know what the Creator One's Son has done for me. Do not cry for me'* is what he told us." I replied.

"There are only two people in my life that I have ever seen die well. One was my father, Totopwi and the other was my older brother, Wikipai. When I first heard you teach us about the Creator and His Son Yesusi I never truly took it all seriously. But then I saw the confidence that both my father and then Wikipai had even in death. There was no doubt in their minds that they would go to be with Yesusi. They were happy to die and they told all of us that they couldn't wait to go to the good place above the sky. That is not the way our people usually die."

Paatoma continued, "Most of us Dao people I have seen die in the past have died in fear, screaming out to be spared from the evil spirits and asking others to kill and sacrifice their pigs to the evil spirits so that they will be spared! When my father and also Wikipai died without fear, I had never seen anything like it. It was at Wikipai's death that I decided this message must be true and it must be worth living for." he concluded.

I couldn't believe what I was hearing. There hadn't been a day pass in the past four months that Jennie and I had not thought and talked about Wikipai. We had wondered out loud over and over again "Of all the people that could be taken, why one of our strongest believers? Why Wikipai?" We wondered if we would ever see anything good come out of his death in this lifetime. Now, for the first time we were seeing that God knew what He was doing after all in Wikipai's death. God knew all along exactly what it would take to turn Paatoma to Himself. He had used the death of his older brother Wikipai as the final straw to bring Paatoma into His family.

Before Paatoma left to continue with the building of his new house that afternoon he said, "After my wife and I learn how to read and write, I want to teach the words of the Creator's leaf book to our people and to my family just like my brother Wikipai did before he died. I have moved here and am building this house here because I believe now that this message is worth living for. I want to live well just like my brother Wikipai did." he concluded and then turned and began walking back down the jungle trail.

I realized in those minutes as I watched Paatoma walk away that God knows better than Jennie and I do what is best for His glory. I thanked God that He knows what He is doing. I asked Him for His forgiveness for thinking I know what is best. Then I thought about the faces of the people we had met from Taomi and the other yet unreached areas of the Dao territory. I thought about the many people in Indonesia and other parts of the world that are still dying in fear, crying out to be spared because they have no hope of eternal life. I thought specifically about the Dao people and how they still needed Jennie and I to finish translating the rest of the Creator's leaf book into their language.

And in that moment I realized that if there was any one thing I had learned during those past few months as I had watched Wikipai spend his last days trying to carry God's message to the people in Taomi that had not yet had a chance to hear, then in the midst of his efforts slowly waste away in his sickness but never stop smiling and giving God glory despite his suffering, I had learned what it looks like to die well. Because when I die, I want my last weeks to have been spent on the front lines. I want my last days to have been spent commending Jesus to the most unreached of the unreached with a smile on my face no matter how much pain I may be in. And I want my last words to have been spent pointing my family, friends, brothers, sisters and all those around me towards our Creator so that He is the One people are left looking at, not me.

Then a smile stretched across my face as I thought about how great it will be to someday be reunited with Wikipai and Totopwi again. How awesome that day will be when this battle is finally over and Jesus has decided that the job is done! Jennie and I will be standing side by side with many Dao people, many of our family and a vast sea of people from every language group, tribe, people and nation as the book of Revelation describes and we will all be together singing out heartfelt praises with everything inside of us to Yesusi for what He has done for us on that crossed wood.

It isn't until then that the best will have arrived because it is then that we will experience more joy and satisfaction in our beings than we have ever experienced before. It is on that awesome day that our great Creator will finally get the glory He deserves. These present trials will be well worth the enjoyment that is yet to come. We haven't barely even begun to experience true life yet!

Closing Remarks

Missions is like scaffolding that is used to erect a building. It is just temporary to lend support until the structure can stand on its own.Then it is pulled away and moved to another location where it is needed.

Steve Saint,
The Great Omission

When Paul carried the message of Jesus to new groups of people that had never heard that message before he had a clear goal in mind. As he packed up his things and tearfully said his goodbyes to a group he had been living among in the book of Acts he made a very important statement about that goal and his strategy. The statement being *"I have not shrunk back from declaring to you the whole council of God."* In other words, "I have not kept back from telling you all that God wants you to know."

If the conditions remained peaceful in the places where Paul was teaching and he was physically able to stay in a place, it was Paul's goal to teach the people there the whole message. Then finally, when he had come to the end of the Creators words, when he had taught through everything that God had given him to teach and the people were ready to stand on their own he would move on to a new place.

In the same way, this is the strategy of Jennie and I in the Dao tribe. Even right now as you are reading the words on this page we are likely either in the Indonesian jungles in a Dao village teaching, in our little solar powered jungle house translating new portions of "the Creator's leaf book" into the Dao language, or we are preparing to soon return to the jungle to continue with this work until it is completed.

We have a goal in mind, which is to teach the Dao people "Everything that God wants them to know" and in order to do that we must first translate the entirety of the Bible into the Dao language. We do already have most of the key stories of the New Testament and Old Testament translated. It will likely take a number of years however to complete this project of translating the entire Bible and to in addition to that also teach the entirety of the Bible from cover to cover in the Dao people group.

Even though because we live in a politically and religiously sensitive country we have chosen not to mention in this book the names of most of the organizations that we have worked alongside, we do want you to know that there has been an incredible group of people standing behind us since the very beginning. From our schooling and training days in America to our first survey and language learning days in Indonesia and even up until now for that matter we have been extremely fortunate to have many people encouraging us along the way.

From many of our family members, such as my mom who kept every single letter we ever wrote from Indonesia and gave copies of them to me so that I could compile this book, to the teachers at the schools we attended before coming to the field. From the people that have prayed for us regularly to the pilots, doctors and their families that live in the cities here in Indonesia and support us from those locations, we have been incredibly blessed. So to our supporters and coworkers, both on the field and off the field that have labored alongside of us we want to say thank you. Thank you for your prayers. Thank you for your support. Thank you for sacrificially giving of yourselves to be a part of this work.

Please pray for the Dao people, for our family and for our coworkers on the field as well as we seek to finish this awesome task of both translating and teaching *"The whole council of God"* here in the Dao tribe and in other unreached places and people groups. And if your not playing a part in the amazing things that God is doing in the last remaining unreached corners of the world, we want you to know that your missing out on being a part of something incredible! Step forward and a play a part! You have the words of Jesus written down with pen and ink just as we do. His last words and command to *"Go into all the world and preach the gospel to everyone"* do not apply any less to you than they do to our family, the Dao believers, or any other believer in this world for that matter. Find a way to get involved and take Jesus at His word that it will be well worth it "Both in this life and in the life to come!"

If you have a desire to play a part specifically through financially supporting our family in our ongoing efforts here in Indonesia and in the Dao tribe, you can contact us or get involved with our work through our website:

propheciesofpaleskin.org

Made in the USA
Lexington, KY
26 May 2013